The Story of Childhood

The Story of Childhood

Growing Up in Modern Britain

Libby Brooks

BLOOMSBURY

For my mother, Susan Anne Riddell, and for
my godchildren, Freddy Haines and
Omni Thiessen Molteno

First published in Great Britain in 2006

Copyright © 2006 by Libby Brooks

The moral right of the author has been asserted

Bloomsbury Publishing Plc, 36 Soho Square, London W1D 3QY

A CIP catalogue record for this book is available from the British Library

ISBN 0 7475 8343 9
ISBN-13 978074 7583431

10 9 8 7 6 5 4 3 2 1

Typeset by Palimpsest Book Production Ltd, Polmont, Stirlingshire

Printed in Great Britain by Clays Ltd, St Ives plc

All papers used by Bloomsbury Publishing are natural, recyclable products
made from wood grown in well-managed forests. The manufacturing
processes conform to the environmental regulations of the country of origin

Contents

Introduction   1

Rosie   19
Lois   50
Allana   85
Nicholas   124
Adam   160
Laura   194
Majid   227
Ashley   260
Lauren   304

Conclusion   332
Select Bibliography   337
Acknowledgements   345

Introduction

Sometimes it bothers me that I don't know the way to Troon. It was always my mother who drove us there. Growing up in Glasgow, Troon was the beach we went to for breaks and bank holidays. Two hours from the city, over the Fenwick Moor, it has a famous golf course, but that's not the reason we went. I'm not sure why she picked it as our holiday place. She tells me now that she wanted somewhere she could get home from in a hurry. Alone with a small child, my mother worried terribly about sudden illness and her distance from the familiar.

So the steady seaside town became our wee family's regular haunt. Troon in my mind is mapped through repetition: the places we went in the order we went to them, season by season, year by year. Sometimes it rained, but everything else stayed the same: the gritty car park, the sharp grass dunes, the wide promenade where bigger boys brought their bikes. The treacherous and winding cliff walk, so narrow in places that we had to walk single file. If you don't concentrate, you might get too close to the edge. The distance to the rocks below grew smaller as I grew up, really only a full body's length, but the danger signs stayed red.

Across to the diffident town centre. Regalia, the ladies' dress shop, with a twirling display of coloured plastic clip-on earrings by the cash register. The Copper Kettle, with its sticky plastic banquettes and triangular menu stands. Always cheese and ham toasties and chocolate cake. The sweet shop, an Aladdin's cave of Gibbs barrels. Cola cubes and soor plooms, cherry lips and pineapple chunks, racketing into the pan of the weighing scales by the quarter ounce. Treasure deposited in white paper pokes. And always one sugar mouse from the open glass jar on the counter. I chose the colour then saved it, best until last, eating it slowly like an observance, ears first.

Could I find my way back now? Along the motorway, to the roundabout where you can first see the sea, past the bend in the road where there were horses in a field, through the streets to the threadbare bank with the graffitied shelter. Would the memory be stained and feathery, like the pretend treasure maps I soaked in tea to make the paper look aged? There are footprints in the sand, but now on a foreign shore for me.

Human beings are story-loving creatures. We tell tales as a way of understanding ourselves. But as individuals, and as a society, the most potent story we ever tell is the story of childhood.

This book is made up of stories of childhood as told by people who live there. Each of the nine chapters tracks one child across a fragment of time, through a series of interviews and observations which took place over a number of months. My native guides have been chosen for how they illuminate a particular archetype of childhood experience, or an especial locus of adult anxiety. Woven through the chapters are trips into more discursive territory, but essentially this is childhood told from the inside, in the voice of the small person.

The older children were mostly happy to sit and chat about the events of their week. But with my younger guides, the visits were framed around play and visits to the park.

I was never interventionist, but sat in the corner while four-year-old Allana commentated on the activities of her dolls, or six-year-old Rosie hand-clapped across her school playground. What I hope has emerged is what children sound like when they are listened to.

Of course, I cannot claim that their words are presented utterly without mediation. I'm a writer, and I have moulded the material that I was given to suit the themes that I wanted to address. I asked Lauren, the teenage mother, about sex education and not about school dinners, for example. But I always tried to be guided by the particular preoccupations and mood of my guides when we met.

Nor would I suggest that these nine lives present anything other than an entirely arbitrary selection of experiences of contemporary children. I had archetypes in mind when I began searching for guides: a rural child, a poor child, a child who was also a parent. But their selection was not – and could not be – scientific.

I spent a long time finding these nine children, through friends, colleagues and voluntary organisations. I asked a lot of them and their families – to commit to my regular visits over a period of months, to allow me to shine my torch into the nooks and crannies of their daily lives. In return, they were given approval of the quotes and descriptions that I wanted to use in this book. Although they corrected me on factual details, no one asked for any substantive changes to the text.

Their generosity has been boundless, and my thanks feels meagre. Without them, as you will see when you read on, there would be no book.

In writing about childhood, I have been driven by two ideas.

Firstly, I believe that in listening to the story of what it is to be young at the beginning of the twenty-first century, there is also much to hear about what it is to be older. The Bible says: 'When I was a child I spake as a child, I understood as a child, I thought as a child; but when I became a man, I put away childish things. For now we see through a glass darkly; but then face to face.' The ending of childhood is inevitably suffused with loss, not least the loss of any ability to witness those years with clarity. The contemporary adult vision of childhood has become so distorted as to render it opaque, and this opacity is seriously affecting how children grow up today.

The second idea is this: I believe that the arena of childhood will situate some of the most exciting ideological battles of this century, and that progressive thinkers must begin their interrogation of that territory now. In a secular, pluralist society, where adults and children wear the same clothes and read the same books, how do we reach a consensus on the kinds of morals, ambitions and characters we want to share with our children?

This demands a public statement about what kind of people we want to be. Although New Labour has not been slow to co-opt the language of morality, this is something that many on the left feel uneasy about, fearing accusations of nannying or authoritarianism. Public debate about children and family is still dominated by the right, and stultified by a superficial polarisation between tradition and diversity.

Essentially, this is a travel book about a state of being. It tells the story of contemporary childhood with the help of those who still reside there. All of us lived there once, of course, and many of us know and love people who live there still. But as we age, childhood becomes another country, a disputed territory of memory and meaning. Its true geography is quickly forgotten, giving way to an adult-imagined universe. Childhood becomes a story grown-ups tell themselves, the yarn we spin to explain away personal frailties and to position collective anxieties.

Adults may feel that childhood today is in a peculiarly parlous state. Yet contemporary anxieties can be traced back across history. The Greeks saw youth as a potential threat to the civic project. Twelfth-century moralists debated whether a child's fundamental nature could be altered by nurture. The Enlightenment philosophers proposed the concept of childhood innocence to counter the religious imperative of infant depravity. Social reformers of the eighteenth century believed that children's need for segregation from adults trumped their capacity for economic independence.

Of course, growing up today imposes the burdens of the moment – earlier exposure to the adult world, increasing containment and surveillance, the tyranny of consumer and moral choice. The definition of maturity itself is in flux as the traditional adult milestones of courtship, marriage and procreation recede, and our popular culture reaches back to youth in order to sustain itself. It is a struggle to reach any consensus on the substance of childhood.

But the form remains uncontested: that human young must serve an extended apprenticeship, only after which they are deemed competent to become integrated members of society. Was it always so? The French academic Philippe Ariès began contemporary thinking about the state of being a child. In his seminal work *Centuries of Childhood*, published in 1962, he argued that childhood was not a historical constant but a social and economic construct, first recognised – by the middle and upper classes at least – towards the end of the seventeenth century. In medieval society, he claimed, childhood did not exist: children mixed with adults as soon as they were physically capable, and the private sphere of the family held little sway.

According to Ariès, between the fifteenth and seventeenth centuries a new emotional ethic developed concerning the care of children, promoting what he described as 'coddling' in place of traditional indifference. The child, 'on account of his sweetness, simplicity and drollery, became a source of amusement and relaxation for the adult.'

He went on to argue that, from the seventeenth century, the growing influence of Christianity – in particular the idea that all infants were burdened with original sin – and a new interest in education found expression in 'psychological interest and moral solicitude'. Churchmen and reformers came to believe that 'the child was not ready for life, and . . . had to be subjected to a special treatment, a sort of quarantine, before he was allowed to join adults.'

This 'discovery' transformed society: the family assumed a greater moral and spiritual function, while schooling effectively segregated children from adults, imposing upon the young of the middle classes the long childhood that we now recognise as standard.

While Ariès' work was significant in focusing academic attention on the way that childhood was constructed, it has since been subject to considerable reappraisal. What he traced was the development of an upper- and middle-class version of childhood – which affected a minority of children well into the nineteenth century – while poor children's experiences were still shaped by poverty and the struggle for survival.

Other historians have pointed out that, just because a modern concept of childhood did not exist in medieval Europe, this does not mean that a different understanding of it was not present. In particular, medieval scholars have pointed to the inheritance of the Greek and Roman discourses on youth. Indeed, many debates about childhood have their roots in antiquity. Plato could be said to prefigure Locke in his belief that education had the power to transform both society and the individual. And akin to the twentieth century Swiss psychologist Jean Piaget, Quintillian, an influential Roman educator who lived in the first century AD, suggested that schooling should be based on stages of development, from infancy to adolescence, and devised specific lessons for each stage.

However we choose to locate this 'discovery', it is certainly arguable that the Enlightenment philosophers did much to consolidate a modern understanding of childhood. John Locke, for example, refuted the concept of innate ideas, bringing the objectivity of reason to the study of the human mind and contending that knowledge and morals originated from experience. In *Some Thoughts Concerning Education*, published in 1693, he introduced the notion of the child as a blank slate, urging that teachers consider their pupils 'only as white paper, or wax, to be moulded and fashioned as one pleases.'

But while Locke cautioned parents against being overly affectionate towards their offspring, in order that their minds might be made 'obedient to rules, and pliant to reason' from a young age, across the Channel the French philosopher Jean-Jacques Rousseau warned against the early imposition of intellectual structure on the child's nature. Rousseau's *Emile*, published in 1762, was particularly influential in countering the insistence that only a strict and austere upbringing could exorcise a child's inborn wickedness, flouting the Methodist preacher John Wesley's injunction to 'break their wills that you may save their souls'.

In his hugely popular account of how he would educate an imaginary child, Rousseau emphasised instead the primitive goodness of children, who should be left free to respond to the world around them and only later be nurtured by a responsive teacher. 'First leave the germ of his character free to show itself,' he wrote. 'Do not constrain him in anything, the better to see him as he really is.'

As philosophical inquiry turned from strict reason towards a more emotional and organic description of the world, the Romantic writers of the late eighteenth and early nineteeth centuries embellished the ideal of childhood innocence and joy. William Blake followed Rousseau's notion of the primitive purity of the child. For Wordsworth – who pronounced, 'The Child is father of the Man' – childhood was a 'lost realm', a time of mystical communion between the natural and the divine, to be viewed with often cloying nostalgia from the 'prison-house' of adulthood.

Such Romantic enchantments were far removed from the reality of childhood. As Charles Dickens chronicled, for the most part Victorian society brutalised its children, manifestly in its treatment of child labourers but also through the more subtle neglects inherent in the social conventions of the upper classes. Throughout the nineteenth century, reformers campaigned to regulate poor children's employment and introduce a degree of compulsory schooling through a number of factory and education acts. This was a crucial step towards the creation of a universal childhood experience in Britain which extended beyond the wealthy.

Many working-class children – and their parents – resented the curtailment of their economic independence. But as Viviana Zelizer, an expert in the social value of childhood, notes of the debate about child labour in the United States: 'For reformers, true parental love could only exist if the child was defined exclusively as an object of sentiment and not as an agent of production.'

Zelizer documented this shift in the status of the child,

from economically useful to useless but emotionally 'priceless'. And with the advancement of sciences of the mind in the early twentieth century, social focus turned towards children's psychological development, and how that might be influenced by their emotional relationships with adults.

In her fine historical survey of trends in childcare, *Dream Babies*, Christina Hardyment notes how the two world wars affected popular views of children in this country. In the 1920s and 1930s, parents were encouraged to apply a strictly behaviourist approach to their children by the ascendant childcare advocates of the time, Frederick Truby King and John B. Watson. Conditioning was all: feeding and sleeping were strictly regimented, indulgence kept to a minimum, and good habits introduced early and constantly reinforced.

'[The behaviourist approach was] well-suited to a world recovering from but still apprehensive of war, which saw its children as a generation with a military purpose,' writes Hardyment. The Second World War changed all this: 'Once the child-rearing principles of the Third Reich and Stalin's Russia became threats to freedom rather than models of egalitarianism, a reaction set in, a determination grew to allow the children of the free world to be more free than children had ever been.' Child-centric care became the norm, exemplified by the likes of Dr Benjamin Spock and, more recently, Penelope Leach, who advised that parents trust their own instincts and have fun with their offspring.

But the popularisation of clinical theories of emotional and educational development also proved influential. Just as Rousseau had done in an earlier era, practitioners adopted the concept of successive stages. One such theory was offered by Sigmund Freud, in his classic work on psychosexual development, *Three Essays on the Theory of Sexuality*, first published in 1905. He conceived adult sexuality as the outcome of libidinal drives present from birth, with pleasure being derived from different erotic zones at each developmental phase.

As Hardyment notes, although the theory was too overtly sexual to be universally adopted by parents, a diluted version did influence popular thinking about the avoidance of psychological distress. '[Parents] moved from the offensive to the defensive. Rather than directing the infant, drawing upon the blank tablet, they became its guardian against a host of fears and anxieties which could, it was believed, produce deviant emotional growth and neurotic disorder.'

By the late 1940s, uncertainties about applying a strictly psychoanalytical approach to child-rearing led to a renewed interest in behaviourism. In 1953, Jean Piaget offered another theory of successive development, this time concentrating on cognitive and intellectual rather than emotional development.

Piaget identified four different stages and, in order to explain the inevitable exceptions to them, coined the term 'mental age', so a child who exhibited competence beyond her prescribed stage had a higher mental age than her peers.

As Piaget's concepts filtered into the public psyche, Hardyment observes, parents began to take the concept of an elastic mental age as a challenge. While they may now have worried less about their children's secret sexual yearnings, Piaget did not offer them an opportunity to relax. Instead, the focus turned to how parents could stimulate their children in order that they grow up as intelligent as possible. 'They are now handmaids to intellect instead of emotion,' she writes.

Within academic circles, the new discipline of sociology came to challenge what it saw as a deterministic view of childhood. Sociologists have argued that psychologists treat children as incompetent, judging them solely in terms of what they have yet to achieve. They maintain that this standardises childhood, distracting attention from the diversity of ways in which children can develop, often pathologising deviations. Children should be seen as social beings, they argue, rather than as individual developing minds.

In their essay on the sociology of childhood, Michael Lavalette and Stephen Cunningham, both lecturers in social policy, note the growing interest in children and childhood as social categories within their discipline since the late 1970s. They go on to identify the dominant theoretical approach which has emerged in this country as the 'new sociology of childhood'. They argue that this approach makes four central claims: that childhood is a 'social construction'; that children occupy and conduct themselves in worlds that are full of meaning for them, but about which adults understand little; that children are a 'minority group'; and that children are an identifiable social group. However, Lavalette and Cunningham balk at what they consider the central message of the new sociology of childhood: the post-modernist view that 'we have to abandon any attempt to arrive at a full understanding of the world, or to assert that there is any broad directionality to human history.'

They argue: 'When we look at the social construction of childhood we cannot fully grasp this process without looking at changes to the totality of social relations within society – the creation of the modern family form, changes to productive relations, the role of the state – and how these affect the perceptions of and attitudes to children, and the children's responses to all this. Finally, while childhood is not static, it is not the case that there are an infinite range of 'reconstructions' of childhood – indeed, today's childhood in Britain is recognisable as the childhood established for working-class children at the turn of the twentieth century.'

The psychology camp has countered that their endeavours have been misrepresented, that development is crucial and that sociologists risk lumping children together as a homogenous group. This is not the place for a conscientious examination of interdisciplinary wrangling. But what was novel about the sociology of childhood, and the broader childhood studies movement that developed out of it, was a fresh emphasis on rights. The broad consensus was that children should be treated as a minority, and defined as a disadvantaged, excluded group who deserve greater social, political and economic rights. It should also be noted that both psychologists and sociologists are now calling for a more integrated and less discipline-oriented approach to the study of childhood.

Most advocates of children's rights take the United Nations Convention on the Rights of the Child, finalised in 1989, as their guide. It provides for rights to provision, protection and participation for children in all parts of the world, and is designed to take into account their vulnerability, particular needs and 'evolving capacity'. It is also the most widely ratified treaty ever – only Somalia and the United States have not signed up.

Although the UK voluntarily ratified the convention in 1991, it took this country another decade to concede that an independent body was needed to monitor its application. Following appointments in Wales and Scotland, Professor Al Aynsley-Green, the first Children's Commissioner for England, only came into post in July 2005, to widespread disappointment that he was not actually charged with promoting children's rights.

The convention has not been without its critics. It does, after all, present children's needs as defined by adults because, ironically, it was drafted without any consultation with children. Some believe that it presumes that all children experience a Western indoor childhood, and so fails to acknowledge that the capacities invested in children and the transition to adulthood vary widely across different societies. But it remains an essential template, given that children throughout the world continue to be denied fundamental rights that adults take for granted.

In Britain, perhaps the most basic inequality is that children cannot make decisions about their own circumstances – their care, their education, their health. Indeed, it can be argued that to be young is to meet the definition of social exclusion without trying – existing outside the political process, unable to contribute directly to the economy, criminalised for offences determined by your status rather than your actions, vilified by the media.

The body of research which already exists on children's participation indicates that when young people are included in decision-making they don't just demand free Smarties, but respond with often astonishing maturity according to the circumstances in which they find themselves. Studies of children's ability to consent to medical treatment, for example, have shown that young people with chronic illnesses can reason in ways that far outstrip the developmental standard for their age.

But to suggest that there exists such a thing as 'childism' is to risk ridicule. The notion of children's rights is inevitably greeted with hostility in a political climate where young people are most often maligned for their lack of respect for the rights of others or adult authority. There is a common assumption that children will run wild given the chance, and that parents must keep control at all costs.

Many adults nowadays believe that children already have too many rights, perhaps because they confuse rights with consumerism and pester-power. But acquiring expensive designer clothes or state-of-the-art technology is not the same as having rights. Adults fear that children's rights mean refusing to go to bed at a reasonable hour, demanding extortionate pocket money, and divorcing their parents if they don't give them what they want. It is assumed that children will not make rational choices if they are allowed to make decisions.

But this is to misunderstand how children's rights might operate in practice. Children's citizenship looks different from that of adults. The fact that ten-year-olds head households in Rwanda is beside the point – because children *can* doesn't necessarily mean children *should*.

Of course parents and the State are often best-placed to make decisions for children. But the fear that giving children rights will deprive them of their childhoods, or create a generation of mini-militants grabbing what they can from the diminishing pot of adult power, is based on a fundamental misconception about what growing up is really like.

It suggests that childhood is a time free of challenge or difficulty, when rights are unnecessary and would only be used for petty personal gain. As Mary John, a developmental psychologist renowned for her work on children's rights, argues: 'One of the persisting myths is that childhood is somehow stress-free – that children are learning and growing rather than enduring and surviving . . . Maybe such myths serve to order and control in our minds what is mysterious and possibly threatening about the presence among us not of "unpeople", as some might wish them to be, but of sentient beings – witnesses to much of the futility and anarchy of adult lives.'

John believes that for the child to be considered a powerful member of society, she must first be recognised as a person rather than a person in the making. But if children are no longer to be seen as raw material, shaped by adults into social conformity and obedience, then 'the question arises as to what sort of person and what role does that little person occupy relative to us.' The place of both adults and children in society must be re-imagined.

It is not difficult to make the case that children's rights are poorly served in the UK. Children are the only members of British society who can, by law, be hit – perhaps the most vivid exemplar of this country's failure to treat all children with the respect they are due. A defendant not old enough to buy a hamster legally can be tried in an adult court and named and shamed in newspapers, in direct contravention of their internationally recognised human rights.

In the school summer holidays of 2005, for example, over 70 per cent of children in England and Wales were subject to curfew orders that allow the police to send people under sixteen home if they are on the streets after 9 p.m. without a supervising adult. Although the government has committed itself to the elimination of child poverty, the numbers of children growing up without warm beds or hot meals remains utterly unacceptable. And, less immediately, adults could be argued to be depriving children, and their children's children, of the right to a future, as they bequeath them a planet on the brink of environmental collapse.

In June 2005, a report by the Council of Europe's Human Rights Commissioner Alvaro Gils Robles condemned the British government for its record on supporting children, expressing particular concerns about the UK's low age of criminal responsibility, the high numbers of children in custody, and the detention of asylum-seeking children. He reserved his most strident criticism for what he dubbed 'ASBO-mania', stating that 'it is difficult to avoid the impression that the ASBO is being touted as a miracle cure for urban nuisance'. At the time, almost half of all antisocial behaviour orders were being served on juveniles.

As Ruth Lister, former director of the Child Poverty Action Group, has noted, authoritarian policies like ASBOs and curfews do not only circumscribe children's rights. They also expose an agenda that demands a pay-off for investment in children, particularly poor ones: 'social order today and responsible citizens tomorrow'. 'Children count not as child-citizens in the here and now but as citizen-workers of the future,' she argues. 'In a "social-investment state", the child has taken on an iconic status as the prime unit of invest-ment in human capital.' This offers minimal scope for addressing what the building blocks of a happy childhood might be.

Al Aynsley-Green marked his appointment Children's Commissioner for England by querying whether, as a nation, we cared about childhood at all. He warned of a 'deep ambiva-lence' towards children, with adults investing enormously in the young people with whom they were intimately involved, while remaining equivocal about other people's children – espe-cially those growing up on the margins – and disconnected from any broader discussion of the condition of contemporary childhood.

Over the past three decades, worries about children's well-being have been amplified to an excruciating pitch. Concern about the vulnerability of some children has been traduced by an all-pervading child-panic. Childhood has become the crucible into which is ground each and every adult anxiety – about sex, consumerism, technology, safety, achievement, respect, the proper shape of a life. This is a time of child-panic. Our children are in danger, preyed upon by paedophiles, corrupted by commerce, traumatised by testing. Our children are dangerous: malevolent beneath hooded tops, chaotic in the classroom, bestial in the bedroom.

All of these fears are real, but not all of them reflect reality. It is axiomatic that adults worry about children. But in an era defined by child-panic, to be anxious about childhood has become a definition of adulthood. That the process of becoming an adult is changing fundamentally is both a symptom and a cause of this. Childhood is seen to be corruptible or corrupted, and between these poles there lies a shrinking habitat for young people of average virture.

Of course, granting them a central role in society is not a universal panacea for the multitude of challenges that attend contemporary childhood. Children still need limits to learn from, but that is not the same as limiting them purely by virtue of how old they are. Necessary adult authority should not be confused with adult power that is abused. And nor should contemplation of children's rights be seen as an inevitable erosion of those of adults. If anything, offering power to a child augments the adult's role in teaching them how to wield that power humanely.

This is not a book against adulthood. To assume that the majority of children are neither angels nor demons but beings of ordinary integrity is not to discredit adults who face incivility or aggression in the classroom or on the streets. Freedom is much more than the absence of restraint. To call for greater understanding, rights and respect for children is not to undermine parents, or to diminish the strenuous moral, emotional and practical project that raising children has become.

As the philosopher Thomas H. Murray observes in his book, *The Worth of a Child*: 'In the context of parent-child relationships we learn many vitally important things. We learn most of the content of whatever morality we will embrace as adults. We learn some rules, but also the images that guide us and the ends we should pursue. Within families, we also come to adopt our attitude to morality. We learn, that is, whether it is worth trying to be moral . . . Last, in a family where love survives, we come to understand the centrality of relationships in human flourishing.'

I have a confession to make here. I am not yet a parent myself. I do not believe that this disqualifies me from writing about childhood, though others may disagree. Parents are best placed to discuss the welfare of their own children, but not necessarily the welfare of all children. To conclude that parents have the franchise on debates about young people is fundamentally to misconceive the nature of childhood. It is to treat children as chattels, rather than recognising that children are everybody, and that everyone has a stake in their upbringing.

There are as many ways to understand childhood as there are children. But despite numerous attempts, the story of childhood has rarely been well told. It has always been embroidered with myth, steeped in nostalgia. And it has always reflected the prevailing anxieties of the age.

Throughout history, childhood has provided an effective prism through which to reveal social mores. In a secular, pluralistic era, with a widening gulf between rich and poor and a greedy, coarsening popular culture, that revelation is more welcome than ever. It takes us to the heart of what kinds of children we hope to raise, and what kinds of adults we strive to be.

The following chapters explore how child-panic and, more broadly, the way that childhood is constructed in contemporary British society, might affect human flourishing.

Rosie

'Without children, this world would be boring; this world would be empty.'

Rosie writes stories in coloured felt-tip on plain paper. The sheets are bound in clear plastic folders, each with a cover illustration. On the back page she provides a brief summary of the contents. This is headed 'The Blurb'.

In a big green box in the back extension, which she called 'Rosie's Garden' when it was first built, are files containing all the stories and all the drawings that she and her little sister Olivia have ever made. There are pictures there from when Rosie was younger, when she wrote some of the letters in her name backwards. There's a sketch of a baby in a cart, which she can definitely remember doing, a Peter Pan, and a lady with two cats going to a wedding. Now Rosie is six, and she can draw a better Peter Pan.

This afternoon her sister is at nursery. Rosie is a cheeky monkey, oop-oop-ing across the lounge carpet, tail high in the air, half a banana balanced between her lips. She has no front teeth at all. Her cleanly bobbed blonde hair curtains her cheeks. All of Rosie's facial expressions generate from her nose, which is pert like that of a fairy tale heroine. The rest of her features are involved in an ongoing dialogue about whether to be pretty or bold.

Rosie writes about a confused bear called Winnie the

Pooh, aliens in space, some of whom like eating stars, and a girl called Jenny. This story is titled 'Jenny and her Wonderful Family'. The blurb says: 'Will Jenny find her family?'

'Once upon a time there was a little girl called Jenny. One day Jenny decided to start karate lessons. When she asked her mum, her mum said, "No you can't." Jenny looked sad and walked sadly up the stairs to her room. When she came downstairs her mum was gone. Jenny said, "Well that's strange." Then in the middle of night Jenny crept downstairs. Then in the corner she saw something dull and black it was . . . it was the cat. The cat crept out of the corner and purred at Jenny's leg. "Now stop it," said Jenny. "We need to find Mum and Dad." So they left the house to find Mum and Dad.'

'Morning and night they looked and looked, but they couldn't find Mum and Dad but then the cat saw something moving in the bushes. It was something they had never seen before, well that's because it was in the dark of course. But then it started to move towards the cat and it was . . . it was Mum and Dad. "Oh I'm so glad to see you," cried Jenny. "Oh I'm so glad to see you," cried Mum. The family was finally together again. "I'm so glad we're a happy family again," said Jenny and a happy time was had by all. But there was one thing. Jenny was quite happy that she hadn't gone to karate lessons in the first place. She was just glad that they were a happy family again.'

Growing up has always charted dangerous territory. Even Rosie's story of Jenny and her wonderful family takes the safest of psychic risks, drawing on a classic theme of children's literature: the lone child on a quest, abandoned by her parents, with an other-than-human helper. Kept between the covers, a different order of things can be tested.

Children construct their identities at play, through exploration and risk-taking, but their culture has become subject to containment and surveillance. Western young are safer today than at any other point in human history; they are less likely to be killed, to suffer neglect or to succumb to disease. In an era defined by child-panic, however, to be anxious about children has become a definition of adulthood.

Children's independence and mobility is limited in a variety of ways – through fear, exclusion from public spaces, more time spent at school – leading to the norm of the indoor child. But risk-taking is essential to learning how to be safe. And private time, away from adult eyes, is necessary for emotional and creative development. What is the impact of increasing surveillance on the child's internal world? What are the consequences for a generation reared in captivity?

Rosie's mum and dad have never gone missing. But the stories that she tells about them end just as happily. Mummy and Daddy kiss each other a lot. Rosie likes to declare her affection too. Sometimes with a different word for each: 'I wove, wove, wove Daddy, and I love, love, love Mummy.' And sometimes formally, in the letters she addresses to 'Simon, Linda and Olivia'.

Rosie was born on the second day of January. She lives in a small, green, in-between town in Northamptonshire. Her parents landed here by accident over a decade ago when her father was pursuing his career as a secondary school teacher and her mother was working in London. They've been married for fifteen years, which Rosie says is a very long time.

Rosie can walk to school, to the park and to Simon's parents' house, though not by herself. Tomorrow is Friday so it's cake day. Every Friday she and Livvy eat a cake with their nanny. Linda says that when Rosie is ten she can go to the shops on her own. Other destinations are reached mainly by car, and sometimes by train. These are arranged according to memory rather than geography: the pub where Livvy got stung by a bee, or Milton Keynes, where Rosie saw palm trees that were much bigger in real life.

After Livvy was born, Simon and Linda radically reassessed their child care arrangements. Previously, both had worked full-time, with Linda daily commuting the seventy-five miles to London and Rosie attending a local private nursery from the age of six months. 'It just wasn't a life,' says Linda. She now works full-time as a database marketing manager for a local firm while Simon does part-time supply work, caring for both children in the afternoons at first and now only Livvy. Next year, once she has also started school, he will pick up teaching full-time.

Under Rosie's bed there are two boxes, one for fences and another for animals. At the farm she visits, there's a shop where you can buy things, like key-rings and toys. 'And there's a place where you can get the animals food, and you tell the man what animal you want to feed and he gives you the food for it.' The horses eat carrots. 'I like feeding the rabbits too but there's a fence around them so you have to toss it into their garden and they come out and eat it.'

Rosie would like an animal of her own, but the type of pet and what it might be called varies according to her assessment of the project's feasibility. Yesterday her nanny's dog Judy died. Nanny was sad, and though she used to have a rabbit and a guinea pig and gerbils and three pussy cats she said that she didn't think she'd have another pet in her whole life. Today, modestly, Rosie suggests she would like a goldfish called Goldie.

But it's hard not to think strategically. 'The people that's house we're moving to, they have a rabbit and a guinea pig.

I would call the rabbit Nibbles and the guinea pig would be called Jessie or Megan.' Rosie's family are planning to move to a new house down the road. 'I'll be a lot closer to school. I walk to school every day. We've had a very good look around and the solicitor says it's going really, really well. He works on our new house and this house and he tells us if its going well and when people don't want to buy our house.'

She is sitting cross-legged on the bedroom floor, working efficiently through a pile of books. 'I like pretending to stamp my books, especially my poetry and rhymes book.' She thinks she will be a library keeper when she grows up because she like books a lot. When they next go to the library Daddy says she can get more Tracy Beaker books. 'She has very big behaviour problems. She made someone eat a worm. She's ten years old and she was at a care home. And she wants some foster parents. Her real parents just left her at the care home because they couldn't feed her properly. At the care home they look after you and you have your own room. She has a lot of friends.'

In contrast, Ark-like, Rosie's family goes two by two: two children, two parents, two grannies and two grandpas, two cousins. There are occasional wrinkles, different ways of telling the same story. Cousin Joseph is bigger than Rosie. He's seven. Joseph's parents are divorced and remarried, and it's hard to live with someone who hasn't spent your whole life with you. It's very strange living in two families, she notes jauntily.

Rosie is coming to the end of her second year of primary education. This session, her father Simon has been chair of governors. A few weeks later, I visit her at school. Today the top ability numeracy group is sitting on the floor, having a sums competition with Mrs Round. They wear yellow shirts with green jumpers, and grey skirts or trousers.

Numeracy is taught in another classroom, by a different teacher, with the top group from another Year 1 set, and everyone is feeling a little discombobulated.

Mrs Round announces that the morning's task is to Colour the Square. The children scatter round the tables, but it's not easy deciding where to sit and Rosie tries three different places before finally settling. Each table collects worksheets and tins of lead and coloured pencils. Mrs Round explains that you have to colour one section of the square at a time to make it balance. Nobody can understand what she means, and there is mass confusion.

The discussion at Rosie's table turns to relationships. 'Everyone calls us boyfriend and girlfriend. You're just a girl and you're my friend,' says Malcolm, the noisiest boy in the class. He plays his words staccato, and is almost double Rosie's size. She is half-listening, but the red lead in her pencil keeps slipping down. 'You two LOVE each other,' teases one of the class princesses, because she can. 'Stupid girls,' blares Malcolm, 'you should never trust them.'

'You have to make the patterns balance within each square,' insists Mrs Round, meaninglessly as far as the class is concerned. A long line of the befuddled snakes towards her chair. In a final attempt to achieve conformity of purpose, she strides between the desks, peering over hunched shoulders. Rosie turns to look into the teacher's face: 'I made a little mistake.' She has a disconcerting ability to appear both abject and impenitent at once. 'I think we're going to leave this activity,' Mrs Round concedes huffily. 'You don't understand what you're doing.' Malcolm collects in the worksheets.

At the end of the morning, Rosie's group returns to its own classroom second, because they weren't sitting best. Away from the numeracy imperative, back in their own space with their own teacher Mrs Ashley, it is much easier to keep quiet and sit still. They hug the familiar like a blanket. Everybody in the room is white-skinned. Each table takes turns to collect packed lunch-boxes and walk to the canteen. Hardly anyone here takes free school meals.

The canteen is chattery but a prayer is said before eating together. It's for God, to say thank you for all the food and drink we have and we're very lucky to have it. Rosie believes in God. Some people believe in God and some people don't. Rosie is taught about the gospels at school. Mummy and Daddy tell her that it's a story, and only what some people think, which upsets her. Rosie likes these stories, and she likes certainties. She tells Livvy that you have to believe in Jesus to go to school.

Rosie arranges herself next to Emily and Chloe. She has a pink rucksack with a lunch-box compartment in the base. She sticks the straw into her orange-juice carton and eats the yoghurt first, carefully adding Smarties to the pot. The coloured dyes bleed into the creamy dairy. Today she has salami sand-wiches, which she examines too carefully, alerting one of the dinner supervisors. This lady removes the salami and gives Rosie back the plain bread. Lunch is a swift affair, the supervisors implacable, then it's coats on and outside.

The playground is a tarmacked L-shape. Perhaps on account of health and safety requirements, it is also barren, with no area hidden from adult view. The noise is shrill and deafening, like an alarm. An enormous knowledge hangs in the air: that anything can happen now; that rules will be made and broken, reputations won and lost, friendships begun and ended and begun again across the long, long minutes of the lunch hour.

The sky is wetly metallic, and the air is cold, but these children are feverish. Beginning in 1970, the British folk-lorist Iona Opie spent over a decade observing children at play in a state primary school near her home in Hampshire. In the resulting book, *The People in the Playground*, she describes the 'continuous Saturnalia' of break-time. 'Children already seem to know that "human kind cannot bear very much reality",' she writes. '[In the playground] a kind of defiant light-heartedness envelops you. The children are clowning. They are making fun of life.'

Rosie locks raised hands with Chloe, and they push each other back and forth, fierce and snarling, then slow, balletic. Some other girls cluster round to cheer on their favourite, and begin to tangle too. Suddenly the combat becomes a multiple hand-clapping, rhyme-chanting game. A boy runs by and Rosie and Chloe give chase, are chased, half-hoping to be caught. Chloe is one of the princess girls, and the boy wants to catch only her. Suddenly she turns on him and gives him a violent hug, then stalks off, flicking her glossy wedge of chestnut hair, bottom out. Rosie returns meekly to the rhyme with another partner.

Play, of course, is not only about playing. It is identity-settling, hierarchy-refining, gender-constructing work. Although Rosie and her schoolmates organise naturally into single-sex huddles, the most exciting moments come when a boy or a girl breaks across the divide. Another observer of play, the American academic Barrie Thorne, chronicled these contacts, describing such cross-boundary penetrations as 'borderwork'. In her book *Gender Play*, she describes how children would deliberately provoke these clashes, sometimes within an organised game of capture and rescue, but often in the more casual episodes of chasing that punctuate playground life.

In some cases, she noted, catching would result in the aggressive affection that Chloe showed her pursuer, but other times it would involve contamination. 'Pollution rituals', by which certain individuals, often of lowly social rank, are deemed to have 'cooties' or 'germs', were strictly organised according to gender. Both boys and girls could give cooties to one another, but boys did not give cooties to other boys. All girls, no matter what their status, could contaminate boys. In one elementary school, Thorne learned that cooties were known as 'girl stain'.

Rosie swings her arms wide, clapping in the air, slipping away from the group and into her own world. Then someone decides she's under arrest. They're a smelly animal. One boy faces into a corner of the school building. 'I've just got nobody to play with,' he sobs. As time gets short, activity gets wilder. Boys are piling on top of each other. Too soon for Rosie, and not nearly soon enough for others, comes the whistle. They line up by class and file back indoors.

For the first part of the afternoon Mrs Ashley does writing with the Orange Group. The other tables read and draw. Rosie announces that she's going to make a kissing book. 'Who's in it?' asks Jamie, blundering into her mantrap. 'Is Jamie too long?' she ponders aloud, measuring out the letters on the page. 'Oh no!' he groans, hand across eyes. Now she draws an elaborate front cover for another story book. It's to be called 'My Tropical Island'.

Mrs Ashley counts one, two, three and stop talking. Rosie's table misses out on a sticker for being quietest first because she's still chattering about palm trees. 'Rosalind!' curses one boy, but soon they're laughing together again. She's good at bringing people round. She is confident without needing to be noisy. Everyone listens when Rosie talks, in a voice that is soft but prevailing.

It's time to move up to the base, a raised section of the classroom with benches around three sides and a chair for the teacher. There is only room for a limited number of bottoms on the premium space around the edges, so there is pushing. Chloe is sitting with her arms tight around Rosie. 'Chloe, can you leave Rosie alone please?' Rosie isn't Pears-Soap-perfect like the other class princesses, but they enjoy having her close.

This is the very end of the school day and it's sharing time. Announcements are made. One person is adopting a penguin. Another has a new baby cousin. Someone's next-door neighbours are having a barbeque. When Jamie stands up, he explains that his gran has asked him to stay the night with her after her birthday party. He uses wide arm gesticulations, and sometimes strokes his face. It's easy to see why Rosie loves him. 'So it's the Dog and Duck, then back to hers and who knows what we'll get up to,' he concludes. Rosie and Chloe don't have any special news, so they perform their four-and-twenty-blackbirds handclap instead. 'We've been practising it for a long time,' they tell the class. Everyone goes home with forms for the end-of-term trip.

A few weeks later, the summer holidays have set in, and Rosie is adjusting to the wobbly rhythm of play plans that can last all week. Her father is downstairs. She's made a washing line out of a skipping rope tied between the top of her bunk and the knob of the tall bureau in the corner.

Every year at the end of school there are reports. Both years Rosie has been a very good girl, and had excellent art. 'That makes me very proud. It's very hard work.' Rosie has a way of nodding when she speaks to add emphasis. It feels funny not being at school. 'Sometimes I wake up in the morning and I think I need to go to school and then Mummy and Daddy tell me I don't have to because it's the holidays.'

When Rosie plays in her room she makes full use of the space, both horizontally and vertically. She scales the bookcase like a climbing wall, to the top shelf where her secret diary is kept. She bounces on the ladder up to her bunk-bed, and reaches across from the end of it to the bureau where some other toys are kept.

She is fiddling with the end of the skipping rope that is attached to the bureau knob. In the new house her parents are going to have a study, so they'll put all these things in there. The most exciting thing about moving house is that they'll be sleeping on the floor. 'I'm going to be the moving photographist,' says Rosie, clambering along to the other end of her bunk, 'and I can stick them in a special book of my first moving and that's going to be one of my favourite books when I'm really, really old.'

Livvy is idling in the doorway of Rosie's room, frowning beneath her dark fringe. It's one of those days when she wants to be everywhere her sister is and have everything she has. They bounce balls together. Rosie can spin hers between two fingers but Livvy can't.

Livvy laments a disparity. Rosie's diary is hidden in some secret place, but everyone in the family has seen Livvy's so it's not a secret any more. She wants to get another one but Mummy and Daddy won't let her out on her own until she's ten and that's a long way away.

In an attempt at mollification, Rosie counts the money in her Sindy tin. She has 23p. 'And you know what?' she announces cheerfully. 'That's enough to buy two things, one for Livvy and one for me. Maybe some toys or jigsaws or magazines.' Unassuaged, Livvy continues to make sad eyes at no one in particular.

Both girls know that ten is the age when they can walk to the shops unaccompanied. Ten is also when Mummy says they can wear nail polish on special occasions, but just for fun she thinks they should wait until thirteen. Ten was also the age of Holly Wells and Jessica Chapman when they walked to their deaths in the Cambridgeshire village of Soham. Adults understand intellectually that it is impossible to monitor every moment of a young life. But the fierce love of parenthood ushers in fear over risks real and imagined. Childhood is becoming a place of confinement.

In his classic comparative study, *One False Move*, published in 1990, the transport and environment researcher Mayer Hillman found that, in a single generation, the 'home habitat' of a typical eight-year-old – the area in which the child was able to travel without direct adult supervision – had shrunk to one ninth of its former size. Tim Gill, a writer on childhood and former director of the Children's Play Council, has likened this to a generation bred in captivity. Under threat, he concluded, is what naturalists would term survival mechanisms and psychologists would call resilience.

Hillman, who compared children's independence and mobility between 1970 and 1990, found that traffic levels had doubled in that twenty-year period, with cars capable of being driven faster and accelerating more quickly. He contrasted this with what he believed was an over-reporting of incidences of child assault and abduction by strangers, in order to understand why parents had become so much more anxious.

He also discovered that, because of the huge extension in restrictions on their behaviour since the 1970s, fewer children were being killed on the roads. But this had serious consequences for their social and physical development. Lack of exercise was one. But Hillman was also concerned that young people were no longer able to engage in an important aspect of childhood: getting into mischief, making mistakes, and learning from their own experiences. Indeed, as adults come to pathologise the presence of young people on the streets, branding them 'hoodies' and 'yobs', the definition of childhood mischief is itself changing.

It can be argued that, since the seventeenth century, the trend amongst the middle classes has been to subject children to increasing control and surveillance. As children were excluded from the workplace and corralled into schoolrooms, their essential vulnerability came to be emphasised, along with the need to isolate them from the temptations of the adult world. But it would now seem that children have internalised this view to such an extent that they are afraid to venture beyond the front door.

A study undertaken by the Green Alliance and Demos in 2004 found that children's interaction with their local environment is in sharp decline. Interviewing more than one thousand children aged ten and eleven across the country, it found that the majority no longer considered the street a suitable place to play, while beliefs about the inherent hostility of public spaces were commonplace. Danger was often the first thing the children mentioned when talking about being outside the home.

Direct personal experience informed children's fear of traffic, with many being able to give examples of accidents or near accidents they had been involved in. But although fear of strangers was just as keenly felt, they were unable to articulate how that threat might operate in practice. Some children mentioned the risk of being kidnapped or killed, and others implied a sexual dimension to the danger. Many also talked about their fear of becoming lost and therefore more vulnerable to strangers and criminals. For a large number of children, the only outdoor space they were sure was safe from strangers was their own garden.

The traffic concerns that these interviewees expressed seem

to be a highly reasonable assessment of risk. There are over one hundred child-pedestrian fatalities in the UK each year, and motor vehicles continue to be given priority over people on foot, even in residential areas. But most is made of that from which there is least to fear. Children are much more likely to be abused or killed by people they know. The number of children killed by strangers is very small – around eight each year – unless that stranger happens to be behind the wheel of a car.

Confinement isn't only a result of parental – or children's – fear. Under-investment in outdoor play facilities means there are fewer open spaces for children to inhabit. There is a vast disparity in access to green areas between urban and rural children. In the seventeenth century, even children living in towns had fields close by. Now, Britain is the most urbanised country in Europe. It's hardly surprising that levels of child-hood obesity are rising.

Lifestyle changes also impact on children's freedom. As a result of longer working hours, more mothers in employment, smaller families and community fragmentation, there's not always a friendly adult around to mind out for roaming youngsters – and, as the Green Alliance study shows, non-familial adults are nowadays more likely to be considered a threat than a help. Parents who do let their children wander free are considered irresponsible.

Frank Furedi has described this as an 'erosion of adult solidarity' in the rearing of children. 'The relation of trust between parents, teachers, nursery workers and carers has become highly ambiguous,' he wrote in an essay on risk and play. 'Instead of regarding other adults as a potential source of assistance in the task of child-rearing, parents regard them with a degree of suspicion. In particular, adults who are "strangers" are treated with apprehension. Since most adults are by definition "strangers", concern for children can often acquire a pathological character.'

The norm of the indoor child has led not only to fear for children who do venture outside, but fear of them. Teenagers who congregate on street corners are seen a priori as a nuisance and a threat. It is then worth asking whether confinement may also be seen as an adult convenience. If children no longer regard the streets as their territory, their elders won't be disturbed by games or gangs. Nor do car drivers have to think about lowering their speed. And it's also a commercial convenience. If children are spending more time indoors, they and their parents are likely to spend more money on expensive electronic entertainments.

Operating in tandem with child-panic is Western culture's profound risk aversion. The second largest teaching union, the National Association of Schoolmasters/Union of Women Teachers, now advises its members to avoid taking part in school trips because 'society no longer appears to accept the concept of a genuine accident'. It has been estimated that school insurance premiums are increasing by up to 20 per cent a year to indemnify against compensation claims.

Although statistically pupils are safer on a supervised trip than participating in almost any other activity, absurdities accrue. A school in Devon cancels its Shrove Tuesday pancake race after its bill for public liability insurance for the event quadruples. A local council advises teachers against making trips on sunny days because of the possible risk of skin cancer. And once again, children's experience of the outside environment is curtailed.

This risk hysteria also has implications for playground provision. As Tim Gill noted in a paper for the Play Safety Forum: 'Fear of litigation is leading many play providers to focus on minimising the risk of injury at the expense of other more fundamental objectives.' It's an approach that ignores clear evidence that playgrounds pose a comparatively low risk to children. Of the two million or so childhood accident cases treated by hospitals each year, less than 2 per cent involve playground equipment, while fatalities are very rare – about one every three or four years – compared with about 500 child deaths per annum from accidents overall.

Gill argues that risk assessment should involve a trade-off between safety and other goals: 'Given children's appetite for risk-taking, one of the factors that should be considered is the likelihood that children will seek out risks elsewhere, in environments that are not controlled or designed for them, if play provision is not challenging enough. Another factor is the learning that can take place when children are exposed to, and have to learn to deal with, environmental hazards.'

In their book *From Children's Services to Children's Spaces*, Peter Moss and Pat Petrie of the Thomas Coram Research Unit at London's Institute of Education argue that the distinction between 'risk' and 'hazard' is not sufficiently understood when considering children's activities. 'Risk is inherent in human endeavour,' they write, 'and for children not to engage with it is for them to be cut off from an important part of human life in the interests of "child protection". People learn to assess and manage risk by encountering it.'

A few weeks further into the holidays, Rosie is digging around in a blue plastic stacking box of toys, her whole head disappearing from sight as she reaches into the depths. Downstairs her father is beginning to pack away kitchen utensils for the move. She is wearing multicoloured tinsel deely-boppers – decorated springs on a hairband – which she never takes off and which, marvellously, never get in her way. At the bottom of the stacking box she finds two small balls from a game she has thrown away.

Rosie's front teeth are growing now, lessening the slight lisp she had developed in their absence. She is keeping a holiday diary: '28th July Today I went to London. We took the train from Bedford. We went on the underground train to the Natural History Museum and we saw dinosaurs. Then we went outside and had lunch. We had Scotch eggs and some cheese and some crisps and some ham rolls and some chocolate and two bottles of apple and blackcurrant. Then we went back into the museum because me, Mummy and Livvy needed the toilet and then we went on the double decker bus and I went on the London Eye and I saw Big Ben and I felt very big.'

By the London Eye there were people bouncing up and down on strings and underneath them were trampolines. 'It looked like really good fun but Mummy said I was too young to do it so next year we're going back and I'm going to do bouncing.' It's as though the trampolines, and London, only breathe into life when Rosie visits, and will await her return, spellbound, stoically, these twelve months.

Livvy brings in her Pinocchio doll. 'I'm a real boy. I'm not a real boy,' she chants as she makes his lying nose extend and retract. Rosie begins to build a house with the Ello bricks. 'That's the girls' room and now I'm going to make a boys' room,' she confirms to herself. 'That's the alarm that lets the girls know if a boy comes into their room. They get punishments if they go in there.'

Livvy is still singing: 'I'm a real boy! I'm not a real boy! I'm a real boy and I've got a handbag!' She manoeuvres closer and closer to the Ello construction. Pre-emptively, Rosie suggests that her sister play with the doll's house instead. Livvy spots a sticker on the Ello. 'That's my sticker!' she cries. 'That's my sticker!'

35

insists Rosie. Livvy invades further, claiming some of the Ello as hers.

'You can have it!' Rosie spits, finally disengaging the offending block.

'Can I play with your doll's house?' asks Livvy slyly.

'No!' says Rosie, before she remembers her promise from earlier. 'I mean yes.' She puts on a large pout, but Livvy is content to leave her alone, massaging her victory.

Rosie resumes her narrative: 'Well, that's the girls' room and that's the boys.' There are two boys in there and two girls in there.' She arranges four wooden-headed cloth dolls into sitting position, though they are too large for the rooms she has built and lean uncomfortably out of the house.

Although no alarm sounds, and the narrative skips the offence itself, it is soon apparent that the boys are going to be punished. Rosie shivers with excitement: 'I know what's going to be their punishment! Can wood go on water? Can cotton?' She grabs the boy dolls and runs into bathroom. She places an old beaker from the shelf in the sink and proceeds to fill it with water. She dunks the first doll head-first. 'That's your punish-*ment*,' she decrees. 'All boys that go into the girls' room get soaked.'

She runs back to her room and hangs the first doll on the washing line, which is still tied between the bunk and the bureau from my last visit. 'They have to hang upside down as part of the punishment.' She runs back into the bathroom to attend to the second boy. Livvy barrels after her. She really wants to soak a doll too and begs to be allowed if another one misbehaves. Rosie is talking to the second doll directly as she hangs him up: 'You know you're not allowed in the girls' room. But why did you go in there? "Because we wanted to see what the punishments were like." Well you got that right haven't you? You have seen what the punishment are like.'

The other part of the punishment, Rosie appends, is that once they've hung for a few weeks the boy dolls will be treated like babies: 'You nappy change them and they sleep in cots and they have bottles of milk, all the things that babies do. It shows them how wrong it is to go into the girls' room.'

The imaginative life of children is full of violence, noted the late psychiatrist Anthony Storr in his monograph, *Human Aggression*. A child's consciousness of its weakness compared with adults compels her to seize on every opportunity to prove her strength. He believed that children need all the aggressive potential they can muster in order to assert their burgeoning individuality. 'One of the unfortunate features of the human condition,' he wrote, 'is that the natural exploratory behaviour of human infants has to be curtailed, especially in conditions of civilisation.' Within all of us, he argued, there must be reserves of repressed aggression that originate from the restrictions of early childhood.

So hostile play offers a fantasy escape in otherwise contained childhoods. 'I think they really do deserve it.' Rosie is brisk and delighted. 'It hasn't been a very good day for them, has it?' She has filled a toy cup with water and is holding it beneath the suspended heads in order to soak the boy dolls more. Rosie doesn't think that she has ever had a punishment. She's never done anything really naughty: 'Not really naughty anyway. Sometimes I used to splash in puddles. No one really noticed that but then I started thinking that I should stop doing it. And that was the only time I felt a little bit bad. But I haven't done anything wrong.'

It's important not to do something wrong. 'Sometimes you can get really bad punishments and sometimes you can get really bad thoughts and they can stay with you for ever and you always think about it and you think "I'd better not do that again" and sometimes you have bad dreams about it.'

The boys' hair needs another soaking. They're getting very, very wet.

A few weeks after that, Rosie is playing in a new bedroom. Moving-day was the weekend before last. It was really good. She took photographs of their old house and their old rooms, and then of their new house and its wide, sloping garden. For Rosie, the whole exercise really did happen in just one day. She's like a vigorous sweet-pea shoot, deftly transplanted to a sunnier bed. Now there's the holiday-camp thrill of sleeping on mattresses with Livvy while her room is being painted. And the joy of a houseful of new furniture arrangements to crouch beneath and hide behind.

Her tour begins in Mum and Dad's room, with a brief, forbidden bounce across their bed. In their bathroom an unattached uplighter lies by the toilet pedestal. You can press it on then off. Rosie and Livvy's bathroom is wider. Livvy's room is messy with torn curls of wallpaper. There's a shelf in the shape of a green caterpillar. 'I think we'll keep the caterpillar,' says Rosie. 'I'll paint it pink.'

She doesn't know who will stay in the spare room. It's for when visitors come. 'And tonight I can't wait because I'm going to sleep there and I'm going to sleep under the table.' There is a broad shelf across one wall, with a skirt of floral material pinned round its edges that reaches to the floor. It creates a cloth cavern where a child might lie concealed. 'I asked Mummy and she said maybe, and then she said maybe again. In the morning Mummy and Daddy will have to open the curtains to wake me up.'

Back in her new room, Rosie presses herself flat into the floor in the gap between the two mattresses. Livvy wants to make herself disappear too. Just the two of them have been together all summer, and their play is becoming fractious now. Rosie straddles her prostrate sister and bounces heavily. 'Are you OK? My little chair.'

'No I'm not!' Livvy shrieks and gurgles, not sure whether to signal pain or pleasure. Their father attends, drawn by the noise. 'Rose, be careful with that, please.'

He extracts the wriggling younger sister, and tempts her downstairs with the offer of chopping vegetables for dinner. Rosie crawls under the orange chair in the corner. Simon put it in the room for Rosie to sit on. Perhaps her older self will. But for now she's more interested in investigating the spaces around it. She tips it over, throwing the seat cover down, to make a tent. Pushing it upright again, she tries to make it rock like rocking-chair. Rosie has never been on a real rocking-chair, but she has been on a rocking-horse.

She switches on the night-light. 'This bulb is really hot.' She holds a piece of cloth over it. 'It's a lamp, isn't it?' she continues knowingly. 'Well maybe if I rub it the genie will come out. It would be pink and I think it should be wearing lovely trousers.'

She scoots out of the room and, somewhere in the half-unpacked packing, finds her dressing-up outfit. She returns resplendent in fuchsia satin pyjama trousers, a pink cropped top with gold coins hanging to the belly, and purple net wings. She is a tidily proportioned creature, her bare tummy retaining a suggestion of toddler roundness. 'This is what I want the genie to be wearing.' She fiddles with her wings. 'I've got some gold curly shoes that go with it.'

And if she had three wishes? 'To live in a big chocolate house with a nice big garden and a marzipan path. The second is that Livvy would never hurt me again and Daddy would never boss me around and I could go anywhere I liked and my last wish would be that I had lots and lots of art things and lots and lots of money.'

She repairs to the bathroom, and comes back with a white hand-towel which she lays down and climbs aboard. It's a magic carpet. 'I can go anywhere I want to because it's my fantasy world and everyone would live in little flower houses and there would be a really nice queen and princess and they would play croquet a lot and the queen would always win because she was very clever and beautiful and the princess wasn't.'

Rosie weaves the stories she's been told into a story to tell: 'And there would be lots of butterflies and they would be called bread-and-butterflies because they would be made out of bread and butter. And there was a children's play area in this world with little tunnels for the children to go through and sometimes there would be little doors and if you went through them there would be a really big room with lots children sitting on steps and they were watching television. And that's where I go on my magic carpet whenever I feel sad.'

Many of the stories that Rosie tells and writes contain a strong element of fantasy. But others, like 'Jenny and her Wonderful Family', explore more everyday relationships. The Swedish sociologist Gunilla Halldén argues that all children's stories are in different ways dealing with the issue of power. In the early 1990s, she collected drawings and stories written on the subject of 'my future family' from children in three towns in Sweden over a two-month period. The resulting narratives showed how children explored positions within the family, and how they made meaning of adulthood and parenthood.

Halldén discovered that the girls created the fictitious family as an arena for female power. The theme of relationships was central, and conflict occurred frequently, usually to be resolved by a girl protagonist. Their main characters were adults in whose hands responsibility for the care of the family rested.

In contrast, boys often failed to identify any adult, or to give them power. They used the family theme to write stories about a life without constraints, and if conflicts did occur they never explained their resolution, although in most cases everyone got what they wanted.

'In omitting the controlling position,' she concluded, 'the boys' stories gave a lot of power to the children. In girls' stories, on the other hand, the mother was the one who kept order and who negotiated and tried to deal with conflicting opinions. In the girls' stories, the children were cared for, but also controlled, by the mother.' So boys and girls explored different gender positions, as well as their own dependency.

The holidays are nearly over, and this autumn Rosie will enter Year 2. 'I have my teacher and she's really, really nice. And we have this really big classroom and Livvy is going into Reception and when we go out into the playground we have to go past Reception.' Year 2 is a bigger year and the work will be harder. They're going to learn about the Great Fire of London.

'Sometimes it's nice to have Livvy around the house, so I think sometimes it's nice to have her around the school and it's just going to be really, really good now that's she's with me all the time.' Sometimes Rosie talks as though her mind is elsewhere. She's not exactly distracted, but keeping a foot in Rosie-world. She's been tying her purple wings round her knees fretfully.

'Sometimes I wonder if Livvy's as stressed as me when I'm doing my work because its already really hard and I think it's going to be even harder in Year 2.' Rosie finds maths hardest. 'Some of the sums have really big numbers and it's really hard because some of the people in my class kept interrupting even though I was trying.' Rosie has strict views about behaviour, and has been unpleasantly surprised by the antics of some of her peers. She adds further detail lest it be thought that she is feigning the difficulty. 'Really, really big numbers, like 103 and 105, and I just didn't find it easy.'

Rosie will be tested nationally for the first time next March. Her father says he's not particularly troubled at the prospect because, as a teacher, he considers the exams valueless. But Rosie senses something coming. As children are denied the opportunity to learn from their own experiences in the outside world, indoors their education has become further regimented.

Priscilla Alderson, professor of childhood studies, told her audience at an Institute of Education centenery lecture: 'Childhood is controlled and confined into child care and education institutions, and surveyed, regulated and tested at unprecedented levels.' Certainly, children in the UK are the most frequently tested in Europe. And, with the government's 'wraparound' breakfast and after-school clubs, some children are at school for longer than the adult limit set down in the EU working-time directive.

Alderson believes that schools reinforce a child-rearing culture of rigid control by following the ethics of the market-place: 'Today's obsession with outcomes is especially oppressive for children when childhood is valued so much for its effects on future adult earning-power, and not for itself.'

Some commentators have greeted the government's five-year plan to extend school hours from 8 a.m. to 6 p.m. gladly, arguing that it will provide poor children with the care and recreational opportunities that the middle classes take for granted. But is a daily ten-hour warehousing of children – while parents' employers are excused from introducing family-friendly working practices – really an advance? Teaching unions have expressed scepticism that sufficient money is earmarked to do more than offer Coke and board-games. And concerns have been raised about privatisation through the back door, as schools have to buy in extra-curricular activities.

It is notable that Rosie preferred to complete at home the tropical island book she designed at school. Her father says that she now prefers to write here, where she colours in her library carefully. Writing at school has become boring to her, he suspects because the teaching has lately been focused towards SATS outcomes.

One Saturday, Rosie is alone in the house with her mother, because Livvy has gone to a birthday party. She's eating a snack of ham and baguette, grapes and half a banana. Simon and Linda have been painting. The house is beginning to feel more like home. Rosie sits on the couch, channel-hopping. Television is compelling. She has written down on a tiny purple clipboard what she likes to watch so she won't forget. She likes *Lilo and Stitch*, *Teen Angel*, *Lizzie MacGuire*, *Big Bang*, and *Sabrina*. TV offers another world of stories, which often happen in American accents.

Livvy has gone to the Wacky Warehouse: 'It's this big house with two really big slides and a ladder and a really big tube and a play area for little children.' Although Rosie has been there on occasion herself, there is still a sense of inequity about this afternoon.

We go to the park. Rosie discharges from her front door like a bullet. There is one road to cross and she jigs on the edge of the pavement, her trajectory disrupted. She runs, skips, bounces to the swings, but this apparatus is too structured for her purposes. Rosie is fortunate: Audit Commission figures suggest that the average child under twelve has a ration of 2.3 square metres of outdoor play space – about the size of a kitchen table. This park is an extension of her domain, full of unassuming places with wild stories attached. There are dangers too. A witch lives behind that wall.

While defending play as an activity involving worthwhile risk, Peter Moss and Pat Petrie of the Institute of Education consider how children develop their own collective social lives which operate alongside the dominant adult culture. Here, play is not a means to an educational end, but 'a central activity . . . what children do, often on the margins of the adult world, making use of the minutes between adult-directed activities for their own purposes.' They echo the work of the anthropologist Erik Erikson, who cautioned adults against defining play as 'not work', arguing that this was to exclude children from an early source of identity.

Noting how children transform and subvert adult cultural forms, Moss and Petrie give the example of how children's maps of familiar areas may give prominence to features that are inconsequential to adults: 'Children use features of school playgrounds intended for other purposes for their own; flights of steps may become jumping apparatuses, castles, alien dens, shops. In a London suburb, a grassed bank, with scrubby trees, runs for a short stretch alongside the pavement . . . For at least seventy years . . . children have scrambled on to the bank and walked behind the trees for a matter of twenty yards and then clambered down again. They have worn a clear, narrow path. This path has no place in adult culture – for adults, paths are usually taken to reach a destination; yet children endow following the path with their own meanings, it is part of their local culture.'

The creation of private spaces, away from adult eyes and sometimes away from other children, is an essential part of childhood culture. The Green Alliance/Demos report also noted that secret or special places, whether hidden at the bottom of the garden or in overgrown parkland, were particularly important to children. They were places for quiet reflection, storytelling and secret discoveries about the natural world. While they were considered to be safe, the unofficial nature of these spaces allowed children to imbue them with their own distinct meaning.

In his book *Solitude*, Anthony Storr makes a compelling case for intimate personal relationships being but one source of health and happiness, arguing that the capacity to be alone is fundamental to creative development. Storr noted that while there has been a great deal of research into children's relationships with their parents and with other children, there is virtually no discussion of whether it is valuable for them to be alone. 'Yet if it is considered desirable to foster the growth of the child's imaginative capacity,' he wrote, 'we should ensure that our children, when they are old enough to enjoy it, are given time and opportunity for solitude. Many creative adults have left accounts of childhood feelings of mystical union with Nature; peculiar states of awareness, or "Intimations of Immortality", as Wordsworth called them . . . We may be sure that such moments do not occur when playing football, but chiefly when the child is on its own.'

Solitude not only fosters creativity, argued Storr, but relates to an individual's capacity to connect with, and make manifest, their own true inner feelings. When the contemporary childhood experience is one of containment and surveillance, what becomes of self-discovery and self-realisation? Without privacy, both physical and psychological, how do children become aware of their deepest needs and impulses?

It may seem odd to talk of surveillance after discussing the lack of collective oversight of children's outdoor pursuits and how that feeds a suspicion of adult strangers. Now friendly adult eyes have been replaced by webcams in nurseries and tracking devices for teenagers, while community surveillance has been superceded by centralised databases.

This intrusion is not at the behest of individual adults. Many parents would be horrified if they were aware of the extent of detailed information recorded in computer databases without any respect for the privacy of the children it relates to. The universal children's database, planned under the Children Act 2004, which was to hold basic details of all under-eighteens, now appears to have been shelved in favour of the National Pupil Database, which is to be updated by a termly school census. It also seems that a number of other databases, held by agencies like Connexions and Sure Start, will be allowed to feed into this national archive. And in January 2006, the government was forced to defend the storage of around 24,000 DNA profiles of children and young people, despite the fact that none had been cautioned, charged or convicted of an offence.

Privacy campaigners are particularly concerned that these databases will include subjective opinions about the behaviour, well-being, and potential criminality of children, as well as basic factual information. At the time of writing, there is no facility allowing pupils or parents an independent adjudication to correct this. The consequences are far-reaching. A toddler who has been identified as aggressive or bullying will carry that prognosis into adulthood. The impact of such intrusion on children's sense of privacy has yet to be investigated.

Rosie swings her legs from a branch of her special tree, rigorously inspecting a wedding party that has spilled from Rushden Hall, a grand old building set in the bosom of the park. She started climbing this tree last year: 'I came to the park with my grandma and I thought it was a good tree and I thought I could build a little fence around it and put a sign round it saying "Rosie's tree". I am going to have a gate in my fence and other people would have to have a special key.'

She spots the bride. She is wearing a russet gown. 'She looks lovely!' says Rosie approvingly. 'I wonder who she's going to marry. But there aren't any children at the wedding, are there? I went to lots and lots of weddings – well, perhaps three weddings – and they all had children. At first I thought that wheelchair was a buggy but it wasn't. I suppose they gave the children to their nannies or grandads.'

'I suppose they are having chicken and peas,' she adds airily, 'because that's what they normally have at weddings. But I'm going to have jelly and cake. And for dessert we'll have biscuits – party rings! But a wedding like that is really boring. Children bring you toys. Grown-ups bring you wineglasses and bottles of beer.' Still outraged at the adult-centricity of the wedding, Rosie remarks: 'Without children this world would be boring; this world would be empty. Because everyone starts off as children and no children means no people.'

If everyone starts off as children, and those children are increasingly confined to school and home, what sort of adults will they grow up to be? The psychiatrist John Bowlby, who studied the mental health of child evacuees after the Second World War, famously described an infant's 'failure of attachment' to a primary care-giver, and the impact that has on the quality of its future relationships. I wonder if annexing children's territory and fencing its borders with fear will result in an extended failure to attach: to other adults, to the environment, to the capacity to be alone.

In examining how children balance risk-taking with self-preservation, psychologists have found that the capacity to take care of oneself is closely associated with self-esteem. The developing child must internalise the conviction that she is a being of value, and that she is worth protecting. But when that development also takes place in an atmosphere of anxiety, containment and surveillance, what else do children internalise?

If a consequence of child-panic is confinement, then a consequence of confinement would seem to be anxious children who are making unrealistic assessments about the dangers posed to them by the outside world. Most to be feared are the constrained and cautious adults that this generation could become.

One thing is certain: watching a wedding without children is not much fun. 'Let's go and have an adventure in my secret tunnel!' Rosie springs from the arms of her tree and scythes through the undergrowth beyond the maintained parkland. A stream runs behind, and the trees along the broken pathway bend to touch fingertips. It smells of growing and decay. She is hidden, while the world is visible. 'I can hear cars and I can see more wedding people. There are lots of ladies in red dresses. There's a dog in that bush.'

After a time, Rosie returns to her arboreal vantage point. 'Livvy thinks you get married when you kiss so she thinks Mummy and Daddy are married again and again every time they kiss. Mummy and Daddy love each other.' She beads the thoughts together relentlessly: 'And I love my ex-boyfriend, James. But he dumped me. So I found a new boyfriend. Sam – he's ten years old. He's at the school Daddy's going to teach at, and his parents are friends with my parents.' Rosie was dumped because she was nagging

James about going on a date and he didn't want to. 'But we're still friends. So that doesn't matter. I'm just planning who I'm going to marry.'

She kicks against the trunk. 'Look no hands! I'm going to get married in fifteen years. It's in April, because one of my best friends is called April, and I was going to have it in January because that's my birthday but then I thought it's going to be very cold.'

There are other places to visit in the park. Rosie wants to sit in the cage – a bench in a brick shelter with high iron bars around it – but it is padlocked. Instead, she poses still like a statue on an empty pedestal by the Hall. There are gaggles of teenagers arranged across the park, and Rosie observes them surreptitiously. Sometimes they call from one group to another on their mobile phones, and sometimes they shout.

Now she has a stitch. It might be telling her to sit down. It has been a golden afternoon, with late light, She chooses to rest on the bench that can be reached by walking round one flowerbed in a particular way. Perhaps the stitch is telling her it's time to go home. Rosie prefers the long way home.

But on the short way she discovers a huge tree branch, as long as two of her, which she drags along with all her strength until she's exhausted. In the midst of this effort she backs into some nettles and stings her calves. She can't find any dock leaves. Rubbing her ankle, she picks off a smaller twig from the branch. She will take that home instead and label it to remember this day for ever.

Lois

'A snap is what families take, when things are just happening. A photograph makes people think.'

It's Saturday lunch-time, after swimming, at the kitchen table. 'By the way,' says Lois, working her jaw, 'if you want to know why I'm eating strangely, I'm pretending to be a giraffe.' Lois is having pasta. Pasta makes you faster. Her brother Kester is banging round his mother's legs as she stands by the stove. Today is one of those days when it's hard to make a decision. Does he want cheese? 'Uh, 50-50, I want to phone a friend, I don't really know!' Lois and Kester used to fight a lot more than they do now, though they still support different football teams.

Lois is almost into double figures. She lives in a long, slim house in London, with Kester, her father Damian, and her mother Sue. She loves Manchester United, and still misses her grandmother, who died a long time ago. Lois doesn't approve of skirts. She likes to wear T-shirts and jeans and she ties her long hair back at the nape of her neck.

She is medium height in her class and lean, her body braced for the stretch into adolescence, with nothing to spare. Her voice is lower than you expect it to be. When Lois grows up she might be an artist, or a runner, or a footballer, or a detective. Or a photographer, because both her parents are photographers and, basically, so are all their friends.

She is looking through a selection of her mother's prints, and comes across a photograph of a child's face in close-up. Lois's own face, at the age of two and a half. This, says her mother, is the record of when Lois first said, 'Take a picture of me now.'

Her features must have still been setting in the clay soft-ness of her toddler skin. But in the shutter instant they have been fired firm. As she comes towards the lens her gaze is steadfast and searching, thrown out beyond the frame and into the world. She seems to be moving most sure-footedly towards life.

'I was two and a half!' Lois shrieks. 'I look about a million! Some of these pictures I think, "That was me?" It's really weird. It feels like another person.' Her mum has been doing proper photos since she was two or three. She can remember what was happening when she took them, but can't always remem-ber what age she was. 'Sometimes I'll say to her, "this is quite interesting," or, "this is interesting light, take a photo," like there's one of me feeding my leg, and stuff like that. But she decides how, because she is a photographer so she does know best.'

Most of the pictures Lois likes are half in darkness, half in light. 'Like the picture of me hugging my dad. It's like heaven and hell.' She likes the ones that remind her of some happy time. 'I don't know if they remind older people of being little. Say there was a picture of Tintin it might remind them of watching Tintin and that might make them think.' And when she has grown up? 'I think they'll remind me of all the things I liked and all the things I didn't like, and what happened. It's probably hard to remember as you get older.'

Lois knows that strangers see her photographs in exhibitions, and she doesn't mind it. There's a difference between a photograph and a snap and, it would seem, the potential for exposure in each. 'A snap is what families take, when things are just happening. A photograph makes people think. Like there was this one with a clock and a face, and the message was "Don't waste your life".'

Sue uses other models too. But much of her work concerns her daughter. She says she wants her art to ask questions about childhood. As a mother she asks questions of herself. Theirs is a working relationship that is continually evolving, she adds. She is Lois's mother first, her chronicler second. The photographs happen in the gaps between the scheduled significances and unexpected dramas of growing up, between the birthday party and the bloody nose. They show still moments – once tears are dried, comfort administered, explanation offered. So in pictures, Lois clutches a cup of tea, a bruise blooming under one eye, having caught her face on the side of a table. Lois folds her arms fiercely in a blue bikini, after an annoying swimming lesson. Lois stares past the crusts she hasn't eaten (nobody wants curly hair). She is also a girl with a mighty ability for pitching herself into her own thoughts. A number of the images have been taken while she is elsewhere, looking out of the window, or into water, her back curved in concentration.

In fashioning this portfolio of progress, Sue insists that the act of photographing does not intrude on their relationship: 'I started taking the pictures when she was little because I thought she was wonderful and I really enjoyed her and the way she was with herself. But it is a very small part of what goes on between us. We spend most of our time doing other things.'

'The question of privacy doesn't come at the time I take them,' she explains. 'It comes when I start to select them. She reached a certain age where she would say, "I don't want that to be shown." But it's fine between us [that I've witnessed and documented the moment]. It's not a question of whether the photograph should have been taken, it's a question of whether it should be made public.'

At the very base of fears for and of our children is the ideal of childhood innocence, and the terror of what might stem from its corruption. It is images of children that have always made this ideal flesh.

From the inception of the Romantic ideal of childhood, mainstream media has craved, promoted and fetished images of innocence. The form has developed – from eighteenth-century portraiture by Reynolds, Mills and Gainsborough; through the mass-marketed illustrations of Kate Greenaway and Cicely Mary Barker; to cutesy Athena baby posters and toddler advertising. But the substance has sustained. These bodies are physically attractive, but not to be sexually desired. And these creatures inhabit a space that is not only the necessary past of every adult, but a collective past to be viewed with nostalgia and a sense of loss for what may never be returned to.

Images of children rarely reveal the reality of child-hood. Although the most popular commercial images of childhood today are photographs, they do not portray real children. Instead, these images exist to sell, to entertain, and to reinforce fantasies. Adults crave the spectacle of innocence precisely because of what it does not show: the rawness of sexuality, the inexorability of change, the certainty of death.

Consequently, there is nothing so resonant and nowadays, in the case of images of naked children, so dangerous. The recent proliferation of accessible child pornography subverts in the most obscene fashion the pleasure that adults derive from looking at children. It need not be a guilty pleasure to enjoy an image of a child. But we are all culpable if, in censoring this one gratification, we conveniently ignore the locus of adult pleasures that genuinely damage children.

Because here we can see quite clearly how our fears about childhood can divert attention away from genuine threats to children. We have reached a point in public life where the paedophile sets the standard for all of us. And yet, in terms of social policy, we have barely begun to negotiate their existence. For too many, sexual abuse is a reality of childhood. For all our adult looking, we do not see how this might be made otherwise.

In the spring of 2004, Sue Andrews exhibited a series of photographs of Lois alongside the work of an American photographer called Betsy Schneider at the Spitz Gallery in London. Schneider displayed a series of shots of her five-year-old daughter Madeleine which formed part of a project that she has been working on since the child's birth. The photographs, taken daily and then arranged into nine-week blocks, show the child full-length and facing the camera, in whatever corner of the family home she's been caught that week. In almost every frame, Madeleine is completely naked. 'I wanted to show how the body changes over time,' Schneider explained later in an interview. 'I also wanted to record the incidental changes which happen day to day: their cuts and bruises, dirt, drawings on themselves, temporary tattoos and sunburn. With clothes on, the work would have been more about what they wore each day.'

But we all know about the kind of people who are interested in children's naked bodies. A minor scandal ensued. On the day of opening, gallery staff expressed concern about the pornographic potential of Schneider's work. A rumour circulated that a seedy-looking man had been spotted photographing the nude images. The exhibition was immediately closed and advice sought from the police. It later reopened, but with the offending display removed.

Schneider, a former assistant to Sally Mann, whose own photographs of her children have in their time prompted controversy, became the subject of an unpleasant tabloid campaign. Back in Arizona, her family were doorstepped. The *Sun* newspaper printed a shot of Madeleine next to an image taken from a child-porn website under the headline: 'Can you tell the difference?' A few days later, the same paper claimed that paedophiles had 'used mobile camera phones to snap full-frontal images of tot Madeleine Schneider' and uploaded the photographs on to the Internet.

Elsewhere, reactions were less sledgehammer but no less critical. Schneider was mocked for her naivety. Given the global climate of hyper-concern about child pornography, had she not considered for a moment that some people might find her photographs offensive? What about her child's privacy? Her defence that she always discussed her work with her – five-year-old – daughter was sneered at.

Given the furore, it's fortunate that Sue Andrews doesn't always take Lois's advice. She had wanted her mother to include in her contribution to the exhibition a photograph of her standing naked on a beach. In the image that Sue left out, Lois stands nude in the foreground, shading her eyes from the sun, pulling her lips into a grimace the better to show the recent loss of a front tooth. The shot halts just below her belly button. In the middle ground, a number of other figures paddle on the shoreline. They are blurred but clearly naked too. It was taken in Devon, on the day after Lois's family met to scatter her grandmother's ashes at St Ives. It was a hot day and, not having thought to bring costumes, the group decided to strip and swim.

When Lois shows me this photograph she examines it

carefully. 'It should be cropped a little bit higher, above the tummy button.' Lois was six when it was taken, four years ago. 'We just decided to take our clothes off because we wanted to play around on the beach. It didn't feel funny stripping – it felt normal.'

Would it feel different now to be photographed like that? 'Yeah. But I don't know the difference between then and now.' Is it because the way that she feels about her body has changed? She thinks carefully. 'It's like the story of Adam and Eve, when they eat from the tree of knowledge. They already knew they were naked, but then they got embarrassed.'

A week later, Lois is sitting outside at the round patio table, alert for pollen falling in her tea. She wears a purple sweatshirt and jeans. This is how she has changed over the past year. When she was nearly nine, her hair was shorter, and she was probably drinking orange juice instead of cranberry and raspberry. Next Sunday, Lois will turn ten. Sometimes it feels different. She's looking forward to it, because she's going to be a two-digit number.

Her sixteen-year-old cousin has been visiting. She's very, very grown up. She wears miniskirts, and likes pink. She has this boyfriend called Charles. He collected her and went on the train with her. But in some ways she was quite childish, like she enjoyed burping.

It's hard to tell whether sixteen is old or young to have a boyfriend. 'I saw these people on TV and they looked about my age but they had boyfriends and that was really weird. No one in my class has one. This girl in my old school said, "I just divorced my husband", and he was fourteen and she was eight. It was quite funny but of course I didn't believe her.'

Her cousin is different to the girly girls in Lois's class at school. 'They're really extreme. They're trying to be like teenagers and they're really mature.' She treats the word suspiciously. 'They wear things off the shoulder, and have handbags as schoolbags. My friend Amy asked one of them, "Why are you so mature? You should enjoy being a kid." And she goes, "It's not my fault you're stupid." And Amy goes, "All we're trying to do is be a kid. I don't want to be older than I really am." But that's what girls in my class do.'

Lois can't imagine being twenty or an adult. 'Adults have to look after younger people. I just like being a child because you can do whatever you like really. Not *whatever* you like. You can't drive a car, you can't smoke, but you can't do much funner things when you're an adult. You can get a job but that isn't really fun, apart from if you like it. I wouldn't like to be at an age when I could smoke because I don't think people should smoke. And you can go to jail. You can't as a child before you're ten. And then you go to children's jail.'

Lois used to like dressing up, but now she's a tomboy. 'Personally I think I'm ugly, but I don't care how I look at all,' she declares. 'I get these shadows under my eyes I really don't like. On other people I can't see them but on me they stand out.' Curiously, Lois doesn't think she looks ugly in her mother's photographs: 'It's just different.' She does look different on a gallery wall. In life, Lois is busy trying out who to be. On film, that stare cuts cleanly through all the awkward guises and poses and they fall away.

'If I look really bad in photographs I do mind. But I don't normally.' Really bad is hard to define. It's not the same as how she looked in the camera fight she had with her cousin, where they snapped each other wearing silly faces. 'That was funny. But if I look really tired that will remind me of being

57

really tired, and that just makes me feel weird. Like on *Holby City* when someone's having a heart attack, if their chest hurts then your chest starts to hurt.'

Lois doesn't think it's important to be pretty, and being pretty is associated with the girly girls, of whom she is not one. 'I don't really care. I just think, "Have a fun time." Normally if I look in the mirror and I don't look right I don't care because I can't be *bothered* to make myself look right.' It's not about the way that people look in magazines, she says. It's more about brushing your hair.

Lois says that she always looks really serious in her mother's photographs. It's true that she's seldom smiling, more often shown drifting off into contemplation. And when she does confront the camera it is with that serrated stare. In another image, one of the few to include her brother Kester, they stand side by side in football kit at the edge of a pitch. Lois has her arms by her side, fists stretching her cuffs; Kester is touching his tummy, the place where his hands often rest in life. They look wary. 'The one of me and my brother, I heard someone say it reminded them of Holly and Jessica because they were wearing their football shirts, but Kester was wearing an Arsenal shirt. Also it's two girls about the same height and they weren't sisters. I'd seen it on the news and I was very interested, because it said on the news once: "Why those two people? They were once innocent little babies." I always think of that when I think of someone evil, they used to be babies. Maybe they've had a really sad life.'

The photograph of Holly Wells and Jessica Chapman, posing in their Manchester United shirts hours before their disappearance, has become instantly recognisable across the world. It was one of many released during that torpid summer fortnight before their bodies were found: holiday snaps of Jessica, posing with feigned languor, cropped top riding up over slim tummy; bright, blonde Holly, grinning wide and toothy, a little Marilyn. There was an appetite for the onslaught of imagery that followed their disappearance and it went beyond any altruistic desire to assist the police investigation. The public feasted on the family albums of the nearly dead girls. They confirmed what tragedy, and what childhood, ought to look like.

Western culture has been looking at children for centuries, in particular since the Enlightenment heralded a rejection of the Augustinian doctrine of original sin and infant depravity. Phillipe Ariès based much of his thesis that childhood existed as a distinct stage only from the seventeenth century on contemporary images of children. He argued that prior to this time the young were solely depicted as miniature adults, or in biblical or mythic contexts, as the Child of the Madonna or as cherubim.

Critics of Ariès have noted that only aristocratic children were thus portrayed, and that often their depiction in mature finery was related to future marriage arrangements. Portrait painters were commissioned to indicate a child's potential power and wealth in order to achieve a good match. It has also been suggested that the change in the way that children were painted was due to a new emphasis on physical realism in art. But what is clear is that, as the idea of childhood transformed, images of children made that manifest.

By the eighteenth century, portrait artists such as Sir Joshua Reynolds, Thomas Gainsborough and Sir John Everett Millais were bringing their craft to bear on the visual representation of childhood innocence. Even then, the images were equivocal, drawing out the desirability of those who were thought to be unconscious of desire. Millais's

Cherry Ripe, for example, portrayed young Edie Ramage in an ill-fitting, adult-styled dress, her gloved hands neatly pressed between her legs and towards her vulva, eyes at once appearing hazy with adult satisfaction and widened in childish ignorance.

While many of those artists dismissed their efforts as genre painting, the market for child portraiture was expanding, as the middle classes took to the form. By the end of the nineteenth century, their paintings had entered the mass-media market, with portraits like *Cherry Ripe* being reproduced in popular magazines. Another Millais painting, *Bubbles*, which captured a dreamy boy dressed in a velvet jacket and knickerbockers, appeared on Pears Soap advertisements.

The appetite for commercial publication of images of children was growing, and illustrations of innocence began to be mass-produced. The artist Kate Greenaway became renowned for her watercolour depictions of children, which first appeared on greeting cards. Mabel Lucie Atwell designed a whole host of child-related products, from posters to handkerchiefs. Cicely Mary Barker, creator of the Flower Fairies, became a sensation with her first set of postcards, drawn when she was only fifteen. The advent of photography further democratised the genre, eventually allowing adults to make images of their own children.

The Romantic poets, particularly Blake and Wordsworth, are believed to have greatly influenced Charles Dodgson, the celebrated photographer of children who, under the pen-name Lewis Carroll, wrote the Alice books.

Dodgson was fascinated to the point of obsession with what he termed 'child nature'. From 1856, when he purchased his first camera, he embraced the developing art-form as a means not only to achieve proximity to children, but to capture their essence. Over the next two decades he took hundreds of photographs of children, some classic portraits, some featuring props and costumes, and others naked.

This devoted amateur became one of the finest photographers of children of his age. 'Child photographic portraiture was still in its infancy,' notes Dodgson's biographer Morton N. Cohen, 'and he showed the way to capture innocence and youthful bloom. Not even [Julia Margaret] Cameron's photographs of children challenged Charles's superior art. His studies of children reached the apex of the genre in the earliest days of photography and retain their authority today.'

Dodgson's pursuit of intimate friendships with children, in particular with beautiful young girls, has latterly been the subject of unfavourable speculation. Perhaps it was the case, as Virginia Woolf wrote of him, that at the core of his being was 'a hard block of pure childhood [that] starved the mature man of nourishment'.

In *Child-loving: The Erotic Child and Victorian Culture*, James R. Kincaid revisits Victorian images of children, including those taken by Charles Dodgson. He suggests that their latent sexuality was a function of the way that innocence itself had become desirable, at a time when adults and children were thought to be separated by one's corruption and the other's purity. By continuing vociferously to deny children any sexual feelings, he argues, contemporary society similarly eroticises them.

Kincaid believes that, because we won't acknowledge any collective involvement in sexualising children, 'a form of allowable cultural pornography' has developed – the best-selling memoirs of abusive upbringings, the fictional renderings, the titillating media coverage of paedophiles. 'Such frenzied denunciations of the villains, such easy expressions of outrage, such simple-minded analyses of the problem of child-molesting as we love to repeat serve not simply to flatter us but to bring us once again the same story of desire that is itself desirable, allowing us to construct, watch, enjoy the erotic child without taking any responsibility for our actions.'

Childhood, André Breton once observed, is the only reality. And it was photography's claim to realism to which Charles Dodgson deferred when he insisted that his pictures of 'child friends' – including those *sans habillement*, as he put it – were in essence innocent. As he wrote in a letter to the mother of two sisters he photographed naked, posing as castaways: 'Their innocent unconsciousness is very beautiful, and gives one a feeling of reverence, as at the presence of something sacred.' And so it is that images of children often manufacture a reality of childhood that only exists in adult fantasy.

Sometimes Lois remembers images instead of realities. When her grandmother died, at first she found it easier to remember the photographs that Sue had taken of her mother when she was dying, rather than the living woman. 'Now I can kind of remember what she looked like, but I remember the photographs too. She had white hair. She was really tall for me and most of the time I saw her knees because I was a baby.'

Lois's room has an elevated bed, with a desk space underneath it. It's cosy like a cave, and thronged with stickers and drawings. There are cat ornaments everywhere. They all belonged to Lois's Granny Cats, her mother's mother. 'We called her Granny Cats because she loved cats. She had about nine.' Lois quite likes cats but she doesn't have a favourite animal. Granny Cats died when Lois was four. 'It probably takes a year to get used to it. I still think about her a lot, and I still cry about her. When she died, I felt like it was everyone else's fault.'

The night before her grandmother's funeral, Lois was bouncing on her mother's bed. She fell and cracked her eye socket on the bedpost. The swelling grew large and livid. At one point her eye went red. The injury has left a tiny dent below her right eye that you only notice if you know to look for it. The death and the mourning, the fall and the healing, are documented in a series of photographs. In Lois's mind's eye they are the same.

She keeps the cats because her granny gave them to her. She will never throw away anything that her granny gave her, even if she's grown out of it. She spreads open the *Animal Did-You-Know?* book she made on the floor of her room. They're not her best drawings, though. She just did them really roughly. There's a penguin, koala, grizzly bear, giant panda, lion – which she did really, really roughly – and a fox. Lois designed one for the mosaic in the community garden at the end of her road. Kester designed a rabbit, which sits calmly beneath Lois's leaping effort. They once had a real rabbit as a pet, but it died of scaredness when a real fox got into the garden one morning.

Lois likes to keep diaries, but her new one has practically nothing in it. This entry is from her first diary: 'It was my mum's birthday. I went to the hairdresser, then we went to Jane's house on the train. Here is my ticket.' She reads out an experiment she tried: 'Babies find it hard to write so I tried writing with my foot. Do you think it feels the same for babies if they write by hand and we write by foot?' She translates the scrawls below: 'My name is Lois. I am nine years old. Hello. This is me writing with my right foot. This is me writing with my left foot.' The transition from babyhood – which, for Lois, ends at four when her grandmother died – into childhood is a recurring subject of speculation. Innocent babies are spoken of indulgently, even the baby who becomes a murderer. And emergence from babyhood feels like a challenge well met, in contrast to the snare-strewn path through adolescence.

She takes another diary outside into the garden. It's a sunny afternoon. Her mother gives her a bowl of chopped-up orange and grapes. She doesn't like orange but, when she was in infant school, she would rub a piece of apple against a piece of orange and the apple would taste really nice. Lois reads on: 'Bank Holiday Monday. It's not fair. I have to wear a T-shirt that says "Girls Rule".' She adopts a prissy voice. 'It's not like I'm a girly girl. I'm a tomboy. In the summer holidays I'm going to Spain—' she laughs, '—I've written Spair – so I'm going to get my real passport. We're supposed to be going to Cambridge today, but Dad has lost his wallet so we might not go. YES! But if we don't go I hope he finds his wallet.' This is Top Secret.

'26 May 2003. This is really bad. My dad can't find his wallet. The day he lost it he went to the fair. Someone could have stolen it and used his credit cards. If he cancels them it will take ages to get it back, and he lost it on Friday so someone will have already used it. If he finds it I will write back . . .

'He found it! Today we went to Lee Valley Park Farm and Mum bought me a sheep called Bleet and Kester a pig called Max.'

Later, Lois takes a walk down her street to the community garden. She is wondering how trees know only to grow one ring in their trunk each year. On the way she spots a snail shell. Once there was something on the ground and it was a syringe and there might have been drugs in it. She's not allowed to play in the street on her own, because of cars, but not because of strangers. 'I know this is a weird thing to say but not many strangers come down our road.'

On the walk back, she finds a ladybird on a wall, and

coaxes it on to her finger. It runs quickly across the plain of her palm and she has to move hand over hand over hand in order to give it enough surface area. When she gets back to the house, Kester wants to hold it too. She lets him. Lois and Sue make their photographs in the gaps between the 'smile' moments. 'All of us experience difficulties growing up,' says Sue, 'and that's natural and part of it. Not representing them seemed very strange to me. It made the difficult moments seem even bigger because they were things you couldn't look at or talk about.'

It is just those 'smile moments' that pervade commercially today. But there is another style of image that pillages the viewer's interior sense of what childhood ought to look like. Photojournalism is adept at using children to tell the story of collective suffering, from the bulbous-bellied infants of the Ethiopian famine to the desolate orphans of the Asian tsunami. And, while these pictures are far removed from the Romantic vision of childhood, they share with it an understanding of adults' desire for innocence, and their vested interest in preserving it.

Sometimes, one image of a child can sum up an entire disaster. The shot of nine-year-old Kim Phuc, photographed naked and burning as she ran from a napalm attack on her Vietnamese village in 1972, is now genuinely iconic. Phuc spoke as an adult of how she had later felt exploited as an anti-American propaganda tool by her government, before she fled to Canada: 'I realised that the picture is a really powerful tool to promote peace and that in a free country I could control the picture, rather than being controlled by it.' She now works as a UNESCO goodwill ambassador and runs a foundation supporting child victims of war.

Phuc survived, unlike Mohammed al-Durra, the twelve-year-old killed by Israeli bullets as he crouched with his father behind a metal drum in Gaza City in 2002. His death was charted in a series of shocking stills that circulated round the world. Venerated as the first child martyr of the second intifada, his photograph still appears on posters across the occupied territories.

Perhaps most memorable in recent times are the images of Ali Ismail Abbas, who became the child face of the second Iraq war. In April 2003, during the final, frenzied days of Saddam Hussein's regime, Samia Nakhoul, the Gulf bureau chief of Reuters news agency, was visiting Al Kindi hospital in downtown Baghdad with her photographer. The place was swamped with casualties from the coalition bombing campaign that was devastating the capital. Nakhoul asked a nurse to show her the worst case they had received, she recalled later. She was led into a side room. There, a woman was keeping vigil by a low bed where a young boy lay under a curved metal cage. His head was thickly bandaged; both his arms had been roughly amputated at the shoulder. His torso was horrifically burnt, the remaining skin crisped darkly around exposed and weeping flesh.

Nakhoul learnt that twelve-year-old Ali had been asleep when an American missile hit his house, killing his father and pregnant mother, and fourteen other members of his family. He implored the journalist: 'Will you help me get my arms back? If I don't get my arms back, I will commit suicide. I wanted to be an army officer when I grow up, but not any more. Now I want to be a doctor – but how can I? I don't have hands. What can I do?'

The following day, almost every British newspaper, as well as many others around the world, carried Ali's pleas alongside his agonised image. An unedifying scrum ensued around his hospital bed, as reporters clamoured for further heart-breaking soundbites. Within days, four British newspapers had launched separate fundraising appeals, and when he was finally airlifted to Kuwait, it was reported to have been authorised following a personal intervention by the British Prime Minister Tony Blair.

Still it is impossible to unravel why it was Ali in particular, of all the children horrifically maimed during the conflict, who generated such a powerful response. His injuries were catastrophic. He was a beautiful and articulate victim. He was not the only one. But a concatenation of circumstances suddenly placed him at the very top of the hierarchy of suffering.

In her book *Compassion Fatigue: How the media sells disease, famine, war and death*, what journalism professor Susan Moeller writes about starving children might also be applied to Ali: 'An emaciated child isn't yet associated with the stereotypes attached to its colour, culture or political environment. They personify innocence abused. They bring moral clarity to the complex story of famine. Their images cut through the social, economic and political context to create an imperative statement.'

Children like Ali offer the opportunity to tell a story – perhaps even one with a happy ending – in a context where no straight narrative exists. It is a story that prompts feelings rather than thoughts, which can be a relief when the political circumstances are intractable. The newspaper appeals on his behalf were hugely lucrative, raising hundreds of thousands of pounds. Those donors witnessed the corruption of childhood innocence, and they acted upon it. In doing so, they took up a moral position that is far from clear. Because it is only the children who are arbitrarily deemed blameless for whom sympathy is felt.

In the occupied territories, for example, the brutalising effects of the second intifada on children have reached far beyond malnutrition, loss of education and family breakdown. Before the Israeli Army's disengagement in 2005, the Gaza mental health programme believed that the majority of local youngsters were suffering emotional problems as a result of the conflict. In early childhood, this manifested in speech disorders, bedwetting or uncontrollable crying. But as the children grew older, their fear and distress distorted into rage. They displayed far higher levels of aggression than their peers brought up in peaceful environments.

In a place where ordinary dreams withered, children aspired to martyring themselves for the cause. Play mimicked the activities of the Palestinian fighters. Throwing homemade bombs at Israeli troops became a rite of passage. And, in displaying too much knowledge, and insufficient innocence, those young people crossed the Rubicon, turning from children we feared for into children we were afraid of. Similarly, had 'Little Ali' lost his arms in an Iraqi resistance attack on Western troops, the donations would not have been forthcoming. Images of childhood are appealing because of what adults project upon them. A child who is an active subject is impervious to projection, denying the fantasy.

Lois remembers the Ali photographs vividly, and describes his injuries with mild relish. 'His family had died and he was lucky to be alive but he actually wanted to be dead,' she recalls. 'I think that was because all of his family had gone and he felt really upset so he thought, "There's no point in being alive if I'm really upset." I felt sorry for him because I thought I'm lucky to have a family. I think he was going to get some plastic arms in London.'

*   *   *

On the morning of her tenth birthday, Lois woke at a quarter to seven, though she wasn't supposed to get up until half past eight. She's wearing the stripey dungarees that her parents gave her. They bought her a Red Hot Chilli Peppers CD too. She's been to Sainsbury's to choose a cake, a scarlet-iced dragon with a thick body curving round a treasure of bright lollies. Her auntie and uncle sent fifteen pounds, instead of the normal ten, because today she's a two-digit number. She got a lava lamp from her brother, though it was actually her mum who chose it for him. Time is moving more slowly than normal. On a day that's been thought about and waited for so intently, how can there ever be enough of the now to fill up the minutes? It's a day that feels ever so slightly precarious. If something were to go wrong, as all manner of things might, would it spoil everything?

Grace calls. Grace is Lois's best friend, but she moved away to Devon. There is a photograph of the two of them in her mother's portfolio, arms around one another, heads bent exclusively. 'I'm wearing her clothes and she's wearing mine. They used to call me Grace and her Lois, and they used to say, "You're sisters right?" No-o-o-o [we'd say]. "So you must be cousins." No-o-o-o. "But you look so alike." But I think we look very, very different.'

They chat a little awkwardly. Lois is distracted. Then Grace asks her what she wants for her birthday. 'Mum, what do I like?' she calls. Lois asks this often, whether it's about pasta sauces or presents. There's comfort in someone else having your needs listed in their head. Sue always starts off by saying that she doesn't know. But Lois is certain that really she does.

When she comes off the phone she explains that she didn't actually expect Grace to give her anything. 'She lives such a long way away that the post would probably cost quite a lot.'

Someone else has given her a card-making kit, with stick-on beads and shells. Lois examines it as carefully as she does all her gifts, and starts about making Grace a card of herself, wearing her new dungarees. She fiddles in her mouth. This morning, she woke up with a wobbly tooth as well as a birthday.

Last week, the Easter holidays ended and Lois went back to school. 'I was quite excited in some ways, because I saw all my friends, but we could just have lots of sleepovers instead.' The last sleepover Lois went to, she had only half an hour's sleep. 'Normally we play Xbox, Xbox, Xbox, mess up each other's beds, eat sweets secretly, Xbox, Xbox, Xbox.'

Lois is in her final year at primary school. Sometimes school is boring and sometimes it's really exciting. 'I don't think they pressure you enough. I'd like it more if they pressured you. You can't work when they say, "If you get really high marks it doesn't matter, it's just different people." She mimics a trendy teacher. Lois tries out lots of different voices and she's very good at them. 'At my old school I got pressured more. This school is much more comfortable.' Unlike Rosie, Lois revels in competition.

Her party friends Sotira, Nicky and Amber arrive all at once, bringing parents and presents. The next stage of the day begins. The girls jostle round her, examining each other and each others' gifts, touching, pushing, snatching, laughing. Lois has known Nicky since she was two and a half. 'She gives me teddy-bear huggles now and again and she squeezes the breath out of me.' Now Nicky wants to hold the puppy that Amber has given Lois. The puppy's fur is very soft and Lois scrunches it into her face, breathing through the bobbly pile. She can hold it once Lois has written a name on the collar. Nicky creeps up to tug it away. Lois shrieks.

Nicky runs down the garden. Amber says she has one just like it except it's a golden retriever.

After lunch at the café in Highgate Woods, Lois thinks she feels phlegmy. Perhaps it's because it's such a hot day. She's been worrying about getting ill for her birthday all week. The girls run across to the playground, but on the way Lois trips over and makes grass stains on the knees of her new dungarees. She cries quickly, briefly. Everything is too much. She wanted to wear them tomorrow and now she can't.

Sue says she might be able to get the stains out overnight, but Lois still doesn't want to go on any of the climbing frames. It's too busy in the playground anyway. It's time to go home and watch the video that she chose. On the walk back to the car, the girls swing downhill arm in arm, poking and hugging each other. They talk about living in different countries, football teams, and brothers and sisters. Amber likes being an only child. Her sibling is her cat. You can actually feel really close to animals.

Next weekend, Lois is the only girl at football practice. She wears a professional strip. She runs with her elbows out to take up more space, but she's still slighter than the smallest of the boys. Nobody will pass to her. Her team loses.

Back at home, she takes her tea in the Manchester United mug that Grace sent her for her birthday. She is righteously indignant at her treatment on the pitch. 'Loads of people said I was rubbish and they kept shouting at me to run up the pitch when they'd said I was in defence. I couldn't score because they never pass to me. This boy said I was rubbish and then a second later someone passed to him and he was about an inch from the goal and he couldn't score.' She takes a lolly from the bowl of sweets left over from her birthday cake.

Boys are rude about girls who play football because they don't know any better. 'Arsenal girls team is actually the best in the world, but all the professionals are men so they think that girls can't play. Girls football is much bigger in America.' She knows that from the film *Bend It Like Beckham*.

This week, she has been looking through her mother's portfolio again. There are some exquisite images of Lois taken in the shower. Wet hair flat against her scalp, a welter of possibilities contained in her slick limbs, she could be boy, girl or amphibian. In one, a droplet of water hangs from her earlobe like an earring. She is naked, obviously, though not shown below the chest. As a viewer, you want to wrap her in a towel and keep her in this charmed moment. You know that she will slip through your fingers, down the drain, and out into the ocean.

Can Lois see a link between these photographs and the ones of Madeleine Schneider that caused so much trouble at the gallery? Lois says she wouldn't like to be in a newspaper with people writing nasty things about her. She worries that Madeleine might have felt ashamed of the photographs afterwards, or ashamed of herself.

'I'm actually copying this from mum a bit but I think [Betsy's] pictures are a bit cold and in other pictures children are naked but they're really warm loving pictures and I think it's the same [with the ones of me]. But Betsy didn't make Madeleine take her clothes off and it's the same here.'

Lois says she doesn't really think about strangers looking at her photographs. Basically, photographs are fine so long as the person being photographed is fine. How would she feel if her mother had tried a project like that with her? 'Weird, but she wouldn't have done that,' she says confidently.

Of course, Sue can only insist that she is not taking advantage of her daughter, or their intimacy. 'She's not a grown-up and she doesn't understand all the implications. So all I can do is respond to what she feels comfortable with, and hope that I'm looking at things that are worth looking at.'

Not only through design but also through circumstance, Sue takes the pictures that fall outside the parameters of family snaps. 'When I'm at her birthday party, because I'm organising it, I'm not the person taking pictures. I deliberately started thinking about the pictures that aren't in family albums.'

Photography, Susan Sontag once observed, does queer things to our sense of time. Before the advent of the camera, the vast majority – those who could not afford to commission portraits – had no record of what they looked like as children. 'To be able to see oneself and one's parents as children is an experience unique to our time. The camera has brought people a new, and essentially pathetic, relation to themselves, to their physical appearance, to aging, to their own mortality.'

But family photographs do not only exist as a faithful record of time passing. Many of the most typical scenes tell fibs. The beaming group around the turkey will be bickering by plum pudding. Picnics don't only happen when the weather is dry. It isn't natural for everyone to be looking in the same direction at the same moment. Family albums keep secrets, and weave staged episodes into a true story. You could buy one at a jumble sale and invent a whole new history for yourself.

Since the camera became affordable to all, photographs have emerged as the dominant record of family life. People describe their favourites snaps as 'irreplaceable', as though they were memories themselves, rather than images of remembered events. As Roland Barthes argues in his book *Camera Lucida*: 'Not only is the photograph never, in essence, a

73

memory . . . but it actually blocks memory, quickly becomes a counter-memory.'

And it is through this simulacra of memory that we use photography to create an ideal image of family, and of childhood. With film and iPhoto, we shuffle reality and lay down what fits best with who we want to be. Memories are made, not experienced. When we enclose snapshots of our children in Christmas cards we are reinforcing the positive domestic identity that we want the world to see. Implicit in the criticism of photographers like Betsy Schneider whose work pertains to the domestic is a sense of betrayal. In subverting the genre, they are exposing this daily manufacture of memories, revealing the unreality of the reality that families so carefully construct.

The American photographer Sally Mann is probably the most celebrated – and most controversial – of the photographer-parents who have introduced their children to the public gaze. For Mann, the home is not a protected place. It is the private realm that renders us most vulnerable, the potential for violation, injury or death stalking every frame. The presence of an adult offers little protection, indeed the position of the parent seems to be largely one of impotent onlooking.

The nudity in Mann's work is equivocally sexual. Her daughter Jessie at the age of five is photographed in rouge and lipstick, hips cocked, her chest naked but for a string of pearls. In another image, Jessie is asleep on a sheetless mattress, fully naked this time, legs splayed, with a stain blooming wetly at their join.

The art historian Anne Higonnet believes that Mann's work has aroused controversy precisely because it deals with aspects of the child's body that the Romantic idealisation of childhood sought to deny. In her book *Pictures of Innocence* she argues that Mann's photographs participate in 'a widespread revision of childhood which is not at all exclusively about sexuality . . . One of its principal differences from Romantic childhood is precisely that it refuses to treat the child's body only in terms of its sexuality, or lack thereof. Childhood now appears to be embodied in many ways.'

But regardless of artistic attempts to expand the definition of what childhood can look like, it seems that society has now reached a point where images of naked children are viewed only through a sexual filter and where, in strict legal terms, one definition of obscenity is youthful nudity. As Higonnet notes, '[T]he only reality a camera can record is light bouncing off surfaces. Knowledge supplies the rest. And perhaps the least reliable knowledge of all is sexual.'

Images of naked children have never been more scrupulously monitored. While adult nudity is unsensational these days, barely meriting comment, in the case of children it is the notional paedophile who dictates what we may look at. It is ironic that a genre devised to manifest childhood innocence and to celebrate what adults value most about youth has come to facilitate one of the greatest threats to children. But still, in attempting to combat child pornography, we seem to be looking for it in all the wrong places.

In a case similar to that of Betsy Schneider, police were called to the Saatchi Gallery in 2001 to investigate the work of American artist Tierney Gearon, who had photographed her children naked and wearing masks. The inquiry prompted the intervention of the then Culture Secretary Chris Smith, who warned against the dangers of censorship.

In 1996, the Hayward Gallery in London left the portrait *Rosie* out of its Robert Mapplethorpe retrospective following advice from the police. Taken in 1976, the photograph shows a three-year-old girl sitting on a bench in a smocked dress. Her knees are bent and, as she looks towards the camera, her skirt is hiked up to expose her naked vulva.

Meanwhile, commercial photographic labs have a new role as unqualified arbiters of the obscenities that may lurk in a roll of family film. Most famously, in 1995, the partner of newsreader Julia Somerville was investigated and acquitted after taking some nude photographs of their child in the bath. Yet paedophiles have been known to find children's clothing catalogues arousing.

Young children take their clothes off all the time. Rosie has been caught at the only stage in her life when she will feel wholly comfortable with her body. That is what makes the photograph so beautiful. How sad it would be if grown-ups eventually denied themselves the chance to look on that and remember.

Responses to images of children are further confused by the prevailing culture. It has become increasingly hard to tell older women from their juniors in the mainstream media. Fashion models take to the catwalk at thirteen, while famous actresses starve themselves into pre-pubescence. At a moment when the faces and bodies of mature women have never been deemed less desirable, the Western beauty aesthetic is constructed around a paradigm of synthetic grapefruit breasts grafted on to a childlike, hipless frame.

The panicky reactions to pictures of naked children have entirely legitimate roots. In recent years, the abuse of the Internet by child pornographers has accelerated with astonishing speed. A click of the mouse separates every one of us from real-time footage of a father raping his own daughter. It is a phenomenon that demands an elemental shift in the way we consider images of children.

A redefinition of what genuinely constitutes a threat to

children is necessary. At present it would seem that surveillance of images of childhood is occurring at the expense of children themselves. Not least there is the danger that, in rendering all images of naked children taboo, we collude with the paedophile who manipulates his victim's feelings of embarrassment or shame in order to keep abuse secret. Beyond this, as a society we have to acknowledge the full extent of abuse that is ongoing in this country. Children can't be expected to talk freely about experiences that have alarmed them when adults won't.

In 1995, the Obscene Publications Unit of Greater Manchester Police seized about a dozen images of child pornography in a year, all in stills or video format, as Professor David Wilson documents in his book *Innocence Betrayed*. In 1999, the team recovered 41,000 images, almost all in computer format. By the end of 2001 they had stopped counting. The scale is staggering. In 1998, when police broke up the Wonderland Club, a global paedophile network which operated across twelve countries, swapping illicit images and video clips, they discovered that the group's entry requirement had been 10,000 fresh pornographic images of children.

This escalation has resulted in a number of police investigations into those who access web-based child pornography. But many child-abuse experts and senior police officers argue privately that targeting people at the lower end of the spectrum has in fact served as a distraction. They believe that focusing on the wrong type of offender – those who download images rather than those who produce them – has had no significant impact in terms of child protection.

Given the lack of resources and volume of offenders, it is inevitable that police forces end up concentrating on securing a conviction for possession of child pornography only. It's easier to prove evidentially, and still merits placement on the Sex Offenders' Register. But it is an approach that lacks nuance. Should people who look at pornographic images of children be treated in the same way as those who create them? Should these images be scaled somehow, given that not all of them depict acts of abuse? Is there any difference between looking at real images of children being abused and computer-generated ones?

All looking fuels the market, but looking does not always lead to doing. There is a correlation between the use of pornographic images and abuse, but estimates vary wildly – from one in three to three in four. Within the professional community, some have expressed concern about the policing of private fantasies. Others support it wholeheartedly, arguing that viewing images normalises antisocial desires, and that the extremity of material available accelerates progression towards offending.

What we do know, according to the most recent study by the NSPCC, is that between 16 and 20 per cent of all children in the UK experience some form of sexual assault before they reach the age of sixteen. Of those children, three quarters tell no one. It is not an exaggeration to conclude that child abuse is at epidemic levels, most of it going undetected and unconvicted.

Yet, there has never been greater public discussion of the paedophile threat. Every generation has its sexual demons, and communities are bound together by what they revile. But the parameters of this discussion are grossly limited. There is no information about how abusers 'groom' parents as well as children. There is no debate about prevention rather than punishment. It has been estimated that 90 per cent of paedophiles remain outside the criminal justice system, but still we concentrate on the minority.

The NSPCC statistics suggest that the majority of paedophiles are well integrated into the fabric of society, living among us. It is estimated that 80 per cent of victims know their abuser. People who abuse children are friends, neighbours and parents, who are loved and trusted. The banality of domestic abuse is too uncomfortable for us. Tabloid campaigns like the *News of the World*'s infamous naming and shaming exercise – following the murder of eight-year-old Sarah Payne in July 2000 by the known paedophile Roy Whiting – confirm the myth that abuse is carried out by other people, and must be dealt with through exposure and ostracisism. But those working with abusers believe that naming and shaming makes paedophiles more likely to reoffend. It drives abusers underground, thus removing them from police and probation monitoring. Fear of exposure and harassment creates extra pressure which may well hasten a return to offending behaviour. This does not amount to child protection.

Donald Findlater of the Lucy Faithfull Foundation has argued that the sexual abuse of children should be treated like any other public health issue, and that a massive public education campaign is needed to inform all adults of the realities of sexual abuse. Approaches based on prevention and non-custodial as well as custodial treatment are gaining governmental support, but require a corresponding shift in public opinion to be ultimately successful.

Findlater is the former manager of the Wolvercote Clinic, Britain's only non-custodial residential treatment centre for paedophiles, who were referred there by social services and the civil as well as criminal courts. Despite being hailed as the most effective treatment programme in the country, the clinic was closed down in 2002 after protests in the area it was moving to by local residents concerned about their children's safety.

Professionals in the field believe that in many cases treatment does work. Research indicates that between a third and half of abusers can be taught to manage their sexual arousal to children. But at present, this is only available via the Sex Offenders' Treatment Programme (SOTP) in prison and the community sex-offender treatment programmes operated by the probation service. Thus only a minority are helped, nor do they receive the ongoing intervention necessary to reinforce their treatment.

The government has funded a handful of projects supporting the integration of abusers back into the community on release from prison. Modelled on a Canadian scheme called Circles of Support and Accountability, each abuser becomes the core member of a group of six befrienders, who offer daily telephone contact and regular meetings, as long as he or she maintains a covenant not to reoffend. Less than half of the abusers in the Canadian Circles scheme had reoffended two years on from release.

The Lucy Faithfull Foundation has also been involved in another Home Office-supported initiative, Stop It Now! UK and Ireland. As well as providing information about the reality of child sexual abuse to all adults, Stop It Now! operates a freephone helpline for abusers and potential abusers, and their friends and family. Those experiencing inappropriate sexual feelings can speak confidentially to trained counsellors who offer risk management strategies.

Paedophiles are not a homogeneous group. They are more likely to be supporting a family than organising an international porn ring. Shifting the emphasis from getting caught to getting help takes into account the different patterns of abuse that occur and the impact on the child of their abuser being exposed. But normalising discussion of sexual abuse is not the same as normalising the abuse itself.

It is impossible to know whether more or less sexual abuse of children takes place today than in previous ages, but we are certainly more aware of it. According to one apocryphal tale of mass hysteria, this awareness caused a mob to attack a paediatrician's home because they mistook her job title for an admission of guilt. But it does not encourage parents to picket the high-street fashion chains that sell padded bras and 'Pop My Cherry' T-shirts to ten-year-olds.

Perhaps this is not a helpful parallel to draw. Do the legions of ten-year-olds dressing like Britney Spears really encourage potential paedophiles to act upon their fantasies? Would a return to high-necked smocks eradicate child abuse? It's a dangerous path to tread, akin to that old rape myth that it was women's responsibility to consider the way they dressed and acted in order not to excite the unpredictable male libido. In fact, research suggests that the majority of paedophiles prefer young-looking, vulnerable-seeming children.

What is more relevant is the question of whether tight tops and miniskirts encourage children to see themselves as sexual beings from an inappropriately early age. Children are eager mimics, but clothes that reveal rump or cleavage speak to highly subjective adult definitions of what is sexually appealing. Of graver concern is whether dressing like this enables those who would exploit children to blur boundaries more easily – in the same way that some paedophiles show pornography to children as part of the 'grooming' process. And, on a purely practical level, it's much harder to climb trees in a tight skirt.

Of course, concern about the sexualisation of childhood is premised on the assumption that children do not have a sexuality of their own, however distinct that might be from the adult version. But children are extraordinarily sensual beings, who flirt and seduce and explore their own and others' bodies.

To acknowledge the presence of these inchoate impulses is not to invite their exploration according to an adult template.

Freud believed that civilisation in the West was accomplished only through a 'sacrifice of instincts', in particular the proscription of the sexual life of children. He argued that this denial severely impaired the sexuality of the civilised adult, creating 'a permanent internal unhappiness, a sense of guilt'

But an understanding of the childhood sex instinct is near impossible when so much is invested in the construction of the child as desirably naive. First, we need to understand why it is that adults need childhood to be innocent, and what they fear will result from the loss of that innocence.

This is the conundrum. Is the antithesis of innocence experience, or is it corruption and guilt, and how are they related? Is adult knowledge inevitably polluting? In his memoir, *Boyhood*, the novelist J. M. Coetzee identifies the curious roundelay when describing his discomfiting attraction to another young boy: 'Beauty is innocence; innocence is ignorance; ignorance is ignorance of pleasure; pleasure is guilty; he is guilty.'

Another Saturday, and Lois is in the kitchen, finishing off the card she's been making for Grace. A box of her mother's photographs is on the table, and she reads from the text that accompanied one of Sue's exhibitions: ' "These photographs all relate to a period around my mother's death and shortly afterward. They are particularly about Lois's feelings towards her grandmother and her first experience of loss." '

Lois turns to Sue. 'It wasn't my first experience. Actually in a way it was grandad.'

'But you were only eight months and you didn't really experience that, did you?'

Lois continues: ' "Lois loves her grandmother Enid. She still talks about her often and although her almost daily crying has subsided Lois feels that if her grandmother were still alive her life would be somehow better. All problems would evaporate. Enid has become a figure with mythical qualities and an ability to transform life's difficulties and make a perfect day. Lois has a portrait of Enid behind her bed, a magic spot by her bedroom door, and frequently has conversations with her grandmother in her head." '

Lois doesn't remember the spot.

'You said when you touched it you could talk to Granny,' Sue reminds her.

'Really?' She wants to know where the spot has gone. It's been thrown away. Now she sounds bothered. 'Someone who doesn't know Granny might try to talk to her!'

One of the photographs shows Lois's grandmother sitting up in a hospital bed towards the end of her life. She stares non-commitally at the camera. 'I like that one better even though she looks like she's really desperate. She looks like she's trying to smile but deep down inside she feels really scared.' Another image shows her grandmother's hands folded across a clinical sheet. 'That's the ring that she gave me.'

This is the set of photographs that also charts the fall from the bed. 'It's a black eye,' she says. 'It's actually a purple, red, blue, orange, multi-coloured eye. It was the night before my grandmother's funeral and I was bouncing on the bed and I slipped. I was actually trying to bounce off. It was really unlikely the way I did it. All the ways I've hurt my head have been really unlikely.'

Lois also has a scar above her eye, the result of an altercation with the edge of a coffee-table during a game of front-room football with Kester. One image shows her clutching a mug, the evening after the injury was sustained. 'I remember that night they gave me a cup of tea, and it was quite late. The thing I remember most was thinking, "I get to go to bed without having brushed my teeth, after having drunk a cup of tea!"' The voice she uses for her younger self's thought is high up the scale. 'It was really, really deep. I needed fourteen stitches and then it went yellow above my eye and then my nose went really wide because of all the fluid.' She squirms. 'I hated that word because it was like blood. My nose kind of widened and my mum said I looked like a lion.'

She still gets teased about her scar at school, but she doesn't mind. 'They call me Frankenstein's monster. They actually call me Frankenstein, which isn't so bad because he was a scientist. They just laugh at me because I bang my head all the time.' Is she clumsy? 'No,' says Lois wearily, 'I'm just wild.'

Allana

'Go in the bushes! There aren't monsters. My
mum gone in there.'

Allana says her doll has ticklish eyes. She is playing in
the turquoise hall of her mother's second-floor council
maisonette, stuffing the raggedy girl with exaggerated irises
behind the radiator. Allana is four years old, and she's not
a big talker.

Her half-sister Sienna, who is two, is the chatterbox. They
live with their mother, Gloria, on the Blackbird Leys estate,
south-east of Oxford. It's not as bad as people say, not if
you've lived here all your life. Gloria moved away once, to
a place by the river, but that didn't last for long. Her own
mum still lives just up the street, and helps with the girls
whenever she can.

Gloria's colour is almost ebony, but Allana's skin is lighter.
She has her mother's strong nose and a rosy cupid's bow.
She wears shiny gold hoops in her ears. When she smiles,
her two front teeth arrive first. She gets frightened of
monsters, especially in the night-time. She knows how to be
naughty, and likes to test how naughty she can be before
consequences accrue. But mainly, Allana likes to watch. And,
because she won't tell, it is hard to know what she makes
of what she sees.

Sitting on the top stair, she manages a considerable

cacophony for someone who finds words surplus to requirements. This doll is a talking one. She feeds her some carpet
fluff. Dora says, 'Will you help me find my friend?' in a
cherry pie accent. Allana tries to copy the voice but blurs it
into 'da-da-da'.

'Sit here now,' she orders. When she speaks the sounds
are brisk but unconfident, the phrases collected without
relish. 'I turning off now.' Dora's freckled head bangs on the
landing floor.

At nursery, Allana has a best friend called Kayleigh.
Kayleigh is a chatterbox too. The teachers have explained
to Gloria that her daughter lets Kayleigh do the talking
for both of them. That's one of the reasons why Allana
won't be starting Reception for another term. They say
her behaviour can be aggressive too – a bit of pushing, a
bit of kicking.

The teachers are hoping that, apart from Kayleigh, Allana's
own verbal skills will improve. Gloria isn't sure why her
daughter is so quiet. At home, she and Sienna talk plenty to
her, but she knows from her own mum that she wasn't talk-
ative at that age, and she thinks that Allana takes after her
in a lot of ways. She just doesn't seem to like it. But kids
develop in their own way, in their own time, don't they?

What the nursery teachers don't know is that the friends'
separation may soon be more permanent. Kayleigh's mum
is being evicted because she owes nearly three thousand
pounds in rent arrears. Gloria is struggling too. She reckons she has fifty pence left over at the end of each week,
if that. She's always borrowing money off her mother, who
works for a local supermarket. The benefits she gets just
aren't enough, she says. Her friends who have their kids'
dads around find it easier, but she's never gone to the Child
Support Agency herself because she doesn't think it's worth

it. She knows that many people who've given up on it because they never got any money and it just caused lots of stress.

This is the hard stretch of afternoon between the end of nursery and the serving of tea. Gloria is downstairs in the living-room, watching a *Supernanny* episode which she videoed last night. The eponymous TV child care expert is marshalling twins who won't sleep through the night. Sienna is journeying between her mother and her sister, a large pink rucksack strapped tightly on her narrow back.

Allana narrates her activities on the top stair: 'That goes *down*.' She is throwing coloured plastic balls from behind the low bannister. 'I can climb up here. I won't fall 'cos I'll hang on.' She climbs up one, two wooden bars then jumps down heavily with a piercing shriek: 'I fall down!' She does this again, and again, and again. She finds more balls to dispatch. 'They all gone down now. Look, it's all.' Gloria calls up not to play on the stairs in case Sienna falls.

Allana and Sienna's bedroom has two bunks, two chests of drawers, two boxes of toys and a Winnie the Pooh frieze that stretches almost all the way round the walls. There are a handful of books – mainly illustrated Disney fairy tales – but Allana isn't interested in them. Gloria thinks she's a bit lazy. She doesn't have the patience to sit down and read, or to write her name.

The more that childhood has been examined, the more it has been debated how the quality of care people receive when they are young, especially in the earliest years of life, influences their capacity to cope in the world. For previous generations, most of this care was the unremarked though utterly remarkable work of mothering. But a historically private occupation is now of huge public concern.

Inquiries into the existence of innate character, and the influence of upbringing, stretch back to Plato. In his *History of Childhood*, Colin Heywood suggests that one of the reasons why medieval writers did not dwell on childhood was that they did not share the contemporary conviction that care is critical to development: 'To the medieval mind . . . the nature one is born with is the most important influence on life, the raw material without which the finest nurturing will be wasted. It suited the hereditary aristocracy all too well to promote this line on lineage.'

But with the Enlightenment came a growing interest in the impact of nurture, and in particular the benefits of education. John Locke confidently pronounced that, 'of all the men we meet with, nine parts of ten are what they are, good or evil, useful or not, by their education. 'Tis that which makes the great difference in mankind. The little, and almost insensible impressions on our tender infancies, have very important and lasting consequences.'

Locke believed that because education was responsible for these differences between individuals, 'great care is to be had of the forming of children's minds, and giving them seasoning early, which shall influence their lives always hereafter'.

Rousseau's rejoinder, that 'nature provides for the child's growth in her own fashion', was not the return to ancient notions of nativism that it might seem. Rousseau firmly believed that a child's morals and thinking could be shaped through nurture, but was concerned with the way that educators interacted with their charges. He believed that a child was born with the capacity to learn at her own pace, and wanted teachers to be directed by this, rather than imposing adult 'reason' on children before they were ready.

Rousseau was one of the first thinkers to divide childhood into discrete stages: the Age of Instinct, in the first three years of life; the Age of Sensations, up to twelve; and the Age of Ideas, at puberty. He believed that children only developed their ability to reason during the third stage, rejecting Locke's imperative to reason with children from infancy. 'Those children who have been constantly reasoned with strike me as exceedingly silly,' he observed. He suggested that, rather than training the child out of its natural state, educators should 'leave nature to act for a long time before you get involved with acting in its place'.

Rousseau thus provided a foundation for the ideal of childhood innocence. The opposition of innocence and corruption continues to inform the adult-inflected version of childhood today. But the development of sciences of the mind and body at the end of the nineteenth and beginning of the twentieth century embedded another opposition which would go on to influence contemporary thinking about children: that of nature versus nurture.

As the children's culture theorist Stephen Kline points out, the position of families and schools as the locus for nurture gained currency during the intense social and economic upheavals of the nineteenth century: 'It was the industrialising Victorians who took this new attitude [tracing back to Locke and Rousseau] seriously, who worked at undoing the feudal matrix of socialisation with its strict definition of children based on the family's property rights.'

But the belief that character could be moulded through learning was challenged by advances in the biological sciences. When Charles Darwin posited his theory of natural selection in 1858, the science of genetics was in its infancy. Darwin abolished the Cartesian distinction between people and animals, arguing that both humans and apes shared a common ancestor. He described the process whereby organisms which inherit traits that make them better adapted to their environment tend to survive and produce more offspring.

According to the concept of natural selection, evolution results over time from the selecting out of traits that do not assist environmental adaptation. Darwin theorised that these inherited characteristics were passed on by minute entities he called 'gemmules'.

Though radical in the way that it challenged the teachings of the Church, not everyone welcomed Darwin's theory. The German socialist Friedrich Engels dismissed it as a conjuring trick: 'The whole Darwinist teaching of the struggle for existence is simply a transference from society to living nature of Hobbes's doctrine of *bellum omnium contra omnes* and of the bourgeois doctrine of competition together with Malthus' theory of population.'

Darwin's findings were also implicated in early eugenic thinking, originally espoused by his first cousin Francis Galton. Galton believed that the proper evolution of the human race was being thwarted by misguided social philanthropy, which encouraged the 'unfit' to bear more children and ran counter to the mechanism of natural selection. He argued that a kind of artificial selection was necessary; he called it 'eugenics,' from the Greek word for 'good birth'.

But running alongside this academic emphasis on heredity was a growing popular obsession with how parents might influence their children's intellectual and emotional development. From the fashionable behaviourism advocated during the 1920s and 1930s, to the affectionate indulgence that followed the Second World War, belief in the importance of nurture was ascendant in care manuals of the time.

The absolutist positions of child as tabula rasa or child as adapted ape are no longer tenable. The more that is learnt about the human genome, the more is being discovered about how genes influence human behaviour and vice versa. The focus of investigation has shifted to the manner in which this symbiosis is played out.

As neurobiologist Steven Rose has pointed out: 'Simple-minded claims that there are "genes for" this or that trait . . . without understanding that how a gene is expressed depends both on the active cooperation of many other genes, and on the cell within which the genome is embedded, are misleading. Nor is "the environment" a simple concept, embracing as it does everything from the entirety of the cellular DNA via the organism as a whole, to the ever-changing physical and living worlds in which all life is embedded.'

So how might 'interactionism' inform the way that children are brought up? In 2002, researchers presented some startling results as part of a cohort study of young men born in Dunedin, a city on the South Island of New Zealand, in 1972. A proportion of the boys in the study were maltreated during childhood, and many of that group went on to exhibit antisocial and violent behaviour themselves. Taking an interactionist approach, the researchers tested the boys for differences in one particular gene which controlled an enzyme in the brain, and then compared this with their upbringing.

What they discovered was that those with the gene for developing high levels of the enzyme monoamine oxidise A (MAOA) were virtually immune to the effects of childhood maltreatment. But boys with a less active version of the same gene, and lower levels of MAOA, became significantly more antisocial if subject to abuse. Neither a poor upbringing nor a poor genetic inheritance were alone responsible for an unhappy adult outcome; this required a combination of the two.

Longitudinal research projects like the one from Dunedin

demand time and resources, but they reveal findings which those that only examine a specific gene and outcome fail to do. As Professor Richie Poulton, who presented the 2002 study, noted: 'The key that unlocks genetic effects is a good life history. Looking at genes is the easy part; you then need thirty years of good, broad, detailed information about the participants.'

As more sophisticated investigations like this one are conducted, the bitter feuding between the nature and nurture camps shows little sign of abating. While protagonists on both sides now wisely qualify their positions, they continue to berate the opposition for putting up straw men in order to caricature their stance as naive environmentalism or genetic determinism.

The hybrid discipline of evolutionary psychology, which proposes that human behaviour may be best understood in the light of evolutionary history, has caused further entrenchment. From its popularisation in the mid-1990s, adherrants made controversial pronouncements on gender differences, in particular with regard to mating preferences and strategies. One such thesis was that rape in humans is an evolved adaptation to help males pass on their genes, which was bizarrely extrapolated from evidence of forced copulation in scorpion flies. Critics countered that such thinking discredited the notion of human nature, just as the Social Darwinist reliance on self-interest had done previously.

In policy terms, the debate about early years tends towards nurture: are young children best looked after by parents or professionals, and how should that looking after be done? The present Labour government's emphasis on early-years provision has earned it the moniker of 'secular Jesuits' (an order that declared: 'Give me the boy at seven and I shall give you the man'). Still it remains unclear precisely what the government thinks public child care is for. To get mothers back to work? To ready toddlers for the labour market? To save children from poor or feckless parents?

There is a risk here that the government will end up holding individual families responsible for structural inequalities. But, as academic factionalism continues, there is precious little clarity about how we should weigh and balance the multifarious factors that can shape a young life. When will Allana's fate be determined, and by what?

Allana wanders into her mother's room with the nonchalance of a practised intruder. There's another television there, a portable CD player, and a pile of unsorted laundry. Allana sits on top of it. She finds a screwdriver, which Sienna says belongs to her daddy. Allana likes to call Sienna's father 'Daddy' too. When he moved out, Gloria admits she enjoyed the extra space in the bed.

Allana also discovers a dummy which she sucks energetically. She didn't have one as a baby but she loves them now. 'Is that your dummy, Sienna?' she asks companionably, as though she might actually relinquish her find. She quickly scotches hope: 'You've already got a dummy, in't you?'

The dummy becomes a theme. Allana compresses herself into her Baby Annabel pram, sitting up on top of the frame, her knees tight against the handlebar. Sienna, who relishes the order of bags, begins packing toys and food into her rucksack for a walk in the park. Allana is now fully a baby, grizzling and kicking her legs. She throws a doll out of the pram. She is almost too heavy for Sienna to push.

They swap roles. Allana counts toys for the baby up to nine, then gets lost and starts making up numbers. 'You want milk baby?' Sienna sucks hungrily on an empty liquid soap dispenser that has become an improvised bottle. 'I think her wants some lunch. Let's go home.' She makes a nest behind the chair in the corner of the bedroom and navigates Sienna in there with her.

After a while, Allana picks up a brush and starts attending to her sister's hair. This is an enterprise of dubious intent. 'That not hurt, that not hurtin',' Allana soothes as she rakes the bristles through Sienna's tight curls. Both girls have difficult hair to keep, says Gloria, but Allana will never sit still long enough for her to oil it. 'Don't brush my eyes!' Sienna pleads.

Later, Allana washes her dummy in the bathroom. She is fascinated by the taps, and pretends to be brushing her teeth in order to turn them on then off again, on then off again. She needs to pee. She closes the door discreetly but Sienna bursts in on her. 'No! No! No!' They are fighting over the door-knob, Allana still with her trousers down. She starts whipping her sister away with a towel, eventually reclaiming possession of the knob.

Gloria calls them down for tea. Allana and Sienna sit opposite each other at the small oblong table in the corner of the living-room, by the arch into the kitchen. They are deadly opponents in the contest of clearing plates. Gloria passes through chicken nuggets, chips and beans. She administers salt and ketchup judiciously. On the local television news there is an item about a sculpture which sounds like a waste of money. Allana eats all her meat. Sienna eats everything but. There are Munch Bunch yoghurts for afters.

Whenever they go food-shopping, Allana asks for spaghetti bolognaise and Sienna wants macaroni cheese. It can be a struggle to buy them what they like, but Gloria usually asks her mum to get some things for her, since she gets a discount because of her job.

On another day, Allana is out on the walkway, hanging off

the arm of a neighbour who props her baby son on her hip. She had him when she was sixteen. Gloria didn't have Allana until she was twenty-six – it just worked out that way. She left school at thirteen, and spent the intervening years working in a college kitchen. Now the neighbour is trying to stop Allana following Gloria down into the yard. Gloria thinks the local council is pretty awful. After Allana ran away they had to wait two years to get a gate on the top-floor landing. She was only two, but she went all the way to the shops on her own. Everyone on the estate was out looking for her. She'd found some money and wanted to spend it.

Back in the flat, the girls roll around on the sofa while Gloria hangs out the washing on the balcony. She calls down to another neighbour below, and they exchange plans for Saturday night. Gloria doesn't get out much, because baby-sitters are so expensive, but sometimes her mother takes them and Gloria will relax with whatever's on telly and a bottle of wine.

It's a sultry day of heat and cloud. Allana wears navy shorts and a yellow T-shirt with pink sandals. Her nanna bought them a size too big so they keep coming off. Her hair is wild today.

'Going to the park, Mama?' she asks. Gloria concurs. Back down in the yard, she gets Sienna's pushchair and Allana's pink scooter out of the pram shed. She says Allana's been doing her head in today. Sometimes she just won't listen. She's tired.

On the short walk to the park, Allana zips along the pavement. Her balance is even and the scooter glides smoothly. When she crosses the road, she announces that nothing is coming before proceeding. She stops at bushes along the way and scours them intently. Gloria warns her off. She's been picking up insects lately.

When they arrive at the park, Sienna disembarks then

runs ahead towards the swings and climbing-frames, but waits for Allana to decide what to go on first. Sienna still totters, but Allana strides with torso thrust forward and hips at the best angle to get her legs marching.

She has one twirl on the curly yellow slide, then runs across to the swings. She doesn't like to be pushed. After five minutes of dawdling, tummy then bottom to seat, trying each one in turn, she returns to the big climbing-frame. She tries the rope ladder but can only manage two rungs. The footholds are too far apart for her legs' reach.

She goes back on the slide, and tries to crawl up it. She enjoys the daft backwardness of it. But when she attempts to go up the ladder that will return her to the top of the slide, a little boy pushes her out of the way. She turns in her mother's direction. 'Push him back then,' Gloria calls from her squat on the grass verge, but Allana is cowed. The boy's mother scolds him in Turkish. The sun is passing in and out behind thick puffs of cloud.

Gloria has bought Ribena cartons and little packets of mixed sweets. Allana takes the straw for the juice out of its plastic and pops it in her mouth, sucking before she has even punctured the top of the carton. She drops a tiny jelly baby and a luminous yellow caterpillar without noticing. The sweets cause a stir back on the climbing-frame. The pushing boy wants some, but Allana isn't offering.

Gloria smokes a cigarette. A woman down the street drank a whole bottle of vodka last night and was taken away in an ambulance. Allana keeps asking her mum to buy a garden. It might even be a possibility if the family below them moves out, because the downstairs maisonettes open on to a green.

As the trio turn for home, they pass a gaggle of teenage girls gathered round a bench. They are passing a newborn baby between them like a parcel and it's impossible to tell who he belongs to. There are high shrieks of derision when someone calls the infant 'it' instead of 'he'. They compete with each other for a turn of feeding with the bottle. Gloria worries about that baby. A week later she sees the same group helpless with laughter by the roadside, after inadvertently tipping their charge out of his pushchair and into the gutter.

Gloria doesn't like to see people not taking mothering seriously. It's not always easy to be patient, especially when you're on your own, but she wouldn't want to leave them with anyone else. Gloria got a lot more confident about looking after her girls when she went to the PEEP project. It taught her how important it was to talk to them and read to them, even when they were little babies. She liked the singing and the book-sharing, and she keeps in touch with some of the other mums she met there.

The Peers Early Education Partnership (PEEP) is not specifically a parenting class, though it is available to all parents of fives and under living in the area. The essence of PEEP is this: that parents are their children's first and most important educators, that children are competent learners from birth, and that everyday life offers the best opportunities for teaching. PEEP believes that young children don't need to be prepared like string beans before being thrown into the education pot, and that it is feeling secure about yourself and your relationships with other people that creates a disposition to learn.

Initially developed in the mid-1990s in the catchment area of a local secondary school, the project has now expanded across the country and is highly regarded. Initial evaluations have found that PEEP children made significantly more progress in their preschool learning and, more fundamentally, exhibited greater self-esteem than non-PEEP children.

Gloria has taken both Allana and Sienna to PEEP, and

she also studied there for an accreditation in child development. It was a lot more reading than she's used to, but she felt proud when she'd done it. The reason she liked PEEP best, though, was because it didn't feel like people telling you what to do.

The basis of PEEP, and other government-funded initiatives, is that parents can make a fundamental difference to their children's development. However, the independent psychologist Judith Rich Harris begged to differ when, in 1995, she arrived on the nature/nurture scene with an arresting new theory. A suburban grandmother, who had failed to complete her doctorate because of illness and was not affiliated to any academic institution, Harris had a paper accepted by the prestigious *Psychological Review*. In it she argued that parents do not make as much of a difference to children as people think, and that peers are more important to an individual's development.

Although doubters fixed on her lack of professional status, Harris was soon being championed by the likes of Steven Pinker at M.I.T., the poster professor of evolutionary psychologists. Harris later expanded her thesis into a book, *The Nurture Assumption*, which teased apart the way that human beings had come to understand themselves over a century of psychological inquiry. 'They fuck you up, your mum and dad. They may not mean to, but they do,' wrote the poet Philip Larkin, articulating a conviction that had launched a thousand analysts' couches. Not so, argued Harris.

She suggested that the correlation of good parenting with certain personalities was meaningless, because it did not distinguish between cause and effect. Are children who are cuddled a lot nice, or are nice children cuddled a lot? Harris believed that what developmentalists had assumed were parent-to-child effects were often child-to-parent effects.

Harris used the example of two children, five-year-old Audrey and seven-year-old Mark, who she encountered when her dog ran to the curb barking as they walked past with their mother. Despite the fact that the dog was barking in an unfriendly fashion, Audrey veered towards it, asking her mother if she could pet it. She was swiftly cautioned: 'I don't think the dog wants you to pet him.' Meanwhile, her brother retreated to the other side of the street, and had to be encouraged at length by his mother to return to the group. 'Come on, Mark,' she soothed, 'the dog won't hurt you.'

Here was a parent who, depending on which child she was interacting with, could be seen as overprotective or permissive, argued Harris: 'Their parents treat them differently *because* of their different characteristics. A fearful child is reassured; a bold one is cautioned. A smiley baby is kissed and played with; an unresponsive one is fed, diapered, and put in its crib.' A parent's treatment of a child was not a cause of their behaviour, but a reaction to it.

In addition, Harris posited, since children share 50 per cent of their genes with each of their biological parents, surely for genetic reasons alone children born with a predisposition to be timid are more likely to be raised by timid parents, and children born with a predisposition to be aggressive are more likely to be reared by aggressive parents.

Harris believed that the influence on children of peers, teachers, neighbourhoods and culture were too readily given second billing. So peers were considered important, but parental influence was seen as primary because early experiences with parents supposedly influenced later relationships with peers. Culture was similarly thought to have an impact, but the nurture assumption held that culture was passed on from parents to children.

But if that was really the case, Harris asked, then why do

children of immigrant families quickly acquire and feel more comfortable using the language of their peers? Telling the story of Joseph, the son of Polish parents who arrived in the United States at the age of eight, she observes: 'He categorized himself as just a kid, a second-grade boy, and adopted the norms of behaviour appropriate for that social category. The norms included speaking English.' Parents do not have to teach their children the language of their community, she wrote: 'In fact – hard as it may be for you to accept this – they do not have to teach their children any language at all.'

In a paper responding to criticisms of her book, Harris noted: 'Every published report of a correlation between parental behavior and child outcome now contains a disclaimer admitting that the direction of effects is uncertain and that the correlation could be due in part to what I call a *child-to-parent effect*, a type of evocative gene – environment correlation. It is never admitted, however, that the correlation could be due *entirely* to the child-to-parent effect and that the parent-to-child effect could be zero, even though that possibility cannot be rejected because neither effect has been measured.'

This is a theory of parenting that must hold some appeal for those confounded by the babble of child care 'experts' currently peddling their wares across the media, and by social policy determined to hold parents to account for their child's every transgression. Parents, and mothers in particular, are told regularly about the harm they can do their children, and seldom about the good. But Harris's theory does have one serious ramification: if parents believe they have a minimal effect on their children's psychology, are they not potentially more likely to maltreat their offspring?

On the other hand, the heart of Harris's thesis may be interpreted as profoundly pro-child. She asserts that the nurture assumption 'has turned childhood into parenthood'. Children are not interested in becoming like their parents, she argues, but want to be successful children. In viewing peers as major facilitators of children's development, she can be argued to be presenting childhood as an end in itself, rather than as a training for adulthood.

But Harris, unwittingly or otherwise, has been corralled into the 'nature' camp. Steven Pinker relied heavily on her thesis in his book *The Blank Slate*, which put forward a gloomy, neo-Hobbsean view of human nature as a set of inherited instructions.

Railing against the 'corrupting dogma' of the developmentalists' tabula rasa, Pinker argues: 'The mind was forged in Darwinian competition and an inert medium would have been outperformed by rivals outfitted with high technology – with acute perceptual systems, savvy problem-solvers, cunning strategists and sensitive feedback circuits. A malleable mind would quickly be selected out.'

Pinker contends that developmentalist dreams of perfectability have been used in the service of the greatest travesties of the twentieth century. It is no coincidence, he writes, that Mao said, 'It is on a blank page that the most beautiful poems are written.'

Yet Mao was co-opting a theory to suit his own ends, just as Hitler misappropriated the findings of Darwin. Understanding our fundamental drives is a worthwhile project, not least because it might allow us to become masters of rather than martyrs to them. But, as the philosopher Mary Midgley wrote in an essay on the subject, although genetics is a physical science, applying it to human behaviour is complex. Different ways of classifying behaviour express different attitudes, which in turn suggest very different conclusions.

'The reason why "the gene" has now become a household

word is not that we have all suddenly begun to understand genetics,' Midgley cautioned. 'We haven't. What has brought the word to public notice is the metaphor linked with it – selfishness – a metaphor that seemingly claimed to resolve long-standing debates about motivation.'

Coming back to nurture, recent findings from the field of neuroscience suggest that the responsiveness of the primary carer to their child, especially in the first year after birth, does have a direct physiological impact on the formation of babies' brains.

Surveying this research in her book *Why Love Matters*, the psychoanalytic psychotherapist Sue Gerhardt makes the case for how a loving and attentive parent can stimulate development of the 'social brain' – the pre-frontal cortex, a part of the brain that develops almost entirely postnatally. Here, key emotional responses like empathy, self-restraint and the ability to pick up on non-verbal cues are organised – the neurological rules according to which we will govern relationships for the rest of our lives. Put simply, says Gerhardt, love facilitates a massive burst of connections in this part of the brain between six and twelve months. Neglect or rejection during this period can greatly reduce the social brain's development.

Gerhardt also details how a baby's stress response – the production of the hormone cortisol by the hypothalamus – is set like a thermostat, usually within the first six months of life. Babies cannot regulate cortisol production at birth, but they learn to do so through repeated experiences of being comforted when distressed. If a caregiver expresses resentment or hostility towards a crying baby, or leaves him distressed for longer than he can bear, the brain becomes flooded with cortisol and will go on to over or underproduce the hormone in future stressful situations. Excess cortisol production is linked to depression and insecurity. Too little can result in aggression and detachment.

The concept of early calibration of emotional responses reflects the work of the British psychiatrist John Bowlby, who developed his 'attachment' theory after reporting on the mental health of children who were evacuated and orphaned during the Second World War. He argued that during the first three years of life 'maternal deprivation' for any extended length of time caused irreparable scarring of babies' 'psychic tissue', creating an 'affectionless' child who would at best go on to become an inadequate parent themselves.

Drawing on studies of higher primates, Bowlby argued that attachment behaviour may have served the evolutionary purpose of protecting the helpless young from predators. He believed that human infants developed specific attachments between the ages of nine months and three years. The mother, or other primary care-giver, provided a secure base from which the child could navigate her surroundings, so attachment and exploration were reciprocal behaviours.

Bowlby identified a sequence of responses induced by the removal of this attachment figure. First was outraged protest, followed by a period of despair, when the infant seemed apathetic. Finally, she became detached and, if separated from her mother for a sustained amount of time, no longer cared when she was again present.

Bowlby's formula was simple: 'Healthy, happy and self-reliant adolescents and young adults are the products of stable homes in which both parents give a great deal of time and attention to the children.' Babies who enjoyed an intimate relationship with their care-giver learnt resilience, the quality of psychological flexibility that would allow them to tolerate challenge and set-backs as they grew up.

Attachment theory has since been much qualified, particularly by those who believe it blamed mothers for everything that became of a child. But Bowlby himself was attuned to the effects of the wider environment on babies. He believed that, even if the primary care-giving connection was imperfect, resilience could be fostered through subsequent relationships.

Conversely, a strong primary relationship is necessary but not always sufficient for successful development. And so it is with Allana that, beyond the intimate influence of her mother, powerful forces are acting to disrupt her progress. The question here is not whether biology is destiny, but how much race and class are. A genuinely interactionist understanding of human development must also take in social inequality.

It is estimated that nearly three million children in this country are living in poverty. Children from lower-income families tend to have worse health, lower educational attainment and earlier contact with the police, while lone-parenthood and ethnicity compound underlying disadvantages. Before the age of two, the attainment gap in all areas of cognitive and emotional development is already evident in deprived communities.

The government's commitment to ending child poverty has benefited many, but its focus on paid employment as the route out of poverty has its limits. Concern remains that families in low-paid, part-time, insecure or transitional employment remain at significant risk – over half of deprived children have a working parent. And, despite the commitment to provide 'security for those who can't work', families for whom employment is not, and may never be, an option are entrenched in poverty.

Levels of income support remain inadequate: 'safety net' benefits for a lone parent with children aged between five and eleven in 2005/6 were only £160 a week – £29 less than the government's poverty line of £189.

Can Gloria challenge all of this with loving kindness and determination alone?

On the following Saturday afternoon, Allana is anxious in a pink gauzy dress with fairy wings. She wears the same alarmed expression that appears whenever she is unsure what the world wants from her. Allana has been at a friend's fancy-dress party across the road. When Gloria went to collect her, the other mums said she hadn't spoken a word, just sat on the swing, not being pushed. Gloria tells Allana to lift up her two arms, and the dress comes off like a stain.

She begins a sedulous examination of her party bag of sweeties and cheap treats. She opens a mini-egg, but the chocolate has softened. It's another hot day, hotter indoors, despite the fan in the living-room. She sucks the chocolatey goo out of the silver foil, unimpressed. Gloria empties the bag on to the floor for her and collects the rest of the chocolates to put in the fridge before they melt too.

There is a small orange plastic bomb, filled with sherbet. Allana empties some on to the table. Sienna arrives at her side, vibrating with curiosity. 'You have to eat it all up,' advises Allana, as though it were an unappealing vegetable, while managing to scoop most of the delicious dust into her own mouth. A little more and a little more is poured until the container is empty and Allana, with the elegant self-deception of an alcoholic, expresses surprise. 'There no more in there Sienna,' she tells her sister sternly. 'You e't it all up.'

It is so hot indoors, and Allana wants to play outside. So Gloria opens up the pram shed for her, and she fetches her bike – pink to match her scooter and with stabilisers – then rides up and down the thin concrete yard. It is bright and breezeless outside. Gloria has taken a chair out on to the landing and watches her from there.

Allana has a green notepad which she leaves by the staircase, and sometimes she stops off to make jaggy scribbles in it. She doesn't try to make letters. Three early-teenage boys wander in from the street. They huddle by the stairs and bang open beer bottles on the metal railings. Allana cycles over to watch them through the bars. They ignore her, and after some minutes slouch off down the alleyway, beyond the sun's glare.

Gloria and some of the other parents had a meeting with the council about building a play area. There are twenty-five kids on the top floor of these maisonettes, and the overgrown concrete square at the back of flats that is designated theirs just isn't big enough, certainly not for a slide or swings.

Malcolm, the new councillor, is helping their campaign. He's a good man. Gloria has always had terrible trouble with damp and silverfish. The council told her that she'd have to pay to get them removed, but Malcolm got on the phone and now the men are coming on Monday to do it free of charge. It's a relief, she says, because she couldn't afford to pay for it herself. Allana doesn't mind them, but Sienna gets really freaked out. When the council refused to remove the abandoned fridge outside the gate, Malcolm came with a friend and took it away himself.

Back upstairs, the party bag is the magic porridge pot, never emptying. Now there's a bottle of bubbles. Allana tries to blow some herself but she can't direct her breath gently or evenly enough and keeps breaking the meniscus across the wand. Gloria takes over and makes an expert string. 'I pop them!' shrieks Allana, jumping up on the spot and clapping her hands together to catch the falling globes.

Gloria holds the wand against the fan, and a bubble stretches and strains huge in the air-flow. 'Do that again!' commands Allana. 'Here it comes . . .' Sienna gets a turn, and proves almost as expert as her mother. It becomes a competition: 'I can do it! I can do it, Mama!'

Back to the sweeties. Two lollypops down, Allana opens a small packet of Gummi Bears. Gloria tells her to eat them slowly, so she repairs to the balcony, where she crams as many as she can into her mouth at once. Earlier in the week, they all went on a Family Centre trip to Bournemouth. It only cost £8.50. Tomorrow they're going to Weston-super-Mare. Gloria isn't even sure where that is, but it's worth it for the outing. The coach leaves at 7.30 a.m., and she's not sure how she'll get these two ready in time.

Allana is becoming increasingly frantic, as she devours a pastel-coloured sweetie necklace out of view on the balcony. Sienna's dad is coming to pick her up. Allana wants to go with him too, but she's staying at her nanna's instead. Gloria is sitting in tonight, getting ready for the early start. As the hour approaches, Allana whispers something horrible to Sienna about the evening's arrangements. Sienna's face crumples and she runs to Gloria for comfort.

Sienna is getting her clothes changed before her father arrives. 'You're a poo-y,' announces her sister. Gloria starts to brush Sienna's hair, and opens a box of hairbands, asking them to name the colours and choose their favourite. But Allana won't be distracted. There is more pushing, then kicking, and Gloria takes Allana to sit on the naughty step until she's calmed down. She always has her naughty five minutes. Last week, she was down the club with Sienna's dad and tipped a full ashtray into his pint. It was hard not to laugh.

Gloria got the naughty-step idea from a *Supernanny* episode. The hairbands game is the sort of thing that PEEP taught her – how they can learn from something that's just happening along the way. Like every parent, she's discovered a lot since her first-born arrived. The most important thing she's realised is that you should give everything a try, even if it doesn't work the first time.

It is all too easy to interpret theories about the importance of early-years care oppressively. Just as genetics-based concepts can be seen as letting bad parenting off the hook, so parent-oriented developmentalism may exonerate society.

It cannot be incumbent on Gloria alone to parent her children out of poverty. Without structural equality, no amount of parenting skills – whether instinctive or taught – can break the cycle of deprivation. To suggest that when poorer parents fail it is purely a question of individual responsibility is to ignore how social disadvantage works.

But it remains the case that genetic theory is more open to manipulation in pursuit of ugly agendas. Take that New Zealand study, which uncovered the interaction between a particular gene and maltreatment in childhood. On one level this is heartening: neither a rotten genotype nor a rotten upbringing need ruin a life. But what about the child who has both? If science can identify individuals as irrevocably lost causes, then is the socially responsible option to lock them up and throw away the key? Society has never been much inclined to help children like this, and if genetics offers an empirical basis for writing them off completely, then the community needn't exercise its collective conscience at all.

The nature/nurture debate may be gaining welcome nuance, with a degree of consensus now that genes do not act independently of environments but respond flexibly to them. But the potential for studies like the one in New Zealand to be employed in the pursuit of regressive and authoritarian policies remains troubling.

Of course, any study can be manipulated in pursuit of a political goal. Moral conclusions do not follow directly from scientific evidence. But traditionally genetics have been used to bolster more conservative agendas, perhaps because nature has been seen as more restraining than nurture. As genetic engineering advances, however, there is always the possibility that biology will end up being more flexible than culture.

Similar vigilance must be exercised when considering the flipside of the law of lost causes: the excuse of exceptionalism. This is the idea that through talent and determination children can transcend their circumstances, trouncing inequality by sheer dint of will, and so obviating the need to tackle social exclusion. Here Stephen Pinker may have a foothold, when he contends that blank-slate theory is just as likely as a theory of evolution based on Darwinism to entrench inequality and determinism.

Exceptionalism is a fantasy that is only ever applied – again – to the children that society is least willing to take responsibility for. There are one in a million Billy Elliots or Samantha Mortons or Tracey Emins. On very few occasions do ability and application alone provide a route out of poverty, and on fewer occasions do children possess such copious gifts in the first place. Inequality is inherent in the capitalist system, and meritocracy is its partner in crime.

The children that this country has most difficulty accepting are those that the sociologist Charles Jenks called the 'unexceptional disadvantaged' – the ones who can't dance or act or paint their way out of the cycle of deprivation. But they are no less deserving of care because they will never go on to thrill the audience at Covent Garden.

A few weeks later, Allana is climbing up on to the bench in a bus shelter in the city centre, kicking against the reinforced glass: 'I break it!' Again and again, she likes to test the boundaries of the physical world – and adult tolerance. Gloria ignores her and goes to check the timetable, leaving Allana in charge of Sienna, who is asleep and gaping in her pushchair. Tenderly, she arranges her sister's blanket and strokes her hair. She does not stir. Allana was in trouble again last night: 'Fuck's sake, I can't do it!' she said as she was struggling to put some clothes on a Sindy.

The journey to the Snakes and Ladders play warehouse is an adventure in itself. The interior of the bus offers a new domain of physical challenge and entertainment. There are also strict rules that must be adhered to.

Gloria finds a nook for the pushchair behind the driver's cabin, while Allana heads up to the back of the vehicle. She's looking for a front-facing seat next to a hanging strap. (The back-facing seats next to straps are positioned too low for her to reach up.) Both seats are taken. She regards the occupants jealously, and makes a few pointed remarks about not being able to reach from her height-retarded, back-facing perch. But the two men are talking into their mobile phones and don't seem to realise that they're sitting where she should be.

She moves off into one of the two-seater rows and buries her face in the seat. Sometimes she looks out of the window. Sometimes she sings: 'Wah, wah, wah.' One of the men alights and Allana dives to claim her position. 'I reach up.' She grasps the strap with firm satisfaction. 'I gon' go on the one next to it.' She tells herself to hold on when the bus starts moving again. 'Bus goin' now.' She refuses to move when the bus is in motion, and won't even slide along from one seat to the next on her bottom.

On the walk from the bus-stop to the Snakes and Ladders building, Gloria keeps calling to her to keep up, but Allana hangs behind the pushchair, grabbing ever more preposterous handfuls of flowers and leaves, only to throw them up into the wind. The boundaries set by walls and other people's gardens don't matter. Anything that can be reached can be ripped at.

It's not Allana's first time here, so she propels herself through the entrance gate while Gloria is still paying. The Snakes and Ladders warehouse comprises a vast, primary-coloured and multi-storied play area, with a scaled-back version for threes and under, and a café space where adults can sit and chat, or even read a book, and wave occasionally to a child up on high. The air is prickly with body heat and plastic. Everything inside is soft and wipe-clean.

Shoes come off. Gloria goes in with Sienna and Allana climbs by herself. She's curious, but cautious. There are bigger, quicker kids, who push past. The top floor is not explored immediately – she climbs one level, returns to the ground floor, then up to the second floor and down again. Even with this studied gradualism, the top level when first reached feels overwhelming, and she starts crying for her mummy. Gloria lifts her up tenderly, and carries her across the intimidating wobbly floor.

Eventually, both girls settle on a route: up the spongy ramp; across the net; along the rope bridge; through the hanging mats with cartoon faces; and down the wide, blue, wavy slide which takes four children at a time. Sometimes they race on the way down: 'Ready, steady, go!' Allana always says it, and she always pushes herself off slightly ahead of 'go'. When the sisters get to the bottom of the slide they're not dizzied for a second; they spring upright and run for the ramp again.

The café sells Slush Puppies. Allana's mouth is turning purple. Sienna has dropped a piece of ice on her trousers. A little girl walks past, crying torrentially, and they both turn from their drinks to observe her with interest. Their mini chocolate biscuits are melted and stuck together. Allana pushes the packet at Gloria. 'You have them, Mum.'

The man came to attend to the silverfish this morning. They went up to Botley last night and spent a lot of pennies on presents for Sienna's third birthday. Gloria has to borrow for things like that – sometimes from her mum and sometimes from the Provident, who come round to the door; you pay them back weekly.

The girls are both tired now and it's not a struggle to persuade them that it's time to go. Sienna says she wants to walk. Allana gets in the pushchair, but the moment her sister sees her there she changes her mind and demands her rightful place. Now Allana wants to be carried.

As she grudgingly walks back up to the bus-stop, Allana is again seeking foliage. She picks up a huge, brown, leathery horse-chestnut leaf. It's as big as her face. She finds a lavender bush and picks some scented stems. She gives one to Sienna and one to Gloria.

Summer ends. On the first day of school after the holidays, the class is truncated. The majority of the children have moved up a year and are starting Reception today, while the new nursery intake has yet to arrive. Allana walks with her nanna along the road towards the sprawl of low school buildings, fiddling with a heavy ring on the hand she is holding. She finds her name peg for her pink hat, and strolls out into the playground once nanna makes it clear she isn't staying.

So Allana begins a new term – without Kayleigh. It's hard to know if she's missing her, or whether her absence will make a difference to her talking. Everyone is feeling funny today, missing home, remembering playmates and where the toys are kept. The nursery assistants are unobtrusively alert to the tension under the sunny sky.

Allana is playing with Mr Toad, a wrinkled, unpretty creature who will be her constant companion this afternoon. She discusses his movements on the climbing-frame. 'He climb up. He slide down. He go under.' Sometimes she looks around to check whether anyone else is listening to her, but mostly she aspires to conduct herself unwitnessed. She shows no interest in the other children, who are mainly competing with each other for grown-ups' attention, sometimes with tears and sometimes with tantrums. Allana prefers to be away from adult eyes.

She commandeers a bike with a long wooden trailer and trundles over to her favourite part of the playground, an avenue of thick bushes that connects with an unlandscaped area beyond. 'Go in the bushes!' she calls excitedly. 'There aren't monsters. My mum gone in there.' She pauses to savour the isolation before peddling round to the other side of the tarmacked cycling area. 'Monsters in there,' she reveals, pointing to the primary-school building. 'He say "I'm gon' eat you".'

Indoors, the classroom is quiet, and empty but for one boy who would like somebody to read him a story. Allana walks round to the seating area, which contains a small sofa and a big bucket of toys. She removes the toys one by one, naming them as they come: the dinosaur is a monster, the bear a teddy, the dolly a little baby. 'Sienna, Sienna,' she croons as she pauses to cradle it for a moment.

By the door, the assistants have set up a table with pink play dough. It's home-made and sticky, leaving a wormy residue on people's palms. Allana takes a lump. 'I break it!' she challenges. 'I roll it.' She presses Mr Toad's limbs into it. 'Him very naughty.' Allana has taken her neatly rolled sausage and torn it to bits. 'Him very, very naughty. Him allowed to do it again?' The other children round the table don't care if she's ruining her dough. Lack of censure can frustrate her as much as its imposition. She seems to have difficulty distinguishing between the intrinsically bad and what is merely self-defeating. 'See him do it again! Him sad, him sad.'

Now it's fruit time. Everyone goes outside and sits on squares of carpet on the almost-too-damp grass. There are plates of chopped apple and banana and cups for milk. The assistant suggests they count the number of adults and the number of children. A little boy is squirming, worried about his plastic comb, which doesn't fit in his pocket when he is sitting down. The plate is passed from hand to hand nearly flat, and only a few slices of fruit fall on to the grass, when one girl is distracted by a fly.

Allana has chosen an orange cup for her milk. Would she like a little bit more? She nods and nods, but Miss puts her hand to her ear with an encouraging face until a small 'please' emerges. By the third refill, she says 'yes, please' without prompting. The other children are talking about what they'll be when they grow up, but Allana isn't paying attention. Sometimes it seems that it is the communal expectation of speech rather than the act itself that bothers her most. In the next playground, the Reception class comes out. Some of them approach the fence and call over to their friends in nursery. Someone calls for Allana but she doesn't go to them. It's not Kayleigh.

At the end of the day, one of the nursery assistants bets that they've all forgotten how to tidy up. There are new green drawers to put the toys away in. Allana goes to the table of bricks and sweeps some off into the box on the floor. They make a mighty clatter and she turns around to check, unsure that something so noisy can be approved of. It is. She repeats the motion carefully, over and over, until all the bricks are cleared away. Her sticker says: 'I tidied up.'

Mrs Harrison just about has time to read a story. It's

called 'My First Day at Nursery', because it's their first day back after the holidays. Allana sits cross-legged with the other children. She looks carefully at the book being held up, though she doesn't call out the answers to the teacher's questions with the rest of the class. When asked directly, she says her favourite colour is purple.

They sing 'Old MacDonald Had A Farm', and for each verse a different child is invited to choose an animal. Allana picks a cow and, even though someone picked that only two verses ago, Mrs Harrison says it's OK. She asks Allana if she knows what noise cows make, but she doesn't want to say. The first day without Kayleigh, her personal spokesperson, is nearly over. Halfway through the verse, Allana begins to sing along. They finish with 'Twinkle, Twinkle Little Star'.

Although they're separated at school, Kayleigh still comes round to play. Next weekend, the atmosphere is hot and high in Allana's room. Her visitor is cooking in the plastic microwave. She's making cake and hot chocolate, actually. You've got to be very careful with it, actually. Kayleigh bosses Allana briskly, while bringing out foodstuffs for an imaginary guest: 'Don't draw on the walls, actually, your mum's already told you.'

Gloria and Kayleigh's mum have been friends for years. Hardly any of the mothers they know with young children are out at work. Gloria would like to get another job eventually, but she knows that for now Sienna won't be left. Gloria hasn't had any trouble herself, but a friend of hers with young children was told that if she didn't get back to work they'd stop her payments. She lasted two days in her new job.

It has been suggested that the government only started to take an interest in child care when it surmised that one way to tackle this country's appalling levels of child poverty was to get poor mothers into the workplace. But 'welfare to work' has its limits: more than half of children living in poverty already have a parent in employment. This is also a question of culture. The upper and middle classes have historically paid other people to look after their children to an extent that is anathema to a working-class – and particularly ethnic minority – mother. (More often because of structural imperatives rather than personal choice, child care in the UK remains a woman's province, though this is slowly changing.)

It can seem that policy is based on the assumption that all mothers are desperate to return to work. This presents another culture clash. Gloria is not a middle-class professional anxious to get back to the well-paid job which fulfils her sense of self beyond the home. Once she has paid for child care, returning to work in a college kitchen will barely offer more financial incentive than the benefits that keep her on the poverty line. And she certainly wouldn't have the time to take Allana and Sienna to Snakes and Ladders any more.

The motivations behind the government's ambitious ten-year child care strategy – which aims to provide free nurseries in every community and will compel local authorities to provide care for children up to the age of fourteen – remain ambiguous. It would seem that the emphasis has lately shifted from getting mothers back to work to the impact of early-years intervention on child development.

So what kind of children do the government want adults to raise, and what kind of parents are deemed unable to do it by themselves? A belief in the possibilities of nurture is far from progressive if it is applied only in order to populate the workforce of the future. Granted, a happy, resilient child will probably go on to enjoy a fulfilling working life as an adult. But that's not all that a life is for.

I remember at a Daycare Trust conference in London the look of blank incomprehension on the face of a Swedish delegate who was asked about the 'later social benefits' of her country's much-vaunted approach to preschool child care. As she struggled to answer, the Chair stepped in. Perhaps, he suggested, she found the question difficult because she wasn't beholden to the Anglo-American obsession with outcomes. Eventually the delegate offered: 'We don't regard preschool as preparation for school or work, but as a place to have a happy childhood.'

Similar to the Swedish approach is that of the Italian city of Reggio Emilia, home to a body of pedagogical theory and practice that is admired throughout the world. In 1964, the influential educationalist Loris Malaguzzi founded a network of municipal early childhood centres for children aged from a few months to six years old. (Britain is one of the few European countries where children start school as young as four.) Parents and other members of the local community actively support these municipal centres. Malaguzzi's approach has been described as no less than part of a civil strategy to win back society for children.

Malaguzzi's vision of the child was capacious and optimistic: 'A gifted child for whom we need a gifted teacher.' He rejected the narrative of schooling transforming children into adults, and believed that children were active constructors of their own learning. Malaguzzi saw teaching as a democratic process – rather than making children fit for school he wanted to make schools fit for children – but found that too often a child's potential was 'cut into pieces' by the conformity of educational expectation.

Peter Moss and Pat Petrie of London's Institute of

Education point out that Reggio's philosophy was embedded in a particular political context. They note its origins in postwar Italy, quoting an interview with the mayor of Reggio in the 1960s in which he described how the Fascist experience had taught the community that people who conformed and obeyed were dangerous, and that 'in building a new society it was imperative to safeguard and communicate that lesson and nurture . . . a vision of children who can think and act for themselves.'

Centres like those in Reggio require enormous financial and human capital, as well as a local community and a political administration that is willing to sustain them. But, celebrating the fortieth anniversary of Reggio's children's services, Harvard professor of education Howard Gardner suggested another reason why this model had not been replicated throughout the world. There are almost anarchic overtones to Malaguzzi's insistence that children can be guides in the teaching process, he wrote. It was a threatening vision: 'It means that you abandon an approach to life that is purely instrumental, purely financial . . . in favour of one that recognises the rights of children and the obligations of humanity.'

Nevertheless, elements of the Reggio approach are being integrated by some practitioners of early-years schooling in this country. But if child care is genuinely to centre around children – rather than the employability of their parents – and all children rather than those whose carers are deemed feckless, then much has to change. This country would do well to adopt the Scandinavian model of early-years provision, where child-caring has genuine professional status, with meticulous training and high pay.

Embracing the culture of the pedagogue is one thing. But unpaid child care has an even lower status than the paid kind. And meanwhile, new research is showing that one-to-one care for very young children is a central determinant in raising happy, secure, resilient children.

In 2003 and 2004, two large and significant longitudinal studies both reported that high levels of nursery care, particularly for the under-twos, led to an increase in emotional insecurity. In the United States, the National Institute of Child Health and Human Development, which had been following more than one thousand children since 1991, concluded: 'The more time children spend in child care from birth to age four and a half, the more adults tended to rate them as less likely to get along with others, as more assertive, as disobedient and as aggressive.'

A year later, a UK study – the Effective Provision of Preschool Education project (EPPE) – noted the benefits of early-years education for three- and four-year-olds, finding that nursery care advanced children's cognitive and social skills, especially in those from deprived backgrounds. However, it warned that 'high levels of group care before the age of three (and particularly before the age of two) were associated with higher levels of antisocial behaviour at age three'.

Then, in 2005, Penelope Leach presented the initial findings of her Families, Children and Child Care (FCCC) study, a five-year follow-up of 1,200 families in north London and Oxfordshire. She found that, at eighteen months, the development of children cared for by their mothers was better than the development of children who had received any other type of child care, including those looked after by nannies or grandparents.

The FCCC study suggested that nurseries are the worst child care option for children up to at least eighteen months, while home-based care by nannies or child-minders is 'significantly' better than that provided by 'informal' carers such as grandparents. But the study also emphasised that the differences were small, and that toddlers whose mothers were depressed or otherwise insensitive to their needs benefited from high-quality nursery care.

Given the sensitivity of the debate about the care of young children, it was inevitable that these findings caused controversy. The results were swiftly filleted by that insidious element of the British media that delights in pillorying working mothers. Alternatively, the authors of the studies were accused of being unsympathetic to the realities of women's lives, much as John Bowlby was a generation ago. Discussion of the role of fathers was conspicuous for its absence in all studies, though the FCCC researchers planned to publish a paper on fathers at a later date.

But the important data contained in detailed studies like these demands that we do more than endlessly polarise positions – the right insisting that women belong at home; the left, along with many feminists, making the historic mistake of assuming that every woman is a careerist at heart.

As Penelope Leach commented when she was interviewed about the findings: 'These days it isn't a choice between having an "at-home mummy" or a "working mummy". Most people have a bit of each and child care is the backbone of many people's lives, which is why it is important to get it right.'

The inference is not that every mother must stay indoors until her child starts school. Taken together, the data shows that for children under three, high levels of group-based care can have damaging effects on emotional development, while beyond that age the situation reverses and nursery care benefits all aspects of development. For very young children, it is best if the majority of their care is provided one-to-one by mothers or high-quality carers.

The studies also highlight the significant differences in

care needs between babies, toddlers and preschool children. Although not included in the initial release of findings in 2005, the FCCC research also covered older children and was expected to show that, from around three, children benefit from spending some time in nursery education.

Child-minders and nannies are prohibitively expensive for many, and Leach noted that the government must look at ways of expanding child-minding to make it more affordable. She was also critical of plans to extend free early-years education to two-year-olds – a move prompted by the EPPE findings about the impact of group care on the educational development of poorer children.

Leach also said that children's centres – undergoing a rapid expansion to include one in every community – should not end up as little more than 'nurseries with add-on', but should offer drop-in centres where infants would come with a parent or other carer and not be pressured towards group play too early.

And what about the Glorias of this world? Will the next ten years see poorer parents having their toddlers wrenched off them, because they have been deemed incapable of providing the appropriate emotional and intellectual stimulus to bridge the early-years attainment gap? Or will universal children's centres – like the PEEP project – consolidate the involvement of parents in their children's learning? Interestingly, when discussing how to tackle the escalation in adolescent depression, many mental health professionals have advocated putting parenting classes on the National Curriculum.

Meanwhile, Gloria keeps talking and waiting for Allana to talk back. Though she may not manage the same precipitate patter, Allana is not entirely mute around her best friend.

She is an active meaning-maker, if not yet a skilled communicator. They are dividing up Barbie dolls. Which one do you want? You can have that one. You can't have this one, this is my favourite. Allana begins to make some conversation between her male and female dolls: 'I'm not wearing any shoes'; 'That's OK, I'll carry you.' But although she keeps them talking, the noises degenerate into a jumble of sounds because she can't find the words quickly enough. It looks frustrating.

Kayleigh is putting her doll to sleep in Allana's Barbie castle.

'Someone's knocking on the door,' says Allana, outside.

'Hello, my name's Cinderella, who are you?'

'Pony.'

'Oh, so if you want to come to our tea party, it's our tea party.' Kayleigh opens the drawbridge to Allana's doll.

'Hello. What your name, what your name?'

'Cinderella, now who are you?'

'Batman.'

'You can come to our tea party.'

Allana starts jiggling the castle and a bed falls into Kayleigh's face.

'Don't play with it!' she screeches.

Sienna marches in, pink rucksack on her back as usual. 'I got lots of bags,' she announces with satisfaction. 'I gon' tidy up in a minute!' she adds efficiently. 'Me need two bags to put the packed lunch in.'

Gloria brings in some socks to put away. Sienna folds hers away in her drawer. 'Shall I help?' asks Kayleigh. 'I wan' help me one', Allana insists. She puts some away in her drawer too. 'Are they my ones?' asks Kayleigh, confused. 'I think you've got lots of socks at home,' says Gloria.

'Do you want some of this?' Kayleigh offers her the microwaved cake. 'I made it for you.'

'Nau'y, nau'y gill,' says Allana to Sienna once their mother has retreated, 'I'll smack you.' The crime is undefined and Sienna is unconcerned.

''Lana, I found the dummy. We got new bag. I've got a new bottle.' She is fondling the special bottle that belongs to Allana's Baby Annabel doll. When you tip it up the milk drains, and when you right it again it refills.

'Can I have it?' asks Kayleigh slyly, immediately discerning the superior quality of this plaything.

'No, it's 'Lana's,' says Sienna with hostility.

'Let me feed it!' cries Kayleigh, snatching the bottle from Sienna's grip and turning to cradle Baby Annabel. Allana flicks the switch at the back of the neck. The doll emits a pre-recorded burp and both snigger loudly. Kayleigh turns to Sienna triumphantly: 'Annabel burped!'

Allana tries to get her hand on the magic bottle but Kayleigh moves it away, gently but deliberately. She can't operate Annabel properly and it's making her crotchety. 'Stop it! It's not working.'

'Because YOU broke it!' shouts Allana.

'She's thirsty ain't she?' says Kayleigh, into the air.

'Bye, see you later . . .' Allana has gone back to playing with the Barbies, feigning disinterest.

Then comes another round of noisy evacuation. 'Allana! Annabel's burping!' The pair can't contain themselves. They make a staccato impression of an adult laugh: 'A-ha-a-ha-a-ha-ha-ha!'

Nicholas

'Once there was a programme that was an hour long and I counted twenty adverts, and they were all about a minute long, so that was twenty minutes.'

Two crepuscular portraits of dark-dressed ancestors hang in the sitting-room. The gentleman by the fireplace bears a certain resemblance to Robert Burns, with the same milky-blue complexion and wanton sideburns. In the background of the painting is a bookshelf, and on it can be made out the spine of Adam Smith's *Wealth of Nations*. It is a dry, cold Sunday afternoon towards the end of November, and Nicholas has been to a bowling party for a classmate's eighth birthday.

Himself newly eight, Nicholas is, in all matters, an empiricist. It is rare for him to resist the opportunity to mathematise. He has lived here for two and a half years, with a mum and a dad, one sister, and one au pair. His father is a shipping lawyer. His mother teaches languages at an independent girls' secondary school, near the major London preparatory school which he attends. He has three grandparents, an aunt and three cousins, two uncles and some older cousins.

His house has eight rooms, if you count the sitting-room which takes up most of the ground floor as one, and three bathrooms. 'Aaaah,' he sighs, for the sake of making the sound.

He has tufty blond hair and scrupulous consonants. His sister is five and a half, and her name is Emma. 'It's quite hard to explain what she's like. She's quite like me in some ways.'

Nicholas's bedroom is on the first floor, next to his sister's, and their shared bathroom. He has recently had a new carpet fitted. His box bed, bookcases and sofa are all in place, sinking their shapes into the fresh pile, but the shelves and surfaces are empty of clutter. It smells of clean.

On the cork board above his pillow are drawings by him, secured with the pins from the pot on his bedside table. There are pictures of pandas, fish, several coloured-in patterns, and a drawing he did this week at school about Christmas. The forthcoming festive season is his favourite time of year, apart from his birthday. 'I would like my birthday a bit further away from Hallowe'en because it's the next day and I get invited to Hallowe'en parties. I get invited to about four and then I can't go to any of them because it's my own birthday party.'

Nicholas has finished all his homework. He had a lot to do because on Fridays it's double. 'Probably it takes about an hour and a half, when normally it takes about twenty minutes. At the weekend I have geography, double spelling and reading, but normally I just have reading and maths, or reading and spelling. I'm good at spelling but I'm very, very, very good at maths'. Because he's so good at maths his teacher has put him up two sheets in the times-table tests.

Numbers can tell us a lot about childhood. It has been estimated that the total under-sixteen market in the UK adds up to £30 billion per annum, and that children receive an average of seventy new toys a year. It currently costs more to bring up a child than to purchase a house. Just as we have come to bemoan the corruption of Christmas by commerce, so we worry that childhood is uniquely at risk from the gluttony of market capitalism.

Children's changing status in the economy reveals much about their position in society. The young have always been active economic participants, whether as producers or as consumers. But their exclusion from the labour market over the past century and a half has caused their direct economic value to diminish, while their indirect economic value – as pesterers of parents, or as human capital for the future – has increased.

Viviana Zelizer, professor of sociology at Princeton University, who has written extensively about the social value of childhood, argues that the elimination of child labour 'is key to understanding the profound transformation in the economic and sentimental value of children . . . The price of a useful wage-earning child was directly counterposed to the moral value of an economically useless but emotionally priceless child.'

So children's 'work' was gradually reconceived as education and play. Their essential innocence was seen to be under threat from the adult world of employment, resulting in confinement at home and at school for the purposes of appropriate nurture. But here, they are left vulnerable to a damaging culture of competition, as both education and commerce thrive on separating children into winners and losers.

Meanwhile, Nicholas remains very good at maths, and undertakes a variety of other activities at which he is variously good, better or best. Last Friday, he sat his Grade One piano exam. He was quite nervous but he thinks it went well. You had to learn three pieces and do scales. He has piano lessons out of school, but flute lessons in school. 'And me and my mum always put on a Christmas concert 'cos my mum plays the organ, cello, guitar, piano, and I play the flute, piano, recorder. I normally just play about three pieces on the piano, one on the flute, probably a few on the recorder. Mum will play one on the piano, one on the cello.'

There is a wide poster of the solar system on the evenly painted wall beyond his bed. He's not really interested in space, not now. 'I used to be, one or two years ago, but now I'm into things like chess, and making crosswords and reading.' He started to construct a crossword earlier today. It took over two hours and it's not finished yet. One clues reads: 'Chess is one of these (5)', and the answer is 'games'; another is 'a parent (3)', and the answer is 'mum', but not 'dad'. It's quite hard to find a way to make all the letters fit.

Next March Nicholas is going to a chess tournament to play in the under-nines section. He may go on to play matches out of London. He likes to play chess with his granny. He normally beats her but she's quite good. 'I do get competitive,' he admits. 'It's a competitive game.' In the corner of his bedroom is his electric chess set. It's a thick, seventies-style board, plugged in at the mains. 'It used to be my mum's, and when I started to beat her she said that I should play the computer.' He switches it on, and it lights into life. A monotonal voice greets him: 'I am Intelligent Chess Challenger, your computer opponent. Select your level.'

Nicholas talks about his school, which he knows by the initials. It's all boys. 'You have to wear a tie which is striped, and you can wear a short-sleeved shirt or a long-sleeved shirt, and shorts or long trousers, and grey socks and you have to have black shoes.' He prefers a short-sleeved shirt and shorts. He doesn't get chilly knees. 'For a start, when it's very cold we have play inside, and I have a fleece.'

He's not certain what's different about a private school because he's never been to an ordinary school. An adult would know. You have to pay. He doesn't know anybody his own age who goes to a state school. The only difference between the kind of person who goes to a state school and the kind of person who goes to a private school is that to go to a school like his you have to have more money. People might have more money if they work very hard, or they might have more money from their ancestors.

His days are steadily ordered. The routine is solid and incontestable, a shire-horse of a week. 'Monday I have after-school club karate, on Tuesday that's when I have my piano lesson after school, Wednesday that's when I have my flute lesson in school and we have Golden Time and then after school I'm free.'

Golden Time is twenty minutes of free play, but minutes can be taken off as punishment for misbehaviour during the week. Once Jonathan got nineteen minutes out of twenty taken off, and the last minute is spent on tidying up so he missed it all. Nicholas normally has a game of chess or draughts with his best two friends George and Thomas, or maybe Charlie T. ('I've got two surnames and two first names in my class: James and James, and Charlie T. and Charlie O.' He offers a lot of his speech in parentheses. There is such a lot to observe and ennumerate.)

Nicholas is older than both George and Thomas, but only ten days older than Thomas. 'Thomas is taller than me. He likes chess but it's not one of his favourite games. George is very good at suicide chess. (There are lots of different sorts of chess: baby chess, suicide chess, Greek chess, Scottish chess, Irish chess.) I only know Greek chess and suicide chess and normal chess, and George is really, really good [at suicide chess] and no one in my year can beat him. No one in my year can beat me at normal chess.'

The routine trots onward. 'On Thursday I have breakfast at school because it opens really early and I get there at quarter to eight and then after school we collect Emma. Me and my au pair have to walk up to her school, wait for about half an hour while I do my homework, and then Mummy comes. After school on Friday I have two hours of chess club 'cos I like chess, so I never do my homework on Fridays and I save it for the weekend.'

He is manoeuvring the mince pie, which his mother has brought him, into his mouth. 'And because we've got the Christmas play coming up we've got these after-school rehearsals and last Monday I had to go to that instead.' He sits upright on the two-seat sofa, the plate on his knees. 'Oh my!' A morsel has fallen into his lap.

The Christmas play is not the story of Baby Jesus. 'I'm a citizen. There are twenty shepherds, twenty citizens, twenty angels, twenty travellers and there are six children's songs. It's for all of Year 3 and there are supposed to be a hundred pupils, although there are actually ninety-six. I just have to say my line when it gets to the scene that I'm in, scene three. I have a copy of who I am and everyone's words and one of the songs.'

He can't really explain the plot. It's the story of Jesus but it's not the story of Jesus at his birth. 'As a citizen I'm selling things, so I say, "Spiced wine, hot snacks, buy your hot snacks here!"' He sing-songs it in a clear treble. 'And I don't actually only know my own words. I know quite a few other people's. For instance, I know: "I'm freezing", "I'm exhausted", "It's freezing", "It's not been properly organised", "So this is Bethlehem".'

Christmas is fun, but it doesn't really start until the holidays begin. 'There are three weeks now and another three at Easter.' He drops in another casual calculation. 'Last year it was two weeks at Christmas and four at Easter for some reason.'

* * *

A week later, Nicholas is completing his practice at the grand piano. He has only just started learning 'Good King Wenceslas' but his sight-reading is keen and he stretches his fingers to span the three-note chords. He grins equably when his mother praises him. Emma loiters around the piano legs, darkly ignoring them both.

The play was on Thursday. Loads of people came and it was videoed, which was pretty nerve-racking.

By the window in Nicholas' bedroom is a print of the Rembrandt painting *Belshazzar's Feast*, in which a mysterious hand writes a message on a wall foretelling the destruction of the King of Babylon. 'I've had it ever since I read this,' he explains, knee-shuffling from the sofa to the bookshelf. He pulls out a hardback illustrated Bible. 'It's got 360 pages which is quite long. It's quite good to read but it does take a long time.' It didn't really teach him any useful lessons though. It's not like going to school.

Nicholas isn't especially religious. 'We have to pray in assembly but that's the only time. My mum's mum goes to church but no one else does.' He went round to his granny's again yesterday, because Emma and his parents had parties to go to. Mainly, they played chess.

This week, his books and games have been reinstated following the carpet-laying, but the room remains preternaturally tidy. His favourite novels are arranged in series order: the Famous Five, Roald Dahl, and Lemony Snicket, Tintin, Lucky Luke and Asterix. He has a collection of *Horrible Histories* magazines in a separate rack. His Top Trumps collection is stored in a drawer beneath his bed. There is nothing on his floor that ought not to be there.

People are coming to lunch later, and Nicholas thinks they may be having sausages because there were lots in the fridge. 'It's one of my mum's old colleagues, and their children who are six and nine. Emma plays with the nine-year-old and I play with the six-year-old, because the six-year-old is a boy and the nine-year-old is a girl.'

Emma's a girl so she likes playing Barbies but Nicholas doesn't. 'She's sometimes not nice to me, so I'm not nice to her. Sometimes she wants me to play a game with her which I don't want to play and then she tries to threaten me with telling my mum and everything. She sometimes pretends to hit me but I'm stronger than her.' He likes being at school with only boys. He did go to a mixed nursery school. 'There seemed to be more talking and I had less friends,' he recalls.

His school breaks up for the holidays next Wednesday, but Emma's goes on until Friday so he has two more days than her. 'My mum's mum is coming for Christmas Eve and Christmas Day, and then we're going to my dad's parents in Oxford for four days.' Otherwise he might see friends from school, but mainly he'll just laze about, and try to avoid doing too much piano practice.

You do more fun things towards the end of term, things to do with Christmas. 'So in maths you had this Christmas tree and there were nine baubles, four going down each way, and you had to fill each bauble with a number from one to nine and each side had to add up to twenty-one. And in English you had to do some writing about Christmas dinner.'

Ever since he started at prep school, Nicholas has had an au pair who stays one year. 'Before I used to have a nanny and she had a daughter who came with her after school and she was called Emma too, so we called her Big Emma and my sister just Emma.'

It depends what sort of person the au pair is. 'If it's some-one who can't speak much English then it's weird. The au pair we have now speaks quite a bit of English. She comes from Germany. She's got her own room. She eats dinner with us, so it's like having an extra mum or dad really.'

'She works twenty-five hours a week (not including baby-sitting), so she's free from seven o'clock onwards. I'm not exactly sure what she does then – watches television in her room or something. She's called Marta. She's slightly shy. She's not really, really chatty. For instance when she's watching television, she's not also talking.' (Nicholas doesn't watch much television, only about half an hour a day and sometimes none at all. He likes *Blue Peter* because it shows you all sorts of different things you can make.)

His nanny looked after him from when he was about three months old, but she didn't live with them. 'We still see her sometimes. She lived in a flat. It's better to live in a house than a flat. In a flat you only have one bedroom, one sitting-room, one kitchen and one bathroom. In a house you have three bedrooms normally, one or two bathrooms and a bigger sitting-room, so there's more room.'

Nicholas hasn't written his Christmas list yet. He doesn't know what he wants. Nor has he really thought about what to get the rest of his family. 'Everybody has the same problem – they all seem to have everything already.'

He got more excited about Christmas when he was younger, he says. 'Now that I'm eight, I've worked out that Father Christmas is just your mum and dad – the same with the Tooth Fairy and the Easter Bunny and everything.' There is the sliver-thinnest of pauses here while he waits for an eleventh hour, faith-restoring piece of evidence to the contrary. But none is forthcoming. 'Because reindeers can't fly and – I mean – there aren't such things as elves, and no one could have that many presents, and no one would come down a chimney really, because some houses don't have chimneys, and it's impossible to go through the doors because they'd be locked.' He is becoming increasingly exasperated.

'I started thinking about it when I was seven. It just sort of made sense to me. I didn't feel disappointed, but it makes Christmas a bit less exciting. Emma still believes.' He sounds almost envious of her unvanquished certainty. 'Mum told me not to tell her.' So why do adults tell children about Father Christmas in the first place? 'Because they have to make up some sort of excuse for how presents get in your stocking.' Or perhaps, less generously, they want to bribe some best behaviour – though Nicholas never really believed that Santa could see whether he'd been good or bad. 'Actually, I'm very rarely naughty. And when I am naughty it's usually because my sister's annoyed me.'

Another eight-year-old, the New Yorker Virginia O'Hanlon, did believe in Santa Claus, until she heard the poor children of her neighbourhood claiming that he didn't exist. When she asked her father, he was understandably non-committal, suggesting that she write to the local newspaper for a definitive answer. Her letter, written in 1897, appeared on the editorial page of the *New York Sun* with a response from the editor, and was reprinted every Christmas until 1949 when the paper went out of business.

'I am eight years old,' it read. 'Some of my little friends say there is no Santa Claus. Papa says, "If you see it in the *Sun*, it's so." Please tell me the truth. Is there a Santa Claus?'

The editor replied: 'Yes, Virginia, there is a Santa Claus. He exists as certainly as love and generosity and devotion exist, and you know that they abound and give your life its highest beauty and joy. Nobody sees Santa Claus, but that is no sign that there is no Santa Claus. The most real things in the world are those that neither children nor men can see.'

Nicholas, being more partial to observable phenonema, might prefer the methodology of the scientist Richard Dawkins. In his book *Unweaving the Rainbow*, he calculates that Santa would have to travel at many thousand times the speed of sound in order to visit every home in the world. Dawkins concludes that the fact no one has ever heard a sonic boom on Christmas Eve disproves the saint's existence.

Finding out the truth about Father Christmas is one of childhood's looking-glass moments: a rude recognition not only that all things are not possible, but that grown-ups may tell lies, even if they are lovely ones. Anthropologists might place this shift in status – between the young child who believes, and older children who do not – within the array of initiation rites which mark the passage into adolescence.

But Christmas-time has always been a precarious fantasy. The modern festival, with its emphasis on homely rituals and lavish spending, was a Victorian creation, a response to the rigours of industrialisation. The domestic sphere was reimagined as a distinct moral realm, in an attempt to shore up family and community against the fragmentation brought on by urban capitalism. At the heart of this haven was child-hood – in the process of being liberated from the exploita-tion of the factory, idealised by the age as a time of innocence and enchantment.

Charles Dickens noted in *Sketches by Boz*, published in 1836, the prevalence of cynics who 'tell you Christmas is not to them what it used to be'. And so it is that contemporary celebrations are frequently denounced as materialistic and unspiritual. Gift-giving and get-togethers have become freighted with social meanings far removed from the simple benevolence espoused in Dickens's *A Christmas Carol*, 'when men and women seem by one consent to open their shut-up hearts freely, and to think of other people below them as if they really were fellow-passengers to the grave'. We even owe Santa's 'traditional' red and white garb to an advertising artist at the Coca-Cola Company, who first depicted him wearing it as he quenched his 'thirst for all seasons' in 1931.

Rather like childhood, Christmas offers a focus for what people most dislike about life: commercialism, fractured families, long working hours. But the dream of a perfect festive time – propped up by the frantic efforts of exhausted adults – is remarkably persistent, a veritable triumph of hope over experience. In the bleak midwinter of stress and excess, it bridges the disconnection between the public display of family we envy of everybody else, and the private disappointments that lurk behind our own turkey and trimmings.

Now it is the day before the day before Christmas Eve. The kitchen table is bright with coloured beads that pop into plastic frames to make pictures. Emma is working on a ladybird. Nicholas has constructed an elaborate geometric pattern. At the piano end of the long sitting-room stands a laden Christmas tree. His favourite decoration is the star, or maybe this shiny green bauble. To the side are the children's advent calendars, the cardboard windows hanging open like broken promises. This is a scene best viewed on a snowy night through a frosted window. It feels rich and snug, as though the whole home has been insulated with red velvet.

Nicholas has been to the cinema with his dad. He might like to be an actor, but he doesn't think being famous would be very good. 'Everyone would know you and everything and you'd have loads and loads and loads of money, too much really.' It is possible to have too much money. A google or millions of pounds would be too much. A sensible amount would be a few thousand pounds, something like three thousand. He calculates. 'Well, more than that really, maybe

£300,000.' Everyone should be able to afford a house and a car.

He retires to his bedroom. It's cold outside, and Nicholas is wearing a smart navy fleece. His thick hair looks warm like a hat. It's a Tuesday morning, but he's here at home because the holidays have arrived. He had a friend round yesterday. They played draughts and watched television together: *Tom and Jerry*, *Scooby-Doo*, *Blue Peter* and *Newsround*. Nicholas doesn't think that people his age know what's happening in the news: 'I don't know anyone who watches it apart from me.' In the news this week, someone has made a robotic dolphin that goes a metre under water and it can do all sorts of tricks.

Outside his bedroom door, Emma is getting in a muddle with her carolling, and a chorus of sweet hallelujahs vowel-slips into 'hallelooloo'. Nicholas laughs hard, twisting on the sofa, aware of how he is laughing and aiming for a note of grown-up derision. 'Emm-aaa,' he calls, 'can you stop that please?'

A tooth is wobbly. He doesn't know how many baby teeth he has left, but he does know that he's got eight big teeth. Two of them are his top front teeth and they look a little large for the rest of his mouth. When a tooth is ready, it gets extremely wobbly and then it comes out. 'I've swallowed nearly all of them. I've swallowed six out of eight. I only realise it when I've brushed my teeth!' He doesn't like going to the dentist, but he's not scared of it.

There is a troop of monkeys at the feet end of Nicholas's bed. He's had George, the biggest one, since he was two. He got nearly all of them for Christmas, except for the smallest one. He definitely used to like them, but not so much now. He would play at throwing them in the air and catching them, and would imagine that they could talk when he was very, very young.

His earliest memory may be that, or it may be this one. 'It was when my sister was born and my mum left me at home with my nanny and I watched videos all night!' It's not every day your sister is born. 'She went at about one o'clock in the morning, and she came back at about eight o'clock the next night, and Emma was born at about one o'clock. I was two and a half, and you get excited about things like that when you're young.'

Ingrid the au pair is going home to Germany today. She's coming back again one day before school starts. He'll miss her a bit, but not as much as when his mum or his dad or his sister go somewhere. He catches himself out. 'Well – my sister never goes anywhere without me!'

His dad sometimes goes away on business. He had to go to Libya once. He brought back this gigantic plate with pictures of camels on it. Libya is next to Egypt. Nicholas does not consider himself widely travelled: 'I've not been far, only to Scotland, and quite a few different places in France, and Crete, and Venice.'

His father's job means that he doesn't have much holiday. He only has three days at Christmas: Christmas Eve, Christmas Day and Boxing Day. He brings work home with him. Nicholas wouldn't really like to be a lawyer. He doesn't know what sort of job would be interesting.

You have to choose what job you want to do when you're about seventeen, he explains, so you can decide what subjects you're going to do at university. 'I'm going to go to university. My mum wants me to so I will probably.' His parents don't know where he should go to university, because his mum went to Cambridge, his dad went to Oxford and his grandad went to London, so they can't decide which one's best for him.

*   *   *

Nicholas can barely imagine a time when he will not be being educated. The number of years children spend in teaching institutions has soared since the introduction of free and compulsory primary education in Britain in 1880. Then, opposition to child labour was a consequence of a shift in how childhood was perceived. The factory and education acts of the nineteenth and early twentieth centuries marked the first instance of the government intervening in children's upbringing. But it was not done purely out of charity, as politicians alighted on a new imperative of better preparing the workforce of the future.

Concern about child labour is a relatively recent phenomenon. Reformers like Robert Owen and Lord Shaftesbury were considered radical when they challenged what was seen as children's necessary contribution to the family wage. In pre-industrial times, it would appear that children in poor households were expected to participate in the family workforce from early on, taking on minor tasks to suit their age and ability, helping around the home and in the fields. Formal training and wages came later, when older children and teenagers left their families to work as apprentices.

Viviana Zelizer notes that in nineteenth-century America, to include children in the household economy of the working class was considered 'not only economically indispensible but also a legitimate social practice'. She refers to children's books of the time, which praised the virtues of hard work, and where the standard villain was the idle child. 'Work was a socializer; it kept children busy and out of mischief.'

There is some dispute about whether industrialisation significantly increased the number of child labourers, or merely extended children's employment opportunities beyond the domestic sphere. In factories, cotton mills and coal mines, mechanical advances allowed children to undertake jobs that had previously required the strength of an adult.

Campaigners against child labour did not have to look far for evidence that interminable hours and desperate conditions were gravely affecting children's health. Miners as young as six risked death in tunnels too small for grown men. Children with nimble fingers who were assigned to clean fast-moving power looms often lost digits. Breathing in dust and cotton fibres led to outbreaks of 'spinners' phthisis' and other forms of tuberculosis. Young girls ruined their sight with the close work of lace-making and embroidery, or developed 'phossy jaw' – gangrene of the jawbone caused by phosphorous poisoning – in matchstick factories.

The plight of child labourers was popularised by Charles Kingsley in his novel *The Water Babies*, published in 1862. The book followed the adventures of Tom the chimney sweep, who fell into a river after escaping his cruel master Grimes, where he was transformed into one of the adventurous underwater infants. Within a year, Parliament had banned the use of small boys as sweeps.

Ultimately, the reformers were successful because they were campaigning with the economic and social grain. As the real value of incomes rose, the need for children to supplement family earnings declined. In particular, calls for a 'family wage' gained momentum – the idea that the male breadwinner should be able to earn enough to keep his wife and children at home. The desire of educational reformers to remove schooling from the purview of the Church further accelerated children's ejection from the workplace.

The nature of childhood was changing. As Stephen Kline argues: 'The factory acts in Britain . . . confirm that throughout the early industrial era childhood was increasingly seen as a stage of growth that in the long-term interests of civilized society had to be isolated and guarded from an abusive world.' This legislation, alongside the introduction of compulsory schooling, did just that.

But Kline is also quick to point out that Victorian state schooling did not provide a children's paradise. 'Brutality was accepted and justified on the grounds that it was necessary to discipline the recalcitrant learner. Learning itself was defined and viewed as a very unliberating process of knowledge assimilation and repetition. Nor was the school completely without an industrial social purpose.'

He also identifies how progressives then turned their attention to children's play. The early twentieth century saw a dramatic expansion of children's organisations – Sunday schools, scouting movements, camps – mostly aimed at the working classes. 'Play, it was argued, was not simple idleness but the "work of childhood" – the moral equivalent of labour . . . Structured game-play and sport were also highly recommended as ways of preparing children for a competitive society and of creating a location for class mingling and negotiation.'

Of course, children of the twenty-first century are not entirely economically inactive, though there is no minimum wage for children, nor are they covered by statutory employment rights. A study by the Joseph Rowntree Foundation at the turn of the millennium found that two in five children aged between eleven and sixteen did some form of paid work outside the home, working for an average of just under five hours a week. One in twenty had three jobs or more, with paper rounds and baby-sitting the most common occupations. Children today tend not to be working to contribute to family income so much as to gain independence from their parents or to satisfy their burgeoning consumer needs.

The demands of industrial capitalism have not abated

since the introduction of compulsory education. Just as adults' time is money, so children's time is valued as an investment in their potential earning and spending power. And – as Nicholas might testify – childhood, like chess, is these days a very competitive game.

In his book *Britain on the Couch*, the psychologist Oliver James investigates the effects of increased, and more competitive, schooling on the self-confidence and optimism of children. He draws on the work of Diane Ruble, professor of psychology at New York University and the most active researcher in this field. Ruble has found that, until around the age of seven, children are indiscriminate in who they choose to compare themselves with, as happy to pick an adult as a peer. But beyond seven, they increasingly use comparison with their peers as the means of self-evaluation, becoming pre-occupied with competition. Ruble argues that many teaching methods exploit this, using techniques that encourage public victories and defeats.

She discovered that, perhaps because they do not compare themselves with their peers and are largely ignorant of their performance relative to them, preschool and primary-grade children showed impressive resilience in the face of failure. 'They maintain persistence, self-confidence and expectations of future success. By mid-elementary school, however, such optimism and positive responses to failure largely disappear . . . with increasing disinterest in school-related activities appearing as children progress through elementary school.' Ruble suggests that, 'Because there are only a limited number of "winners" in any competitive system, children may experience a dissatisfaction with themselves . . . Comparison can promote a sense of relative deprivation and inadequacy, affecting interpersonal relationships and self-esteem.'

James notes that Ruble particularly emphasises that children have no escape from this comparative system of schooling. Although she suggests some mechanisms by which they might avoid it – such as disengagement from school activities or the development of anti-academic cliques – she believes that the most common result is lowered self-esteem.

'The drop in self-confidence and achievement expectancies found during the early school years may be due to the incorporation of comparative standards into the self-concept,' she concludes. Indeed, she believes that children who do badly do more social comparing than those who are succeeding.

'Children may develop a poor opinion of themselves because they compare frequently, or they may socially compare more because they have a poor opinion of themselves . . . They may begin to look for additional information but along the way the perception of the self as poor comes, in part, from negative conclusions they draw from social-comparison information. Taken all together, the data suggest that the period from seven to nine years is a very important one for self-definition and self evaluation.'

It is difficult not to conclude that our own education system perpetuates just such damaging social comparison, seeming to pit student against student in an endless quest for 'standards'. Schools themselves are in competition with each other for scarce resources.

This quest makes a sham of inclusive schooling, as professor of education at Goldsmiths College Sally Tomlinson argues: 'As long as teachers are pressed to deliver higher standards in the form of more children passing examinations and reaching targets, they will understandably be more reluctant to take on the education of all children. There is little time or incentive for teachers to introduce new curriculum practices within mainstream schools, when the emphasis is on achieving at key stages and acquiring the magic five A*–C grades at GCSE.'

The system is destined to create more losers than winners. And it robs children of the chance to learn collaboratively when they are simply delivered a script to be regurgitated at a later date under stressful conditions. As Oliver James observes, it's good news for future employers, guaranteed a wildly competitive workforce, and for the corporations who will exploit these insecurities in order to sell their status-affirming products.

For now, though, Nicholas can forget about homework. He's feeling excited about Christmas because he'll get new toys. 'I asked for a new Gameboy because my last one got lost. I was playing with it and I put it back in my top drawer, and then I think my sister took it out to play with and she can't remember what she did with it afterwards.' He's looked hard for it, but especially since the new carpet all his things have got new places.

His dad has bought presents for Nicholas and Emma to give their mum, and his mum has bought things for him to give her mum, but he has no idea about what to get his dad. His parents won't have stockings, because there'd be no point in them buying tiny presents for themselves. They'd know exactly what was in there and take it out the next morning!

Christmas is a happy time of year for most people, thinks Nicholas. But not all people. It is the year following the second Gulf War. 'If you're in Iraq quite a few of their houses have been destroyed so they won't be having a Christmas tree and lots and lots of presents.'

When I next visit Nicholas, it's the day after the day after the day after Boxing Day, in that peculiar stretch before the New Year that can feel dilatory after the accelerated preparations of Advent. Nicholas's Christmas Day began with him taking things out of his stocking, playing with the things in his stocking and eating some of the chocolates. Then he got dressed, and ate breakfast, which is always bacon sandwiches and eggs. Then he opened his presents.

'I got one or two presents – quite a few actually. I got a snooker table.' He pauses, still impressed. 'It's in the conservatory downstairs. I knew that it began with an "s" but I didn't know that I was getting it. I was told that it was a board to do my homework on but of course I knew it wasn't. It was in this gigantic package and you had to put it together. It took about half an hour, and then my mum taught me how to play.'

He got a new Gameboy and two new games as well. But then when they went to Oxford to visit his grandparents they found the one he'd lost. 'It was in the car under the middle seat, so now I've got two Gameboys. My sister got one for Christmas too so altogether we've got three Gameboys and five games.'

His grandparents gave him a Spirograph that makes patterns, and he got a CD and one or two tapes and of course lots of books. He reaches across the bedroom floor to the pile of most-favoured presents. 'I got the encyclopaedia of everything yucky and it says down the side "including bogies, farts, bottoms, toilets and vomit"!' His high 'hee-hee' strains his neck muscles. 'In here there's probably the biggest fart in the world!'

He reads on, clear and precise, revelling in rudeness sanctioned between hard covers. '"This consists of ants, bats, blood, body odour, burping, eye gunk, farts, fleas, fungi, lice, maggots, pee, poop, leeches, pus, rats, scabs, slugs, snakes, snots, spiders, tics, toilets, vomit." That's what my aunt gave me. It's absolutely disgusting.' He opens it to display a lurid close-up of worms. 'Where's snot?' he muses, leafing through the pages. 'Here's vomit.' His mum told him about the most disgusting thing that's he's ever done. 'When I was a baby, when she was changing my nappy I once accidentally did a wee in her face,' he confesses, merrily aghast.

After he had finished opening his presents on Christmas Day, his dad was really mean and said that everyone had to go out for a walk, at about eleven o'clock in the morning. 'My granny got to stay behind, unfairly. Then we waited for three hours for the turkey to cook, and then we had lunch and I didn't have any pudding, I was so full up with turkey, bacon, stuffing, carrots, potatoes, peas, etc.' Nicholas has a delicious way of saying 'potatoes', as though he's still tasting them.

The Christmas concert didn't go very well because he got every single piece wrong and had to start again. After that he played more snooker. A family friend called Ann was there too. Nicholas went to bed about half an hour later than usual.

The day after Boxing Day, Nicholas and his family went to Oxford to see his dad's parents and his dad's sister and her husband and their children. 'When we arrived my cousin Simon was there and the first thing he did was start punching my bottom. And the twins [who were born earlier this year] were always crying. But Emma played more with Simon, because they're nearly the same age.'

His grandparents like cycling a lot, and they don't like cars, he notes with surprise. They're probably the only ones in the whole street who don't have a car. They're not too old – something like sixty-six and seventy. When he visits, he does a lot of cycling because they live near two cycle paths. Otherwise, he doesn't really like sports. 'I don't like boxing and I don't like rugby that much.' He has a double session on Fridays at school. 'You don't actually tackle each other, you tag each other, but quite often if I

145

have got the ball they pull me down by the thing that holds the tag on and say it was an accident.' 'They' are the mean people from the other classes. Nicholas's worst teacher is his PE teacher. He's *really* mean.

School doesn't start again until 11 January. He has days and stretching days left of what Dylan Thomas called 'that wool white bell-tongued ball of holidays'. His friend George is coming tomorrow, but he doesn't know if it's for a sleep-over. Every single holiday George goes to Canada, even if it's only for one week. 'His father used to live in Canada, so he's half English, half Canadonian, whatever you say.' He's got nothing much else to do apart from boring things like thank-you letters and music practice. He wouldn't really like to be a musician when he grows up, but it's important to do music practice because his mum wants him to and she tells him off otherwise!

He's not sure what he'll be eating with George, but it won't be pizza. 'I don't like pizza. I can make George fall off a chair anytime when I say I don't like Coke, chocolate or pizza. Everyone in my class thinks I'm incredibly unusual not liking Coke, chocolate or pizza and always drinking water.'

Nicholas has a more cosmopolitan palate. He likes mussels, which he normally has with garlic sauce, and omelette. Once, when he was in Italy, he tasted kiwi, and peach and passion-fruit ice cream. He thinks there was even a tomato-flavoured one.

Nicholas isn't sure about whether he needs to make any New Year's resolutions. He hasn't got any bad habits, apart from picking his nose, but everyone does that. It says here in the Yuck Book that there's been a record taken and every-one has once picked their nose. Everyone in the world.

He doesn't really do anything for New Year. His mum will give him a small present like a pencil, but it seems really titchy compared to a Gameboy or a snooker table. He prefers Christmas.

How would he feel like if he didn't get any presents? 'That would depend on whether everyone else did or not. If no one got any then I'd be annoyed. If I was the only one then I'd be really, really cross with my mum and dad.'

Is giving presents a way of showing people that you like them?

'Well, yes,' says Nicholas.

Are there other ways?

'Well, saying it, obviously. Playing with them.'

A major engine in the juggernaut of child-panic is the fear that childhood has been co-opted by commerce, and children integrated into the sphere of avarice. Growing-up has always meant learning the rhythms of wanting, getting and not getting – attention, a biscuit, that toy, now, later. What is new, and profoundly alarming, is the scale and sophistication of inducements to want.

For richer and poorer, shopping has become a leisure activity. The unprecedented increase in consumption over the past fifty years has driven the search for fresh niche markets. Childhood is spliced into numerous needful stages, each requiring appropriate toys, clothes and entertainments. In addition to the teenage market, first targeted during the postwar economic boom, there are now pre-teens, tweens and tinies.

In a major research study released in 2005, the National Consumer Council (NCC) identified a generation of young people aged between ten and nineteen who were avid shoppers. Perhaps surprisingly, it noted that British children were more consumer-oriented than their peers in the United States, usually considered the progenitor of materialism.

Even the youngest in the sample were already keen consumers: the average ten-year-old had internalised between 300 and 400 brands. Brand recognition even amongst infants is astonishing. An earlier study by the *International Journal of Advertising and Marketing to Children* found that over two thirds of three-year-olds recognised the McDonald's golden arches.

A combination of babies born fewer and later, working parents, and the by no means universal increase in disposable income has given children far greater influence over household purchasing decisions. With the advent of 'pester-power', advertisers have learnt to sell to them directly. Around six out of ten children in the NCC study said that they pestered parents for what they wanted, getting annoyed or slamming doors if the answer was 'no'. But children's own disposable income is also rising. According to a study by the Halifax, pocket money increased at more than four times the rate of inflation in 2005.

Staggering resources are mined into reaching this lucrative market, with companies drafting in child psychologists and extending their promotional activities ever more subtly, particularly through sponsorship in schools. Specialised marketing agencies sell advertising space in secondary schools and play areas. Other companies parade altruism in exchange for guaranteed brand recognition, like Cadbury's offering free sports equipment to schools in exchange for vouchers from chocolate bars, or Walkers Crisps giving away free books.

Beyond the playground, as children's leisure time becomes more contained, they spend many thousand of hours each year hopping between commercials on their multi-channel televisions, flipping through pop-ups as they surf the Internet, or clocking the product placements embedded in video games.

And children are now actively involved in the marketing

process itself. Levi Strauss was the first company to recruit 'cool' kids to advise them. Brainstorming amongst young consumers is supposed to have led Heinz to produce its 'E-Z squeeze' bottles. Children can become co-creators of new computer games, testing pre-release versions in online communities. Others are recruited to 'street teams' – armies of underage PRs who are offered freebies and other inducements to promote new bands to their peers.

Stephen Kline argues that it was Victorian concern with the distinct nature of childhood, together with the increasing availability of manufactured goods, that fed the fledgling children's market. A new interest in child development and welfare encouraged manufacturers to diversify into educational and medical products. Soon clothing and furniture – like smocks, pinafores and high chairs – were being designed exclusively for children.

The production of toys followed suit, chiming with a new ideal of modern consumer domesticity that can be seen in the advertising of the early 1900s. Kline writes: 'The child with toys is a symbol of the pleasures of consumerism, of the new objects primarily designed for leisure and fantasy . . . Toys are fitting symbols of economic progress because they direct consumers to the rewards of leisure and relaxation. The recreated atmosphere of domestic consumption takes its emotional cues and mood from the absence of labour implied by a playful child.'

So the children's market had as much resonance for adults. Professor Ellen Seiter, author of *Sold Separately: Children and Parents in Consumer Cultures*, observes how cultural changes throughout the twentieth century – in particular women's involvement in the labour market – have increased the demand for toys: 'In order for the volume of toy sales to have increased, families had to move to houses with space to keep the toys, and children had to have mothers who were so busy that they needed new ways to keep children entertained.' The increase in children's consumption, she argues, has been caused in part by the increasing difficulty in the job of caring for children.

Nowadays, however, that consumption is rising exponentially, and one extremity is swiftly superceded by the next: the toy of the film, the yoghurt of the cartoon, the padded bra of the doll. In the worst light, the industry looks like a monstrous behemoth, pushing sex and saturated fats, creating a generation of obese, promiscuous, celebrity-obsessed automatons, dependent on brands for identity, bullying the poor few who cannot afford the right trainers, unable to appreciate gratification that is anything other than instant.

But this presumes that children are innately free of cynicism, lacking any ability to discriminate. Are younger people especially at risk from the magical materialism that creates unnecessary needs and promises a fantasy world in which they are all fulfilled? Are children essentially more persuadable because they are less competent than adults? Or does some of this panic reflect certain assumptions about what it is to be a child?

David Buckingham, professor of education at London's Institute of Education, has spent fifteen years investigating the impact of the media on children. An authority in his field, he treats child-panic with caution. From the extensive research that he has conducted, he believes that children can be wise consumers – at least as wise as adults – although he admits that just because someone has adequate defences they will not necessarily always use them. He also acknowledges the limitations of discussing advertising in isolation, as the lines between promotional messages and content in the media blur, and corporations employ ever-more-sophisticated means of getting round consumer cynicism.

Crucially, he argues that a false dichotomy has been set up between culture and commerce, with the latter seen to be polluting the former. But consumer culture is not just about manipulating authentic needs which exist in a purer sphere, says Buckingham. Consumer culture, unavoidably, 'is now the arena where those very needs are defined, articulated and experienced.' There is no sacred space, and childhood cannot be made to provide it.

The children in the NCC study certainly come across as enthusiastic but canny consumers. Although they were keen shoppers, most didn't consider themselves particularly attached to promotion, with only three out of ten saying that they liked to watch adverts. Instead, many complained of commercial overload, citing the prevalence of intrusive and inappropriate marketing, which used sexual imagery or offered them overage goods that they were unable to buy.

Seven out of ten children said that they had felt ripped off by the false expectations set by advertising, while others referred to a more direct discrimination when shopping, believing that sales staff viewed them as second-class consumers and potential criminals.

Nevertheless, this sense of a hostile commercial environment appeared to have little impact on the children's desire to buy. One of the most significant findings of the report was that children who have the least want the most. Those from the most disadvantaged households felt more keenly the discrepancy between their own ability to purchase and the possibilities of consumption presented to them. The NCC argued, 'The aspiration gap does have long-term implications. Poorer children are more likely to leave school early. Keen to enter the adult consumer world, they are, compared to better-off children, more concerned to get a job and less concerned to build a career.'

Consumer culture would seem to operate in the same way that schooling can to exacerbate the negative effects of social comparison. It is the *raison d'etre* of advertising, after all, to convince people that without a particular product they are 'losers', and its prevalence offers children no chance to escape this edict.

The NCC concluded that greater regulation of all forms of marketing to children was essential. Much as children have the right to have their choices taken seriously and their capacity to make them respected, they have an equal right not to be bombarded and manipulated. But regulation alone risks falling back on the standard of the incompetent child.

The NCC has also pioneered the case for a national strategy for consumer education, which extends to children. The teaching of 'media literacy' builds young people's skills by working with their interests as consumers, rather than against them.

Ellen Seiter argues that it is a mistake to judge children's desires exclusively in terms of manipulation, greed or hedonism. She suggests that we need to break with the condemnation of children's consumer culture in order to understand it. While acknowledging that children themselves don't originate any of the symbols of this global subculture, she maintains that they can have a creative approach to consuming, making their own meanings from the stories and characters they see. Sometimes those meanings are entirely unanticipated, she says, noting the success of Teenage Mutant Ninja Turtles, which left the toy industry baffled.

While cautioning against a blindly utopian view, Seiter argues that children's consumption can be understood as 'a desire for a shared culture with their schoolmates and friends and a strong imagination of community'. This culture holds an ambiguous position between the domestic and public spheres, she says. 'Sometimes . . . children feel their knowledge and mastery of consumer culture to be a kind of power: something they know, but of which adults are ridiculously ignorant.'

But others contend that this sense of mastery is also being manipulated by the market. Many adults are disturbed by the trend towards selling via inter-generational conflict. The American academic Juliet Schor, an expert on consumerism and economics, argues in her book *Born to Buy* that advertisers have perverted the venerable history of youth rebellion to create a powerful 'anti-adultism'.

By subverting the notion of children as sophisticated and critical consumers, the idea of empowerment has been hijacked in order to sell more products. Schor notes that the world of children's marketing is now filled with us-versus-them messages. 'Marketers defend themselves against charges of anti-adultism by arguing that they are promoting kid empowerment,' she writes. '[But] it's important to recognise the nature of the corporate message: kids and products are aligned together in a really great, fun place, while parents, teachers and other adults inhabit an oppressive, drab, and joyless world. The lesson to kids is that it's the product, not your parent, who's really on your side.'

If children's sense of mastery of consumer culture is being used to sell products back to them, then their power would appear to be voided. The conspiratorial separation of children from adults described here is certainly pernicious. But elsewhere, it is the blending of childhood with adulthood that confounds expectations.

As people of all ages come to define themselves ever more precisely through what they buy, consumer culture has facilitated a strange sort of levelling. Individuals, generations apart, are buying the same clothes, listening to the same music via the same technology, and reading the same books. From under-tens to over-forties, Topshop, Coldplay, iPods, and Harry Potter are binding buyers. Far from offering a self-generated window of rebellion before submission to adult responsibility, the market-devised cult of youth is now sold as accessible to anyone, of any age, provided they have the right model of mobile phone.

Perhaps this is an obvious satisfaction of demand. Just as children, not yet alert to mortality, want to be seen as older, so adults long to be thought younger. Maybe the elongation of 'adulescence' is inevitable as the population lingers further into adulthood before having children, and remains dependent on parents for longer.

But while commerce reaps the pennies of 'kidults', the genuinely youthful continue to find outlets for rebellion, often through subverting the imposed, homogenised 'youth' culture that attempts to usher them into branded conformity. Whether customising clothing or modifying cars for late-night races, creating alternative computer gaming universes in their bedrooms or perfecting their graffiti artistry on the streets, young people are continuing to form cultures of their own. There remains plenty to rebel against when, despite the fetishisation of commercially defined youth, young people's modes of expression remain controlled, trivialised and feared.

Certainly, consumer culture has offered children access to areas of adult life from which they have traditionally been excluded. The desire to get older younger is not new. Adulthood has always meant freedom to the child who feels restricted, power to the child who feels weak, agency to the child who is deemed incapable. But the version of adulthood that it presents is not one of strength, but of conspicuous consumption.

When people complain that our culture has become infantilised, they do not really mean that they are defining childhood as a time of greed, irresponsibility and instant gratification. Like so much of child-panic, this tells us more about our fears for the adult world than about the reality of children's experience. It is adulthood that has been most grossly distorted by consumer culture, and is presented to children, as well as grown-ups, as a venal, vapid, selfish place.

Nicholas, meanwhile, should offer a pinprick of hope that it may still be feasible to enjoy an unbranded childhood. A brand, according to Nicholas, is a sort of mark you make on someone's skin. A slave was branded in the fourth book of his Roman mystery series.

Nicholas has been to MacDonald's only about five times. The food's not very good there and he doesn't like the music. He only sees adverts if they're between a programme he's watching. He only likes adverts for his favourite programmes. He can't remember any others, though there is one for MacDonald's that shows quite often.

Unwitting anti-capitalist that he is, Nicholas ignores bill-board posters, though nobody has especially told him to. 'They're trying to make people buy things or look at programmes. Sometimes they can be saying something's gone down to half-price and that's right, but they can exaggerate. Not all of the time, but most of the time.'

He has never bought something because he's seen it adver-tised. The only logo he can think of is Gap, because it's so big on the front of clothes. Trainers don't have logos, he says. They have either laces or Velcro. He's heard of Nike but he doesn't know what they make.

'When adverts are on the television I either go and get

myself a chocolate biscuit or I pick up my book. Because there are adverts in every single programme!' he explains with amazement. 'Once there was a programme that was an hour long and I counted twenty adverts, and they were all about a minute long, so that was twenty minutes. And they were all advertising different bits to do with the programme, DVDs, videos, cuddly toys of the characters, these plastic toys of the characters, books about the film and everything. That's the sort of thing that makes me mad because it's really, really, *really*, *really* boring!'

This morning, Nicholas and Emma have been swimming. There are seven people in the house: 'the cleaner, my au pair, and she's got a friend round, then there's you, there's me, there's my mum and there's my sister.' Emma is swooshing her wet rats' tails around and sings a song about seven. Nicholas tells her to stop singing nonsense but she says it's real.

Nicholas got a verruca from a swimming pool. The annoying thing is that the ointment puts a white film over it and each night before you put the next lot on you have to peel the film off and that really hurts, because the top of the verruca hurts more than normal skin. He removes his right sock to examine it. 'My mum says I have to wear this sock every single day for a week, so it doesn't get on too many socks. And it will also take three months to get rid of.'

He is damp-haired and droopy, sprawling on his tummy, then his side, across the bedroom floor. His mum brings in an array of chocolate biscuits. He seizes his first KitKat finger. 'My mum shouldn't have really done that.'

It is January now, and today is Twelfth Night. The adult population has given way to the threat and promise of new beginnings. But for still-holidaying Nicholas, the transforming wash of Christmas remains, though it is fading by the hour.

When he goes back to school, he'll see his friends again. 'Oh whoops! Oh bother!' He's been clambering over the sofa with the KitKat, and it's fallen between the back and the wall. He ferrets down the gap. 'It didn't fall on the carpet, amazingly. It fell on that absolutely tiny thin ledge.' He pulls out the sofa. The finger is sitting expectantly on the skirting board. There's also a springing ball down there that he got out of a cracker. He kicks the plate on the floor as he rights himself. 'I'm very careless today.'

But on the other hand, back at school he'll be working again. 'My mum wants me to work especially hard in maths because in Year 4 we get split into top and bottom maths groups and she wants me to be in the top of course.' He probably will be, because he's sheets ahead in tables.

'If there's one thing at my school, they give us too-easy spellings and too-easy times-table tests. I've actually skipped two times-tables sheets – I may have told you that before. And this was our spelling test for the last week of last term – "zoo," "to", "one"; it even had "cat"! We already know those things in Year 3!!' His tone crescendos into outrage. 'Most people in my class know how to spell supercalifragilisticexpialidocious!'

He's glad about his Gameboy. Fifteen out of nineteen boys in his class have got them. Last term he felt sort of left out because he had to borrow everyone else's. 'But you're not allowed them in school, which is annoying.' He pauses. 'But Jeremy brings one in. Somehow he's got a secret compartment in his bag so no one ever finds it.'

He pauses again. 'But – uh – he actually told me, so I told my teacher. But she wasn't able to find it, so she couldn't tell him off, lucky, lucky, lucky for him, otherwise he would have got half his Golden Time off.' (Nicholas has only ever lost a minute off his Golden Time, for talking.)

This is quite a revelation. Why did he tell teacher? 'Well, it's not allowed!' he cries.

Jeremy was cross with Nicholas because he could have got him into very big trouble. But, oddly, Jeremy didn't tell the rest of the class about the incident so nobody called Nicholas a tell-tale.

Even though Jeremy was cross, Nicholas thinks he probably did what was best. But isn't Jeremy his friend? 'Well, not that much. I don't really play with him that much, and now he doesn't want to play with me.'

Would he have acted differently if George or Thomas had brought in the Gameboy? 'I might not have told because the teacher would have found out anyway.' His belief in the teacher's ability to discern disobedience is absolute.

Should friends keep secrets for each other? 'It depends what the secret is. If it's not a bad secret like that.'

So did Jeremy deserve to get in trouble? 'Well, actually I was the one to get into trouble, because he didn't bring it in that day and they thought I was telling a lie. Which was really, really unfair.' Poor Nicholas, carefully balancing the ethics of loyalty and obedience and still getting a row at the end of it.

He says that people learn about right and wrong from their parents, their teachers, and other relatives. Has anything ever surprised him by being wrong? 'Well, my dad is always really cross with me for not hanging my coat up immediately I get in, and I think that's a bit, bit, bit odd.'

If he hadn't told the teacher about the Gameboy, would that have been the same as telling a lie?

'Well, I've never told a lie,' says Nicholas confidently. Not ever? 'Well, not that I can remember. Well, once my dad asked me if I had a vest on because he thought it was absolutely freezing and I thought it was absolutely boiling, so I said I did because I didn't want to wear one. And then when I bent down to do up my shoelaces my shirt came out and he saw I wasn't wearing a vest. He absolutely shouted at me, but it was too late, because he found out at school so if we'd driven all the way back and there again I'd be an hour late and I didn't want to miss a whole hour's work because then I'd be far behind everyone else, etc., etc. That was lie, because it wasn't telling the truth.'

But some lies aren't as bad as other lies. 'You can tell a white lie about a birthday present or something. I was once given a Bionical – a sort of plastic monster, and I don't really like them – and my mum said I had to write a really long thank-you letter, so I had to put in a sentence about me liking the Bionical, and she said that I could do that and I didn't get told off or anything.' And Santa is a lie, but it's lying to make people excited so it's sort of a white lie.

Truth and lies require some hefty negotiation. No wonder Nicholas prefers numbers. Why does he like them so?

'I just do. Because I'm just very good at maths.'

But would he like numbers even if he wasn't good at maths?

Nicholas laughs and shakes his head. The proposition is impossible to contemplate. 'I've *always* been good at maths.'

Adam

'You just break their neck. I haven't done it on my own but I've watched Mum and Dad. After that we cook them.'

Adam's favourite animal up here in his bedroom is a fox puppet called Foxy. His favourite animal in the house is downstairs. He's a bald-headed sea eagle puppet called Beaky. Adam likes puppets, because with normal teddies you can't really move their arms, but with these you can move them wherever you like. His very favourite animal isn't here at all. He's in Spain because Adam lost him there last August. He was a monkey. Monkey's loss was a blow, still deeply felt.

There are other animals about the house: a snarling stuffed badger and a number of birds, preserved with wings spanning grandly. In a perspex box on the landing window-sill there are two stick insects. Adam had three, but one died. He feeds them brambles, and they can eat ash as well. The little round things at the bottom of the box are eggs, but they never hatch.

He peers out of the window into the back garden, which slopes down to a neighbouring farm. 'I've got two goats out there; Coco which is the black one, and Butter the white one. We don't milk them because they're boys. We have a sheep, but not here, at a friend's.'

Adam is seven years old. He has dark hair and pale skin, taut across elfin features. He lives with his mother and father in an etiolated hamlet which straddles the border between Shropshire and Wales. Home is an isolated, oak-beamed house built at the base of a disused lime kiln quarry and reached along a bumpy track. It is not the kind of place you could arrive at by mistake. The scooped-out hill has been densely coppiced, and today the grey white sky is etched with the stick arms of hazel trees, leafless still in cautious early spring. The air is cool and clean.

Adam slips his feet into the wellies that stand ready in the front porch beside two bigger pairs. He goes to the woodshed, where a clutch of young chickens are cheeping under a heat lamp. One jumped out of the pen and froze to death. It's hard to tell which is which so they don't have names.

Beyond the woodshed there are more permanent pens, where hens and roosters strut and call. 'Some in there we got out of an incubator. One of them hatched before everyone else, and we called him Early Bird. There's two Indian Runner ducks, and three Black Sussex, three Bantams and two Apenzellas. The one with the blackish feathers on his tail, he's a male and those two are female.' You can't tell which eggs come from which. 'The ducks had two babies but we sold them. We had four, but one got squashed by the mother or father, and the other froze.' He speaks of death with a light Welsh lilt, without sentiment or surprise. Adam is interested in animals at all stages, breathing and beyond.

Further up the hill, the trees tighten around the path. He's been exploring all through there, where the lime quarry was. In the stone outhouse, where they keep the hay for the goats, is a rusted pail brimming with discoveries. He found a shoulder-blade, some bits of metal, an old tile that says 'France' on it, and – he thinks it was from a house – a padlock. It didn't have a key with it. His favourite discovery is a sheep's skull. It's still got some teeth. He twirls his fingers through the eye sockets. The bottom jaw is cracked.

On a continuum of concern that extends from Turkey Twizzlers to *Grand Theft Auto*, adults worry that children's bodies and minds are being fed the wrong things. As an only child, growing up in a rural community, with his own chickens in the yard, and without access to television, Adam might be thought to embody the last outpost of untrammelled childhood. Anxieties about media violence and nutrition offer two discrete examples of how contemporary child-panic shapes the experience of childhood.

The encroachment of adult knowledge is seen as selective and distorting. So a child can simulate mass murder on the computer screen without understanding how a chicken nugget is manufactured. But what do we mean by 'adult knowledge'? Are children really incapable of distinguishing between fantasy and reality? Or can they manipulate eating and watching to create an identity free of adult assumptions about innocence and dependence?

Back indoors, Adam has a glass of juice and two oat cookies. At school today he did the Romans, literacy and PE. At PE they had dance. There's a lady on a tape who's speaking and you have to do what she says. Because his school is so small, different ages are taught together. It's four to five in the little class, sixes to nines in the in-betweens, and in the older class it's tens and elevens. But they all play together at lunch-time.

The rooms in Adam's house are long and low. Off the

living-room is a play-room, with a worn oak trunk for toys and a desk for Mum and Dad's computer. Normally after school, he comes in here to practise piano on the keyboard by the wall, and after that he watches a bit of telly. It's not a real telly because Mum and Dad don't let him have one – probably because every day he might go down and switch it on, and he might turn it up too loud – but he does have videos.

Adam's parents haven't owned a television licence for over ten years. It was mainly a reaction to the amount of trash they saw being pumped out, and the ease with which people ended up watching it for hours on end. It also gives them a degree of control over what their son is viewing. They can censor videos in advance, and it means that they don't have constant battles over what he wants to watch.

Adam likes *Chicken Run*, and Christmas cartoons. Some of his friends have television *and* DVDs. He'd like to have television so that he could see football matches, and tennis. But he's got every single one of *The Lord of the Rings*. He likes the battle scenes best, but his friend Stephen isn't allowed to watch them because they're too violent. His favourite, favourite character is Legolas, but he likes the ring-cursed creature Golum too. Adam's Golum impression is uncanny, because he too is small and slim, and when he hunches and hisses it's unsettling.

The imaginative life of children is full of violence. It would seem that in childhood a degree of violent fantasy can be beneficial. From Hallowe'en ghouls to *Doctor Who*, children often choose to expose themselves to frightening material, although we do not know whether that has more to do with its taboo, rather than its therapeutic, properties.

Writing in 1968, in the early days of public anxiety about

the effects of violent media, the psychiatrist Anthony Storr concluded in his monograph on aggression that 'to forbid a child to watch television or read stories in which violence occurs is a fruitless prohibition more likely to cause anger than to prevent it'. Surveying the evidence, he found nothing to suggest that mass media provoked delinquency in children who were not already predisposed to it. 'It is the crudity and vulgarity of horror comics, television serials and some pornography which should invoke our condemnation,' he declared, 'rather than their contents.'

Media-related child panics have a rich history. Plato proposed to ban the works of the dramatic poets from his Republic, because the children he imagined educating there would be 'young and tender . . . when any impression we choose to make leaves a permanent mark'. And in nineteenth-century London, social reformers fretted about the popularity amongst poor children of 'penny gaffes' – cheap theatrical productions of murder and melodrama.

But today's panic exists in the context of a broader adult unease about the proliferation of technology, particularly in the domestic setting. It is estimated that three quarters of children in the UK now have their own television, while one third have their own computer. And they are frequently more competent navigators of new media than are their parents.

In his influential book *The Disappearance of Childhood*, published in 1983, the media critic Neil Postman offered a gloomy assessment of the future of youth in an electronic age. His conservative reading of technological change played on growing fears about children's passive consumption of new media, demonising television in particular.

According to Postman, childhood as we know it began with the invention of the printing press in the early 1400s. In the medieval world there was no need for a concept of childhood, he argued, because everyone shared the same information environment and so existed in the same social and intellectual world. But the printing press created a new kind of adulthood, which had to be earned. 'It became a symbolic, not a biological, achievement,' he wrote. 'The young would have to *become* adults, and they would do it by learning to read . . . Therefore, European civilisation reinvented schools. And by so doing, it made childhood a necessity.'

According to Postman, the advent of television traduced this gradual learning curve. He bemoaned the fact that 'not even the ten-year-old girls working in the mines in England in the eighteenth century were as knowing as our own children. [They] know everything – the good with the bad. Nothing is mysterious, nothing awesome, nothing is held back from public view . . . in having access to the previously hidden fruit of adult information, they are expelled from the garden of childhood.'

Responses to new media have always been contradictory, and underpinned by the huge challenge to adult authority they represent. Television was initially celebrated as a means of bringing the family together, and as an educational resource. But, like so many of the media forms that have come after, it was soon viewed with suspicion. Television was no longer seen as a medium for inter-generational harmony, but rather a means of transmitting forbidden adult knowledge to passive youngsters in ways that neither the state nor parents could control.

Even today, despite concerns about children's active engagement – be it their use of Internet chatrooms or the distortion of language through text messaging – the primary focus of anxiety remains on children's position as passive consumers of violence.

And this notion of passivity has an understandable appeal. As children's access to media of all kinds becomes harder than ever to control, either centrally or within the family, adult authority is continually diminished. It is telling that Neil Postman failed to highlight the way that children's use of media not only granted them access to the adult world, but also denied adults access to the child's world. Just as he viewed the printed word as the only way of ring-fencing adult knowledge from unready children, so adults' slower adoption of new media leaves them excluded from the communities that children themselves are creating.

One way of bolstering this fading authority is to argue that children are passive viewers, who can be protected through censorship alone. It is certainly less threatening than the idea that children might be actively colluding in their own 'corruption' – that they are not being 'expelled from the garden of childhood', as Neil Postman would have it, but leaving it willingly. And when that garden contains the ideal of childhood innocence, and the dependency and incapacity that it assumes, who can blame them?

Surely the concept of 'adult knowledge' – as complete, conclusive and essentially corrupting – is just as fantastical as the ideal of childhood innocence. Knowledge is not always dangerous, just as ignorance is not always pure. To argue so is shamelessly to aggrandise the nature of adulthood, and to ignore what we know of the average goodness of children.

The author Lionel Shriver offers an altogether more confronting interpretation of the 'hidden fruit of adult information' that Postman refers to. Her novel *We Need to Talk About Kevin*, which won the Orange Prize in 2005, is narrated by a mother, Eva Khatchadourian, whose son shoots seven of his fellow high-school students dead shortly before his sixteenth birthday. Questioned about her own attempts as a parent to shield Kevin from violent films and games she responds thus: 'The truth is, the vanity of protective parents . . . goes beyond look-at-us-we're-such-responsible-guardians. Our prohibitions also bulwark our self-importance. They fortify the construct that we adults are all initiates . . . Gross with revelation, we would turn back the clock if we could, but there is no unknowing of this awful canon, no return to the blissfully insipid world of childhood . . . The sacrifice is flatteringly tragic.'

She continues: 'The last thing we want to admit is that the bickering of the playground perfectly presages the machinations of the boardroom, that our social hierarchies are merely an extension of who got picked first for the kick-ball team, that grown-ups still get divided into bullies and fatties and crybabies . . . The secret is there is no secret. That is what we really wish to keep from our kids, and its suppression is the true collusion of adulthood.'

Nowadays, aggression on screen and in computer games is regularly blamed for youth crime and delinquency. In a speech to an anti-bullying conference in April 2005, the Oscar-winning producer David Puttnam warned that Hollywood films which portrayed violence as 'devoid of human consequences' were fuelling a culture of aggression in schools. A year before that, the video games industry, now the most lucrative aspect of the toy business, was implicated in the murder of fourteen-year-old Stefan Pakeerah, who was beaten to death by a friend said to have become obsessed with the game *Manhunt*.

Perhaps most memorably in this country, the 'video nasty' *Child's Play 3* was discussed at the trial of John Venables and Robert Thompson, the two ten-year-olds found guilty of murdering the Liverpool toddler James Bulger in 1993. Although there was no evidence that the defendants had ever watched the film, a subsequent review by Professor Elizabeth Newson, then director of Nottingham University's Child

Development Research Unit, suggested that screen violence was tantamount to child abuse.

Newson acknowledged that her concerns about the 'desensitisation to compassion' that viewing such material might cause would confront liberal sensibilities around the issue of censorship. Around the same time, the novelist and poet Blake Morrison – who attended the Bulger trial and documented it in his book *As If* – argued that restriction was not the solution. 'It's no use blaming art, or thinking censorship would solve the problem,' he wrote. 'It's not as though life is so innocent either . . . Copying what you see adults do: it's how children grow up, it's the basis of their play, the dolls, the Matchbox cars, the plastic guns. Copycat, copycat, we taunted other kids. We were all copycats. We still are. No one would need *Child's Play 3* to get the idea of hurting people.'

An increasing body of research links electronic media with a medley of modern horrors. Television viewing has been associated with lower cognitive skills, brain development and academic achievement, as well as increased obesity. One American study reported in 2004 suggested that every hour of television watched by toddlers resulted in a 10 per cent increase in the risk of developing an attention deficit disorder by the age of seven. Another survey suggested that frequent viewing lead to unrealistic expectations of levels of affluence, as well as crime, in the real world.

It is not in doubt that children's access to media, and the prevalence and extremity of violence in such media, has vastly increased over the last fifty years. But the question of correlation versus causality in the research linking media violence with unhappy outcomes remains vexed. Many in the field believe that a critical mass of evidence has been reached, that it is incumbent on governments to legislate for more effective controls, and on parents to survey their offsprings' media diet more strictly.

But others argue that many of these studies are necessarily flawed because they view violence as an objective category and fail to investigate what audiences themselves define as violent. In *After the Death of Childhood*, David Buckingham notes that cartoons – which regularly top researchers' lists of most violent programmes – are not generally perceived as violent by children.

The concept of 'desensitisation' has become loaded, implying a dangerous lack of empathy rather than a healthy coping response. But Buckingham refers to accounts of early film that describe how people would scream and rush from the cinema when confronted with sequences of train crashes or falling buildings. 'Rather than being taken as evidence of "desensitisation",' he writes, 'this apparently distanced attitude to violence could well be seen as a reflection of the sophistication of contemporary audiences.'

And, more than thirty years on, a review in the *Lancet* in 2005 reinforces Anthony Storr's contention that 'it is only when parents or other adults have actually seemed terrifying' that violent stories or images will disturb a child. It found that violent imagery on television and in computer games was more likely to increase aggressive behaviour in children who came from violent families.

The beneficial potential of new media is seldom given as much publicity as its negative aspect. Researchers from the Institute of Education's Centre for the Study of Children, Youth and Media have argued that video games, for example, can assist children's social and educational development, and that the medium deserves to be treated by schools with the same seriousness as books and films. In particular, they noted that the perception of video games as unremmitingly violent is wholly inaccurate. Indeed, the majority of those aimed at children involve imaginative role play. The biggest selling video game of all time is *The Sims*, where players assume the role of city mayor, constructing virtual families and communities.

It is also worth considering some research conducted by the BBC, BBFC and others in 2003, which found that children were far more disturbed by violence or its implied threat when seen on the news or in documentaries than in cartoons or fantasy. They were especially scared by events which they could imagine happening to themselves or their immediate family, like abduction or terrorist attack. David Buckingham suggests: 'As they gain experience of watching fictional violence, children may indeed become "desensitised" to fictional violence or at least develop strategies for coping with it; although the notion that they are thereby "desensitised" to real-life violence has yet to be substantiated. By contrast, however, there may be very little that children can do in order to come to terms with their "negative" responses to non-fictional material, precisely because they are so powerless to intervene in issues that concern them.'

Neil Postman, nevertheless, would have applauded Adam's mother and father. He believed that 'those parents who resist the spirit of the age will contribute to what might be called the Monastery Effect, for they will help to keep alive a humane tradition.' And so, instead of watching endless hours of potentially denaturing television, Adam likes to make things that are kind of messy. He likes cutting-out and sticking, clay and wool. 'There was art that we did at Beavers,' he says. 'Beavers is this club that you go to on a Wednesday, and you have to wear a uniform and a neckerchief and a scarf, and you get to do fun things and play games.'

He has only one week left before he goes off on holiday with his Spanish cousins. 'They speak Spanish but they speak English as well. They're both older, and Sarah does karate and I don't know what Luke does. Together we play football and other things.'

Next week is the class trip to Chester. There's a limit of five pounds' spending money, because it wouldn't be fair if someone brought ten pounds and another person brought less. Adam would like to bring four pounds. He gets one pound of pocket money every Saturday. He'll probably spend it on a little figure, or a Roman helmet.

It will be a whole day trip to Chester. 'We get one hour at school and the rest we get at Chester. So we get twenty-three hours there. Or maybe twenty or ninteen.' He thinks it's in a bus. 'It's exciting really. It gets noisy, especially when we go swimming. Some people sing songs, but I don't. It increases the noise.' Sometimes noise bothers him. 'And sometimes when I'm in bed it can actually be the silence that disturbs me. Because when I was little, I still believe, I know it isn't true, but I think that there's ghosts, but there isn't really.'

When I next visit, it's a dour, misty day, and when Stephen came round earlier they mostly played indoors. There is one more week of holidays left. When Adam's alone, he likes to do archery. He's going to go to an archery club in the summer. He already has his own arrows, which he's got twelve of, and a target.

In the end, Adam took three pounds fifty to Chester. They went round the walls with a man dressed up as a Roman soldier, then they went into the museum, and there was a games area, an excavation area and a gift shop. He bought one little Roman soldier and a plastic sword. You had to bring your own packed lunch. He had some tuna butties, an apple, some juice, some raisins, and some raw pepper.

After Chester they went to Herefordshire, to a cottage. There were nine people staying there in all. They played outside, went up hills and went on midnight walks – which usually take place around half past seven in the evening. 'We take a torch, and some walkie-talkies, and just walk in the dark. We saw foxes, badgers, rabbits, hedgehogs sometimes.' Adam played football, rounders, swingball, and Frisbee with his Spanish cousins. They didn't bring Monkey back because nobody knows where he is. Probably somebody Spanish is looking after him now.

He came back from Herefordshire, which is hard to pronounce, on Saturday, and then it was Easter. 'We went on an Easter-egg hunt up hills. It wasn't really an egg hunt. There were clues and you have to try and look for the thing. We had to find things like feathers or sheep. We got forty-seven points and came second. I got a little chicken with a little Easter egg in it as a prize.'

On Sundays, sometimes he and his dad go to church, though they didn't go for Easter Sunday. On Easter, Jesus was crucified and rose up from the dead. When you are crucified you are killed on the cross. It probably hurt a lot. He came back to life because of God's power. It's something that lots of people are happy about now.

Adam believes in God. If you do, you have to help people and be kind. 'You have to say prayers at night-time and at teatime. The prayers are all different. Sometimes they come from *The Lion Book of Prayers*, which has different prayers for different times of the year, and sometimes we make them up to say thank you, and sometimes we don't say any at all.'

He scrambles up the back of the sofa to watch the hens that are lording around the garden. What became of the chicks in the woodshed? He ponders. 'I think we've killed them all. We've got another set now. You just break their necks. I haven't done it on my own but I've watched Mum and Dad. After that we cook them. There are loads of ways really. Sometimes we roast them, sometimes we make stew. Sometimes chicken doesn't have any taste, and sometimes it does.'

Adam says that his favourite things to eat are broccoli, chips, chicken and chocolate egg. 'I eat five fruit and vegetables a day, and we grow food round where the swing is, sometimes broccoli, rhubarb, leeks, potatoes and sometimes cauliflower.' He rubs a fresh scratch on his nose absently. He can't remember how it got there.

When he goes to the supermarket with his mum and dad, he asks them to buy treacle tarts. But the majority of Adam's food comes from local producers. His parents buy meat, fruit and vegetables that are in season, and that come with the minimum of food miles. There's a non-profit-making organisation that delivers boxes to a house near the school, and the families pick them up every Friday. Most of the villagers avoid big supermarkets if they possibly can.

His mum says it's important that he knows where food comes from, and that their lambs which he pets in spring will end up on his plate. He likes helping in the kitchen, and his favourite thing is chopping. Adam says he doesn't really see adverts for sweeties or drinks because you see them on television. Sometimes he's noticed that after eating jelly babies he feels excited.

When he's at school, the dinners are different every day. His favourite is fish, chips and peas. Again, the food is sourced locally, the sausages are home-made and the pizzas constructed from scratch with fresh ingredients.

This evening it's kedgeree for tea, made with newly laid eggs from the hens. His parents are in the kitchen and the radio is on. This weekend they are going to Durham. It's a golden wedding, which he thinks is fifty years. His own mum and dad are ten years. They'll be in their eighties when they have theirs. They'll be wrinkly then, but they'll still go for long walks because his grandad and grandma still do.

He spots his father out of the window, coming round the side of the woodshed. He's got his helmet, his chainsaw and his clippers because he's been cutting down trees. He's making a fence for the goats from the wood that he's harvested from the coppice. Adam says he can use an axe, and sometimes he sharpens it too. 'Sometimes it's quite heavy when I'm using one hand, but not with two hands.'

Adam returns to playing with his Playmobil figures. One is a flag-bearer, and another is a knight in armour. Where's his shield? Now that notice of tea has been given, there's an urgency to get everyone constructed. He snatches vital seconds, attaching swords to hands as his mum comes in to encourage him towards the table.

The kitchen is heated by an oil stove. Strings of dried chillies and orange slices garnish the sides of the fireplace. Some of Adam's pottery hangs on the walls: an owl with individually moulded clay feathers, a glazed mug and a loving portrait of his mother which presents her with wild, wormy hair. The family sit down to eat together every evening. Before eating, everyone holds hands and thanks God for the food: the fish that gave its life and the chicken that laid the eggs.

They talk about the trip to Durham. Adam is wearing a red sleeveless T-shirt, and when he gesticulates his arm muscles flex vigorously beneath the skin. He describes the games they play in the car, making sentences out of letters on number-plates they see. One of them was Dad's Windy Bottom!

In the spring of 2005, the government pledged £280 million to improve school meals, as a result of the celebrity chef Jamie

Oliver's 'Feed Me Better' campaign. His television series *Jamie's School Dinners*, which exposed the appalling state of school catering, ambushed public opinion, driving an issue that had long struggled for attention straight to the top of the political agenda. The reintroduction of minimum nutritional standards that had been abolished by the Conservative government when they privatised the service in 1980 was also announced.

But miracles take longer. There was suspicion that the Schools Food Trust, created by the government following the Jamie Oliver series, would simply add another layer of bureaucracy to proceedings. It later emerged that some schools were locked into contracts with private catering firms that would leave them unable to implement changes for years to come.

The ban on junk food and drink from canteens and school vending machines announced in the autumn of 2005 was encouraging. But the transformation of school dinners will require a sustained commitment when local authority control over meals is negligible following the compulsory competitive tendering of the 1980s, and when some schools don't even have kitchens.

As Jamie Oliver discovered, adults as well as children resist the introduction of healthy foods. A genuine revolution in school meals will need to tackle parental attitudes and marketing to children as well as the basic foodstuffs on offer.

Although childhood obesity remains one of the clearest markers of poverty, malnutrition and bad diet are no longer the preserve of those who cannot afford to eat better. One in five adults are now classified as clinically obese in this country, and obesity in children has increased threefold in the last twenty-five years. The majority of young people eat more than the recommended amounts of salt, sugar and saturated fats, while consuming less than half the recommended amounts of fruit and vegetables.

Inadequate diet in childhood is laying down risks of cancer, heart disease and diabetes in later life, as well as contributing to behavioural problems in youth. There is convincing evidence linking lack of nutrients – in particular omega 3 and 6 fatty acids – to ADHD and autistic spectrum disorders.

For all the concerns that are noisily articulated about childhood today, it is curious that children's nutrition has only latterly been considered worthy of public action. Perhaps adult ambivalence about food, combined with the stigma that still surrounds obesity, has contributed to this blindspot. Children grow up in a society riven with contradictory messages about food, parented by those who may themselves continue to harbour anxieties around eating habits. On the one hand, what we eat has become a social preoccupation, now variously imbued with messages about status, leisure, love and exoticism. On the other, thinness has never been more prized.

Children are not born demanding burgers. Initial food preferences are biologically driven, the genetic predisposition being to prefer sweet and salty tastes and to dislike bitter and sour ones. These innate preferences are assumed to have served an evolutionary purpose, as sweetness can predict the energy value of foods, while bitter tastes often denote poisonous substances.

Very young children also exhibit a developmental fear of new and unfamiliar tastes, which is again thought to have evolved in order to stop them eating dangerous substances. It has been estimated that approximately ten exposures to a new food are adequate to establish acceptance. Some experts believe that at this stage infants create a 'weaning library' of tastes that will influence their preferences for the rest of their lives.

Researchers have found that children can effectively regulate their intake when surrounded by nutritious foods. Children's poor food choices are dictated by what is made available to them – naturally, they will choose a cake over broccoli – but also by what tastes they have become used to. And here manufacturers have become adept at hijacking evolutionary preferences. The ingredient monosodium glutamate, for example, preys upon the disposition to like salt, but increases the level at which it is satisfied. Because children's preferences are still in flux it is possible to subvert their tastes permanently, creating higher thresholds from which there is no retreat.

While unhealthy, processed foods are marketed as cost-effective and quick to cook, fresh and organic produce remains prohibitively expensive for many people. It takes time, energy and nutritional intelligence to prepare meals from scratch on a daily basis. Knowledge of basic cooking techniques – even the ability to identify different varieties of fruits and vegetables – is no longer passed down through families.

But eating is a psychological as well as a physiological process. Children are more likely to eat foods that they see teachers, parents and peers eating. But, in a generation, there has been a shift to cooking separate meals for children. It has been suggested that, with more parents working longer hours, denial or provision of food has taken on more emotional significance. Studies have shown that when children are rewarded for eating their ability to regulate disappears and their intake increases. Early experience of food being used in a system of reward or punishment has also been linked to the development of eating disorders in adolescence.

Similarly, food is the primary site where children themselves assert control. Refusing to eat certain foodstuffs is how toddlers first differentiate their needs. Teenaged sufferers of anorexia nervosa and bulimia are often thought to be using their condition as a way of controlling their changing physicality or of managing psychological pressures. The sociologist Alison James believes that children can use food to structure their identities in the face of adult authority.

While conducting fieldwork at a village youth club in the north-east of England, James noticed that local adults and children both used the dialect word 'ket' or 'kets', but that adults used it to refer to something diseased or inedible, while children used it to describe penny or cheap sweets. In the essay that resulted from her observations, she suggests it is no coincidence that rubbish and sweets share the same moniker.

James discovered that children used the term only for those sweets at the lower end of the price range. They were comically named and brightly coloured, often in luminous shades wholly absent from adult foodstuffs. They also offered what she neatly describes as 'a unique digestive experience': gobstoppers that fill the mouth completely; Fruit Salad chews that leave the jaw aching; Space Dust that explodes violently on the tongue. They were attractive because they stood in contrast to conventional adult sweets and adult eating-patterns, she argues, not only in their names, their colours and the sensations they induced but also in the timing and manner of their consumption. So kets were munched haphazardly between meals, and sucks on kets were shared, in flagrant disregard of the eating conventions instilled in early childhood.

Interestingly, kets were never advertised. James's idea of children using their food choices to assert their identity becomes muddied when those choices are thrust before them by adult marketing executives. The advertising industry has been quick to reframe its activities in terms of children's empowerment. But how empowered is the average British child who, it has been estimated, views up to 5,000 advertisements for junk food every year?

It would seem that food advertising has contributed to major changes in children's eating habits. In the UK, the Office of National Statistics estimates that children spend more than a third of their pocket money on sweets, snacks and take-aways. In 2004, the food company Organix found that children as young as four were eating up to eighty additives a day.

The food industry would have it that it is parents' rather than manufacturers' responsibility to feed children well. Yet they have historically fought legislation on food labelling, while exploiting parents' desire for healthy products for their children. In 2004, for example, Friends of the Earth discovered that the 'Kids' Snack Pack Carrots' on sale at Tesco were thirteen times the price of the chain's 'Value' carrots.

But the industry is always quick to enumerate other possible causes for the rise in childhood obesity: fewer children walking to school, lack of outdoor play time, the increase in working mothers who have less time to prepare meals from scratch.

It is not only the amount of junk, but the manner in which that junk is promoted, that may prove harmful to children. Many companies now use story books, interactive websites, toys and games to sell their products. It's a strategy known as 'trans-toying': turning everyday items into playthings either by altering their nature – in the case of Heinz green ketchup – or by associating them with other toys, like

Primula's *Scooby-Doo* lunch-boxes or the free gifts that proliferate in cereal cartons.

A report by the Food Commission in 2005 criticised a number of manufacturers employing this practice. Culprits included a Mars-branded arithmetic book promoting M&M sweets, and McDonald's-licensed fast-food toys like play cash registers, plastic burgers and chicken nuggets. At the Frosties Tigercathlon website, children earn points by taking part in races in a virtual stadium, but only if their cartoon characters pick up packets of Frosties to give them power. (Kellogg's, the manufacturer of Frosties, was criticised by the Advertising Standards Authority in 2004 for implying that Frosties cereal was a healthy product when at the time it contained 40 per cent sugar.)

This trend may be impacting on children's psychological as well as physical development. Boston economist Juliet Schor wonders: 'If all children's experiences are geared towards excitement, surprise, and thrills, they may not discover that happiness and well-being are mainly gained through an appreciation of the quotidian. They may never learn to appreciate the taste of good, wholesome food if they are taught that eating is equivalent to playing.' She quotes the Harvard psychologist Susan Linn, one of America's leading critics of marketing to children: 'Marketers would have us believe that the purpose of food is to play with it. Isn't that an obscene value, when there are people in the world who are starving?'

Some consumer activists have called for a ban on television advertising of junk foods during children's programmes. But, like bans of violent media content, blanket gestures like this only move the problem elsewhere, creating enticing taboos where none existed before. It is impossible to insulate children entirely, nor is it worthwhile.

In a comprehensive review of children's 'media literacy', the Institute of Education's Centre for the Study of Children, Youth and Media found that educational efforts designed as 'counter-propaganda' were less successful than approaches that start from an engagement with the capacity and interests of children in their use of commercial media. It is better, surely, to encourage the skills necessary for navigating the changing advertising landscape, whilst moderating children's exposure to messages they are still learning to interpret. Adults may not be able to change commercial culture, but they can change children's position within it, by treating childhood not only as a time of vulnerability.

A week later, Adam is still on holiday, and toasting his back at the kitchen stove. The scratch on his nose has scabbed itchily. He arranges a selection of animals on the hearth beside him while his father makes lunch. He has Beaky the eagle, a spider monkey, who has much longer arms than Monkey, and a small badger.

Bramble the badger is the school mascot, and each holiday a different child is allowed to take her home. They voted on the name, and 'Bramble' got the most votes, though Adam voted for 'Woody'.

It's quiet while his dad chops up vegetables for lunch. The clock is ticking, the stove is throbbing, and Adam reads his comics. He's had four: two *Beanos*, one *Dandy* and one *Bananaman*. He got a free hairy Gnasher badge with this one. At Oswestry Baths this morning he swam fifteen lengths. Each length is fifty metres. He did breast-stroke, underwater with no arms, and floating on his back but not backstroke. There are twelve levels in swimming and he's on level six.

In Durham at the golden wedding he saw a few of his uncles and some aunts. There were about thirty people altogether. 'We had some tea and spoke to a few friends. I played on my own while the others were saying goodbye to people and then we went.' Adam often refers to his parents as 'the others'. They are a gang of three, not divided by generation. Sometimes he thinks it would good to have brothers and sisters, like when he's playing outside and he wants to play a game but the others are busy. Brothers and sisters can annoy you, though.

On the way back from Durham, they went to the pub and to Beamish. At Beamish there was a high street with old-fashioned shops and at the confectioner's he got a yellow sugar mouse and some chocolate raisins. They also stayed at a hotel, which wasn't bad. You got a TV there that wasn't just a video.

It's only two days, Saturday and Sunday, until he goes back to school. 'I don't want to really,' he admits. 'I just like being with my mum and dad. I won't see my dad until six o'clock when we have tea and I'll see my mum when she picks me up from school.' Adam's father is an engineer, who makes the plastic things that you put behind windows. Although his mother works two days a week as a physiotherapist, her professional life is not understood in terms of absence, but rather as something curious that happens when his time is otherwise occupied.

This week he's stayed at home, playing by himself. He likes board-games and jigsaws and doing things, like making planes. Sometimes he pretends to be other people, like the people of *The Lord of the Rings*. 'I like the way they move,' he says reverently. Adam likes to move too. He is limber and precise, and one can't imagine him ever being clumsy. He likes to experiment with facial expressions and different ways of articulating his body. Sometimes it seems unconscious, an absent-minded waggle of the head, or, like now, walking against the walls to get to his bedroom.

He starts to sort the cuddly toys under his bed. Their names are explanatory, often influenced by the maker's tag or place of purchase. This one looks like a person but it's really a monkey finger-puppet. He got it in Seventh Heaven, which is a bed shop where you order beds and they deliver them to you. 'The lady knew that I was very fond of monkeys.'

This one's called Cheeky and he got him in Tesco, so he's Cheeky Tesco. This is his favourite teddy and it's Forever Friends, Made In China. This one is called Monkey's Brother because he does look like Monkey. There are a few without names, who go on a separate pile.

Adam is reading the third *Swallows and Amazons* book. He has the CD of *The Hobbit*, which he listens to on his CD player. He waves the remote control airily. 'Sometimes when I'm in bed I can be quite lazy . . .' He presses the buttons. 'You can do tapes too and I can listen to the radio. I normally listen to classic.'

On his bedroom door is a crafted sign that reads: 'Brave knight sleeping, wake with extreme caution'. 'When I was very ill and had a temperature in the hundreds my dad got me this sign.' The memory is set flush against another of significance: 'Every year we have people from the Eisteddfod, where they have people singing and it's a sort of judging competition. And everyone has to have guests and we had the Turkish people and I was so ill that my dad had to go out with the Turkish people and buy this for me.'

That time when Adam was ill, he got this very bad feeling. 'I had this weird feeling like I was walking twice as slow and I had weird dreams that I was having a boulder thrown at me.'

Last night he dreamt about being stuck in a lift: 'When I went to get my new piano we went into a lift and there was this button outside that the man had to push and he forgot and I thought we were going to be there for ever. Mum had to ring the telephone. It was very weird because last night I thought I was still in the lift.' He was very afraid.

Scary things, he says, that's all he dreams about. Sometimes he even has nightmares. A nightmare is worse, probably ten times as scary as a scary dream. 'Once I dreamt about being in a tunnel with Mum and Dad and other people and we couldn't find our way out and if you fell down there were those skeletons that would eat you.'

But sometimes he has good dreams, even with ghosts in, but friendly ghosts. He's got a ghost in his bedroom called Frankenstein. 'He helps me with my homework and some-times I pretend to play with him. When I had Monkey I didn't have Frankenstein around because I had Monkey to play games with and then when I lost him I got Frankenstein as my friend.'

There is a forlorn grey image of Monkey pinned to the wall, from the time when the pair were at Grandma and Grandpa's and Adam popped Monkey on their photocopier. The day when Monkey went missing is still vivid and he recounts it with due solemnity.

'I was crying when I found out I'd lost Monkey. When we got back to the car the only hope was that he was at the house or in the café we went to but he wasn't in either. I don't know how I lost him. I must have dropped him.' It is a guilty admission. 'I've got two copies of the picture of him, one on the wall and one in the drawer.'

No other monkey toy he could buy would be exactly the same, he says emptily. 'Monkey was my favourite toy. I still sometimes cry because of him. I played with him all the time. I got him as soon as I was born so he was six years old when he disappeared.'

*　　*　　*

Despite the panoply of readily conjured, hyper-marketed toys and characters available to them, children continue to create their own distinctive companions – whether embodied, like Monkey, or invisible, like Frankenstein. First-born and only children are more likely to have imaginary friends and children who have them watch significantly less television. But one study, conducted in America in 1997, estimated that 63 per cent of children under the age of seven had had an imaginary companion at some stage.

Their existence has often been enmeshed with adult creativity. It was the imaginary world of A. A. Milne's son Christopher that inspired the *Winnie the Pooh* books. And the Mexican painter Frida Khalo, describing the inspiration for her painting *The Two Fridas*, credited her invented childhood companion. 'I must have been six years old when I had the intense experience of an imaginary friendship with a little girl . . . roughly my own age.' She contacted her friend by breathing on the glass of her bedroom window and drawing a door in the mist. 'I don't remember her appearance or her colour,' she recalled. 'But I do remember her joyfulness – she laughed a lot. Soundlessly. She was agile and danced as if she was weightless. I followed her every movement and, while she danced, I told her my secret problems.'

But adults remain curiously ambivalent about these companions, worrying that their existence betrays shyness or introversion, a propensity to lie, mental disturbance, or even a connection to something malign and other-worldly. Unbounded invention, while celebrated, also brings with it an element of threat. Although research in this area has been limited, the American professor Marjorie Taylor believes such fears to be unfounded. She surveys the available data in her book, *Imaginary Companions and the Children Who Create Them*, concluding that, 'Although children with imaginary companions might be somewhat advanced in their social understanding, and at younger ages they seem a little less shy and more able to focus their attention, they are not much different from other children in most respects.'

The variety of forms that imaginary friends can take defies categorisation. In Taylor's own work she came across Derek, a 91-year-old man who is only two feet tall but can hit bears; Aida Paida, a girl with a magical ability to make everyone feel safe; and Station Pheta, a boy with big beady eyes and a blue head whose job it is to hunt for sea anemones and dinosaurs on the beach. 'They are all-purpose, extra-ordinarily useful beings,' she writes. 'Not only can they provide companionship, they can bear the brunt of a child's anger, be blamed for mishaps, provide a reference point when bargaining with parents . . . many have design features that appear customised to meet the idiosyncratic psychological needs of the child creators.'

Children usually begin to pretend in the second year of life, and are inducted by adults into a world of fantasy from an early age, through storytelling and inventive play. Taylor praises children for their sophisticated negotiation of the boundaries between appearance and reality. 'Very young children are inundated with fantasy information,' she notes, 'often mixed seamlessly with real-world content. Children interact with adults who talk to stuffed animals as if the toys could understand . . . and react to a child's gentle push by falling violently to the ground.'

And yet, despite their collusion, adults continue to worry that the existence of an imaginary friend indicates an inability to distinguish the real from the make-believe. It is not so far removed from concerns about media violence. Taylor argues that confusions of fantasy with reality occur most commonly when a fantasy is presented to children by other people. Thus it is not surprising that the majority of young children believe in Santa Claus, since family, community and commerce conspire together to sustain their belief.

Perhaps this ambivalence has more to do with an adult sorrow at renouncing the imaginative freedom of childhood. Adult life can feel inimical to spontaneity and playfulness. As the writer and critic Marina Warner once observed, 'The make-believe world of infants and young minds, when perceived retrospectively, often inverts the adult order: it becomes the haven for dreams of unruliness and freedom, for spontaneity and the unrepressed unconscious. Like Alice in Lewis Carroll's great fables, a child instinctively dethrones social prescriptions and accepted ideas through spontaneous lucidity.'

No wonder Peter Pan didn't want to grow up. It's a sense of loss evoked beautifully by J. M. Barrie in his description of Neverland: 'On these magic shores, children at play are forever beaching their corricles. We too have been there. We can still hear the sound of the surf, though we shall land no more.'

But why should adulthood be experienced as a time beyond play? The idea of 'adult knowledge' is a chimera. Knowledge is never complete or conclusive. It need not be antithetical to conjecture and fantasy. It is only fearfulness, convention or complacency that render it so.

A week later, summer term has begun. Adam's primary school, in the nearest village but one, squats in the lea of a wooded hillside. Its limestone walls are fat and sturdy. Further up the rise is a row of newly built classroom cabins that edge a playground, and at the top of the hill are two playing fields. Adam's teacher Mr Bruce is calmly burning off the residual adrenalin of the lunch-hour. He counts óne, two, three and everyone sit up and look this way.

The children are seated in groups, according to ability. Adam sits with three other boys at the front of the classroom, by the computers. They wear yellow shirts, with blue sweaters and black bottoms. In the centre of each desk cluster is a blue plastic tube-tidy with pencils, rubbers, rulers and glue.

This afternoon is observational drawing. The adjective comes from the word 'observe', which means to look very carefully. Mr Bruce points to his two eyes. He has chopped up a selection of fruit and vegetables – which are named and numbered one to sixteen on the whiteboard – into interesting shapes and to show seeds, then arranged them on paper plates. Mr Bruce gives two plates to each table. One boy doesn't know what a papaya is. Adam's table gets some cucumber sliced lengthways and a large head of broccoli. The class has twenty minutes to sketch and, if they've drawn really well, they can sit anywhere they like to do their colouring-in.

'Which one do I want to draw?' thinks Adam aloud. He is turning the plate to get the best angle. The boy opposite him turns it back, and Adam turns it again. It's not antagonistic, just a tease and a test. They settle on a mutually satisfactory position. Adam kneels on his chair to give himself a better purchase on his workbook, and starts measuring the cucumber with a ruler.

There are more girls than boys in the class, and the girls show the greatest variance in height and weight. A few are already budding breasts, but the majority remain neat and doll-like. This is the class with the largest breadth of age, from six to nine. Adam got mostly As in his last school report, and Mr Bruce thinks it's good for him to be challenged by the older children in his group.

Three girls are called out for their violin lesson. Mr Bruce says not to use a ruler but to draw free-hand. Adam strokes the broccoli before he begins to sketch it. At the next table their teacher is demonstrating how to use the aqua pastels. It becomes hard to concentrate on Adam's table so they pause and look on as he gently eases the colour from a pencil score on paper with a wet paintbrush.

Now everyone is colouring in, but they have lost the chance to sit anywhere because they were making so much noise. People are crowding round the bin to sharpen their pencils. As the noise level rises again, it sounds as if there is an under-current of singing in the room. But there is no one secret song of childhood. It's just that when heard together the individual blethers blend into a strange musical hum.

Adam wants to know if this is the green for broccoli. 'It is Adam, it is, trust me,' insists his friend, but he's not satis-fied and goes back to the art corner to find a choicer tone. He returns with a flourish: 'I've got a green at last from the beautiful man!' Sometimes he talks like he's an entertainer, performing as well as doing. He dips his paintbrush in the water – 'Wrong end!' and then, 'Not enough water!' You are as involved with your neighbours' drawings as your own. 'Adam, do you like mine?' He uses a deep red to colour in the seeds of the cucumber.

After break-time, one of the older boys rings a shiny brass bell to signal for everyone to line up in front of their teacher, and three chaotic snakes of children form. Back in the class-room, it's Golden Time for the last half-hour of this Friday afternoon. Adam and three friends share a game of Four in a Row. He sucks the counters in contemplation before drop-ping them into the frame. At one point he puts his face up close to the frame, screwing up one eye to view his opponent through the holes.

With the other boys you can imagine how they will look as men. But with Adam, his bone structure seems so much more ephemeral, as though he might age into someone altogether different or never age at all. 'We won! We won! We won!' He waves his hands side to side, and bobs, like an American cheerleader. 'Fair and square!' he adds emphatically. A huge dimply smile swamps his delicate face.

Perhaps it is because his interior world is so singly imagined that his social contact is this free and confident. At home, he relishes the silence and the gentle community of his others, Mum and Dad. In the classroom, he is jaunty and performative, experimenting with different persona, unafraid of social sanction.

In accordance with the general trend for smaller families in the UK, almost a quarter of British children now are only children. But Adam's self-possession is far removed from the traditional notion of the only child as lonely, maladjusted and spoilt. In fact, there is nothing to suggest that only children are much different from other children brought up with few siblings.

Since instituting its one-child policy in 1975, which restricted birth rates in cities in order to counter an escalating population crisis, China has created a whole generation growing up without siblings. Much has been made of these 'Little Emperors', overfed, overindulged and unable to share. Longitudinal studies on this only-child generation are incomplete, but anecdotally it would seem that Chinese children are struggling with fierce pressure to excel as the expectations of an entire family burn into one solitary child.

Only children do tend to be higher achievers, but this is the same for all children from small families compared with those from larger ones. Contrary to popular belief, only children are not prone to exaggerated feelings of superiority; nor do they have especial trouble forming close relationships.

While they do seem positively to enjoy time on their own, and are less likely to be bored easily, there is no evidence that they are lonelier as children or as adults.

Adam stands up now, one hand in his pocket, surveying the room like a junior cad, then moves off to investigate what some of the other children are doing. He sits down to play Snakes and Ladders with a girl who laughs into his neck flirtatiously whenever he puts on his special voice. He counts the moves out in an American accent. She flutters appreciatively, then loses the dice in the folds of her jumper. Adam begins to tug at the fabric before realising that he is closer to her chest than he ought to be. She coyly dislodges the dice from her armpit. He makes even sillier voices and faces. She deliberately falls across him as she dissolves into giggles.

There's five minutes left, announces Mr Bruce. Adam tries to win with the wrong number of moves. She says it doesn't count but they start again anyway. Now they've got three minutes to put everything away, then get book bags, lunch-boxes and water bottles ready for home-time. At the end of the school day they say a prayer together.

The following weekend, Adam is playing in the garden. The sky is clear and wide and does not look like the same sky that hunches over motorways or shopping centres. He lays out his bows on the path. He's got five. One is professionally manufactured, with a nook for the arrow shaft and a proper sight. Three are hand-made, with string and larch or Scots pine, and one is a crossbow. His dad is still building the goats' fence, and his mum is planting the beds along the driveway. Adam is standing on the seat of his swing, calling above the drone of his father's saw for a brief acknowledgement: 'Mum? Mum! I can swi-iii-ng!'

It's better to live in the countryside, he explains, because you get more space. It's quiet. Quiet makes Adam feel snug. In a city it's quite noisy, and not very green. He thinks that Oswestry is the biggest city close to him, but Oswestry is not really like a city, it's like a village. Most cities have skyscrapers, and villages don't. And cities have more car parks. Posh people, like the Queen, live in cities. Does the Prime Minister live in a city? Some poor people live in cities too. He's not really poor, and he's not really rich. Cities are more dangerous because there's more cars.

When Adam grows up he'd like to be an archaeologist. They find things, like the things in his pail. In his spare time he'd like to do historical re-enactments, like they do at Chirk Castle. He'd like to keep animals too. His mum's a sort of farmer, because they might get some pigs. When you're a grown-up you have to go to work every day.

His mother comes by for some compost, and he asks her for a ham butty. He swings on. Tomorrow he's going to the St George's Day parade in Oswestry with Beavers. 'We're going to march in threes, and one of us is going to be carrying a flag.' St George was a patron saint. 'Most people think he killed a dragon, but I don't think he really did. Because he was in Rome and people wanted people to stop being Christians, and he didn't want this to happen, and he was taken and tortured and whipped and then died. I think he stood up for himself.'

His butty is in the porch. His mum says he should have eaten more of his dinner. He mmm-hmm-hmms a reply through the first overeager-sized mouthful. As he chews, he picks through the items on the porch shelf: some glass bottles he dug up, his mother's sheep shears. Two of the roosters are clucking by the trough of tulips beneath the kitchen window.

A dog kennel has appeared on the paving by the porch,

donated by a neighbour for the chickens. Adam crawls inside on all fours; it fits him perfectly. There is something interesting hanging from the roof, the size of a tennis ball. He tugs it off gently. It's a crumbly ball. He thinks it was a wasps' nest. Opening it carefully, he exposes the perfect honeycomb inside, each egg compartment covered with a fine papery cap. He clambers out of the kennel and runs to show his mother.

Later he sets up his archery target on a stand of three slim boughs. If you're a beginner you have to go on the gravel, but he can do it from the grass. He sets his feet in a line with the target, raises the bow, scrunches shut his left eye and pulls back the arrow. Whack! He hits the board, but out of range of the target. One of the wandering roosters broadcasts a shrill doodle-doo. Normally Adam has six goes with each arrow. The next shot hits the target. That's seven points.

Laura

'When you're younger, you're kept happy all the time. But when you're a teenager it's not so easy.'

Laura had a crap day at school. 'There was this one really stupid boy and he was saying that some of the other boys were saying things about the way I looked, and I had to come home, because I get upset really easily. It's stupid.' She talks very quietly indeed, and her right knee jiggles.

Today was only her fourth at Maple House, a place where people who can't get along in ordinary schools come to learn. There's just Laura in the class, and these four boys. It made her think she's really weak. It made her feel like she's always failing. 'They didn't know about why I was there, but I told the teacher she could tell them if it meant they'd be more sensitive. I suppose to everyone else it must look like I'm a stupid cry-baby. But it just touched a nerve. It's like the one thing they could have said to make me really upset.'

This one boy wrote a note saying the other boys were saying she looks like a man and talks like a man, basically calling her ugly. 'They must think I'm the sort of person who cries loads but before I went into hospital I hadn't cried for about a year.'

It is April, and Laura is fifteen. In January, she tried to kill herself. She was admitted to a psychiatric unit, where she spent three months. During that time, she attempted suicide again. Calling her ugly was the worst thing this boy could have done, because Laura feels very unhappy about the way she looks. She has felt like this since the gang of girls she hung out with turned on her. Since they kicked her unconscious and pulled her trousers down. It takes her hours and hours to get ready to go out, and sometimes she feels so terrible about her appearance that she won't leave the house for days. It might sound just vain, but it's much, much more than that.

Objectively, Laura is a continent away from ugly. She has long dark hair, dark eyes and a neat rosy mouth. Her hips are slim as a handspan. She is pretty of herself, and pretty as all young girls are, purely by way of being fifteen. She looks delicious, and can't see it at all.

Simply being able to word her distress is an advance peculiar to Laura's generation. The extent to which it is considered legitimate to pay attention to feelings, and the accompanying fluency in the language of psychology, are recent phenomena. Advanced by a popular culture that puts a premium on exhibitionism and self-exposure, it it debatable how authentic this understanding actually is.

That young people too experience mental disorder sits uneasily alongside the imperative that the young – like Sunday's child – be 'bonny and bright and good and gay'. Two hundred and fifty years ago, only one in four British children survived beyond their fifth birthday and, in many places, extreme physical deprivation remains a defining condition of growing up. When it's estimated that a child dies of extreme poverty every three seconds in some part of the world, to be concerned with children's mental health could be considered indulgent by some.

But it is not a luxury to feel like Laura, or the estimated 10 per cent of five to fifteen-year-olds like her who use the

Child and Adolescent Mental Health Services. The poet Francis Thompson wrote: 'Children's griefs are little, certainly, but so is the child . . . Pour a puddle into a thimble, or an Atlantic into Etna; both thimble and mountain overflow.' Today, those griefs are not so little. Adolescent mental health has declined sharply over the past twenty-five years, and one in ten children aged between eleven and fifteen have clinically significant emotional or behavioural difficulties.

Given the evolution of medical explanations for human behaviour, it is possible to speculate that what is now interpreted as mental disorder would previously have been attributed to moral laxity or fecklessness. If children and the people who care for them have access to a new language of emotion, are they describing something that was always there or is that language creating a different understanding of childhood? Whatever caveats we lay down, the experience of those working in the field points to a deeply troubling conclusion. At a time of increasing affluence and material provision, children are unhappier than ever, and getting more so.

Is modern childhood affecting children's mental health? Perhaps children's increasing confinement is limiting the development of resilience. Does competition for grades and for consumer goods distort self-confidence and optimism? Maybe children's lack of participation in the decisions that affect their lives is adversely informing their sense of agency. When they gain unmediated access to the adult world from a young age, but remain financially dependent on their parents for longer than ever before, how do they negotiate the transition of adolescence?

For Laura, there is no mystery to the root of her unhappiness. 'I had problems at school a few years ago now, and then lots of bad things happened. I guess they might happen to a lot of people, and worse things happen to a lot of people, but I never really showed how upset it made me and after about four years of holding everything in I collapsed.' Laura speaks in a highly strung register, all Antipodean phrasing and lazy vowels. Sometimes she explains things in neutral words that are the most painless, sometimes in the technical phrasing she's learnt from the unit. Because her voice is so gauzy, it can sound like she is spinning a fairy tale.

'At my first secondary school there were these girls I hung around with, never going to school, smoking drugs, being an idiot. I used to get bullied a lot by them. But when I decided to leave that school that was when they got really angry and started to beat me up loads. I guess they felt like it was me thinking I was too good for them, but I never went into school and I'd never have succeeded if I'd stayed with them.'

There was quite a long time after leaving her first school, and before starting at the second, when she didn't have any friends at all. She started getting really obsessed with her appearance, really distressed about it. During those months in between, the people from her old school still wanted to beat her up so they'd come round and egg her house and stand outside, shouting stuff.

'Then once I did start at the new school, because the two schools are really near each other and everyone knows everyone, they started spreading rumours about me and trying to turn everyone against me, which worked with quite a lot of people. A lot of people don't like me,' she says, matter-of-factly.

The last time they beat Laura up it went too far. 'They knocked me out because someone kicked me in the head. They robbed me and I was quite badly sexually assaulted as well. For hours I couldn't remember a thing. The next morning I was bruised all over and had big lumps on my head. My memory still isn't clear. I just get little flashbacks.'

Despite anxieties about stranger danger and unsafe streets, it is children's peers from whom they require most protection, in the relentlessly familiar environment of the playground. We ask of children what few adults would tolerate: to endure hours of enforced proximity to their tormentors, to manage them-selves – and GCSEs too – in a social environment where the rules are ambiguous and constantly changing. The mother of a boy who had killed himself after being bullied about his weight once told me, 'He just couldn't respond in the way other kids expected him to.'

It is impossible to know whether the problem of bullying is getting worse or whether, as with child abuse, growing public awareness has led to increased reporting of incidents. It is estimated that sixteen children in the UK take their own lives each year because of bullying. The charity Childline receives calls from tens of thousands of bullied children annu-ally and, in a 2003 survey, found that 15 per cent of primary school children and 12 per cent of secondary pupils reported that they had been bullied in the past twelve months. Bullying is implicated in many cases of truancy, and the NSPCC believes that some 90,000 children are temporarily removed from school each year because of it.

Certainly the methodology of harassment is changing. Use of the Internet and mobile phones in carrying out hate campaigns is a new development. In 2005, the children's charity NCH found that 14 per cent of 11–19 year-olds had been threatened via text message. But the intricately conceived cruelties that children visit on one another – for less than half a good reason – the volatility of childhood friendships, and the power of cliques are age-old. As Margaret Atwood wrote in her novel about schoolgirl bullies, *Cats Eye*: '[Children] are cute and small only to adults. To one another they are not cute. They are life-sized.'

Since 1998, it has been the obligation of every school in the UK to adopt an anti-bullying strategy, though critics say this often fails to make the transition from paper to practice. The content of these strategies has also been called into question. First developed in Sweden, the 'No Blame Approach' to bullying has been gaining currency in British schools and, in 2004, was official policy in one third of them. The theory holds that, by encouraging children to communicate in a controlled environment, rather than reinforcing the roles of victim and perpetrator through punishment, chronic bullies will develop sympathy and alter their behaviour accordingly.

A number of organisations – including the major children's charity Kidscape – have criticised the approach, arguing that without punitive sanction perpetrators fail to learn that their actions have consequences. They worry that forcing victims to challenge their bully in front of a teacher may place them at further risk. The dispute would seem to centre around the kind of bullying that this strategy is applied to. Certainly, it can be of benefit for minor incidents in primary schools, but its use is questionable for the more serious cases that Kidscape deals with.

At a time when the criminal justice system, through curfews and ASBOs, is taking an increasingly punitive approach to young people, it is ironic that this strategy persists in some schools. Of course, the 'no blame' approach has worthy roots. A bully who is acting out the violence she has experienced in her own life may well respond badly to further sanction. But just as the courts may employ mitigation to reduce the sentence of a drug addict who is convicted of burglary, so schools need to find a way of making punishment fit both crime and perpetrator. We cannot throw our hands up at children's lack of 'respect' or moral responsibility, while failing to provide a system of sanction and incentive for them to learn from.

Of course, bullying behaviour is not the preserve of childhood. Even with the buffer of maturity, a variety of Acts of Parliament, and recourse to tribunals, bullying does not stop at the school gates. The quest for status, the exploitation of difference and the pack mentality never absent themselves from our social interactions. But it is in the playground, where the relationship between instinct and self-control is still being tested, that the human capacity for cruelty as well as kindness is laid bare along with the old lie: stick and stones may break my bones but names will never hurt me.

It has become an easy adult observation to make, that 'kids can be so cruel'. It is seldom remembered whether 'I was cruel'. The development of moral responsibility seems to happen when we are looking the other way. It is hard to know whether our motivations are pure or practical – because we genuinely want to be kind, or because we are self-interested, and recognise that if we are generally pleasant then people will generally be pleasant to us.

The question is whether there is something in the contemporary experience of childhood that makes bullying behaviour more likely. There is the fear that violence on screen makes children more aggressive towards one another. But if childhood is an experience of disempowerment, perhaps it shouldn't come as a surprise that some children misuse the only power they hold: over each other.

Laura says her teachers didn't really notice what was going on until she left, and by then it was too late. When so many people start not to like you, you have to think it's something about you. 'I always feel like people judge me when they meet me and I always think it must be something to do with the way I look. I maybe don't look good enough or look right for people to like me.'

And this is how the spell was cast: 'When they started beating me up I actually remember thinking to myself, "I want to be pretty." Part of me thought something must look wrong with me for them to hate me so much and part of me thought if I become really pretty next time I see them that'll show them that I don't care what they did to me.' But the more she tried to make herself pretty the uglier she felt. 'I used to spend hours just staring in the mirror and it got quite bad, every morning, every evening. If I wanted to get to school on time I'd wake up at six in the morning, though I didn't have to leave till half-eight and sometimes I wouldn't get in till eleven.'

Laura wears her make-up like armour. It appears impermeable, as though it will protect her from all onslaughts. Beneath, the skin may not actually be able to breathe. Though she is attractive, it is her own cosmetic painting that renders her striking – glossily female, defensively so. Laura still feels ugly enough to die, but the bullies have moved on to the next person. Sometimes she'll see them on the street and they'll look through her like she doesn't exist.

Laura lives in a tall house with many rooms in a nice part of town, sandwiched between an even more expensive area and a rotten estate. She calls this the patchwork. In the other rooms live her sister, who is twenty-one, her brother, who is eighteen, and their mother, a university lecturer, who divorced from their father when Laura was five. They have lived here for as long as she can remember.

She did make some friends when she moved to her second

school. There's a group of nine of them, all girls, and they're extremely close. She'd never found that before apart from with her sister, but with these friends she can be completely herself. They go round to each other's houses, or up on to the common. They have parties when people's parents are away or when they make friends with rich boys with big houses. They buy the vodka and buy the Coke and mix it. She giggles. Not very classy.

She doesn't consider herself a child, but 'teenager' doesn't sound nice either, because teenagers aren't given any credit at all. 'They're made out like these creatures that for seven years of their life stop feeling for other human beings. I think really they're just more sensitive than most people but not good at showing it.'

'That might be a reason teenagers get pissed off with parents is that parents are always asking how you feel and sometimes you don't want to talk about it because you just don't know how to.' When Laura can't explain herself out loud she writes poetry, or writes in her diary. She's been to see loads of psychologists – she attends an NHS child and family psychologist now – but some really aren't good at their jobs. 'When I was in the psychiatric unit the psychology there was really good. But I've been to see a few that were really crap.'

Laura never went back to the school with that one stupid boy. Over the past few weeks she's been sleeping late and feeling low. Today she's wearing no make-up and her skin is peachy and plump. Her voice is still so slight it's as though a wicked fairy has stolen it away, but her mood is more combative. Perhaps it's because she's only just got up. She's sitting outside in the garden by a patio table strewn with empty ten-packs of Malboro Lights. She's still seeing the psychologist once a week, but it's moving quite slowly. Her dad and her psychiatrist want her to go back to hospital, to the intermediate unit that's next to the one she was in before. She's refusing, and her mum's on her side too.

'Like, I do want to get better and I know it is affecting my life in a big way but I don't want to miss out on my whole social life and my summer being stuck in some mental hospital.' She pulls a face. 'There's maybe this other clinic that I would go four times a week, or I might go to this place called Fitzroy House in September which is like a day hospital where you get education and therapy but you don't have to live there.'

She's still dissatisfied with her appearance. 'But it's getting better, because I used to have really bad mood-swings every day and now it's just once a week. And before I'd blank my friends for weeks because I thought I didn't look good enough and now nearly every weekend I go out with them. And that's why I don't want to go back into hospital. If my life's at least OK then I'd rather be outside.' She's very convincing.

Laura is looking slim today. Her weight goes up and down. Before, she was on Prozac. She thinks that it really makes you lose weight and she was seven and a half stone. (Prozac is not usually associated with weight loss.) Then she went into hospital, and she was just lying in bed getting her dad to bring in McDonalds. A few weeks later she was nine stone. 'The whole time I was on Prozac I didn't cry once – Prozac won't let you cry. It blocks your depression off from you, just makes you happy, and that just meant I was bottling my depression up even more,' she states knowledgably.

She just gets so frustrated with the way she looks. 'I think it's unfair that some people are born into life looking so much better than other people and they get treated better throughout their lives because of it.' She's sparring. 'And I feel like people are always going to judge me because I don't look as good.' There's definitely a lot of pressure put on girls and women to look a certain way: 'Because men, if they're not good-looking they can still get far in life just by being intelligent or funny. But girls are told you have to be good-looking as well as everything else.'

Laura has been diagnosed as suffering from body dysmorphic disorder, a recently registered condition which was only reported on by the National Institute for Clinical Excellence in 2005, and which is thought to be a form of obsessive-compulsive disorder. As yet under-recognised and under-researched, it is defined as 'a preoccupation with some imagined defect in appearance', and preliminary estimates suggest that it may be present in up to 8 per cent of cases of depression.

Even in cases less extreme than Laura's, levels of dissatisfaction amongst girls with their bodies are high and rising. Four in ten teenage girls surveyed by the magazine *Bliss* in 2005 said that they had considered plastic surgery. Two thirds of the 2,000 fourteen and fifteen-year-olds who took part in the questionnaire said that pressure to look 'perfect' came from comparing themselves unfavourably with celebrities.

Interestingly, they turned this pressure on each other. Of the one in six who said that they had been bullied, the majority had been harassed because of what they looked like. Only 8 per cent were happy with their bodies, while a quarter had suffered from an eating disorder.

The cultural critic John Berger once wrote: 'A woman . . . is almost continually accompanied by her own image of herself . . . She has to survey everything she is and everything she does because how she appears to others, and ultimately how she appears to men, is of crucial importance for what is normally thought of as her success in life.'

The accessibility of cosmetic procedures, along with a cohort of minor celebrities who are glad to discuss their own surgical enhancement, is gradually distorting not only young girls' idea of what is beautiful, but their notion of what is natural. The more shapes and sizes that become technically possible, the slimmer our inventory of desirable looks becomes.

In many ways, it is the logical extension of the way that capitalism has co-opted the language of empowerment to sell shampoo and mascara, 'because you're worth it'. After more than a century of the women's movement fighting for the right to participate in public life, liberation has been appropriated for the private preoccupation with presentation. What this tells young women is: you can't change the world but you can, and indeed you have a responsibility to, change yourself.

Aside from the physical consequences and side-effects, how does the burgeoning trade in surgical self-improvement shape young women's sense of self? In her 1990 classic *The Beauty Myth*, Naomi Wolf described the inevitable conclusion of what she called 'the Surgical Age': 'Women in our "raw" or "natural" state will continue to be shifted from the category "woman" to the category "ugly", and shamed into an assembly-line physical identity. As each woman responds to the pressure, it will grow so intense that it will become obligatory until no self-respecting woman will venture outdoors with a surgically unaltered face.'

Worst of all, the further we grope towards commodified physical perfection, the further we stray from what makes us individual – the flaws, the scars, the deterioration. The more we define our own attractiveness in terms of what we can construct, the less likely we are to have a truthful discussion about the nature of attraction itself.

* * *

Laura lists her plastic surgery requirements without pause for thought: 'I want a boob job as soon as I'm eighteen. I want liposuction and lip enhancement and eye-bag removal.' There's no point in questioning the motives behind plastic surgery, she says. 'It's so much easier said than done, to just be happy with the way you are. People don't have problems with you wearing make-up, though I know that's not permanent. But if you feel self-conscious about the way you look, what's wrong with paying to change it?'

She's not been feeling so good about the way she looks recently. 'I think that's one of the reasons I'm not getting out of the house much is 'cos it takes so much effort to get ready.' Her routine is extensive and well-honed. 'First of all I have to prepare my outfit, then have a bath, shave everywhere, and exfoliate, then have a shower and wash my hair, 'cos I don't like doing it in the bath, blow-dry my hair, straighten it, moisturise, fake tan, then I have to wait around for the fake tan to dry, then put my outfit on, deodorant, do a hair-style, and then all the stages of my make-up, foundation, concealer, powder, blusher, then eye make-up, eye-shadow, eye-liner and mascara, then lipstick, then accessorise.' She comes to rest. 'But it's the bath and fake tan that takes so long.'

She learned her routine from magazines. She doesn't exactly feel better afterwards, but she does feel like she's acceptable to go outside. She only goes out at night now because it takes the whole day to get ready. It's difficult with magazines. 'Everything always appeals to me. They do make me feel depressed about the way I look 'cos there's a pretty woman on every page. And – this is going to sound so spoilt 'cos I've got loads already – but it makes you wish you had enough money to buy everything. It makes you want to be a celebrity so you could buy everything.'

'In a way I think the magazines are a bit wrong 'cos of the way the women in them are absolutely flawless. And you know you buy cigarettes and it says on the packet "these will kill you"? It's not the same at all but girls look at those adverts and think that's what they should look like and there's no sign underneath saying "these women are completely airbrushed and fake and no one ever looks that perfect".' She looks pleased with a point well-made. The trouble is that the longer Laura stays at home because she feels ugly, the more time she has to pore over those magazine images of supermodels, and the less chance she has to compare herself to other ordinary teenagers, with doughy skin and thick thighs.

Once you have such a set opinion of yourself it stays in your mind and it's hard to change, she says. 'Sometimes, when I'm with my psychologist and she's doing all her little therapy things, it's just really simple stuff. Like she'll give me a thought that I have about myself, like "I look bad", and then give me an alternative thought, like "I look good", so whenever I think I look bad I have to think of the alternative thought. And you can't really imagine that something that simple will actually work.' The delivery is sweet enough, but there's sharpness beneath. Laura is an unhappy creature, but she is tough. It remains to be seen whether she is ultimately a survivor.

The girl gang she ran with, who eventually became her tormentors, were hard: 'That whole period of my life I was lean, smoking so much draw, high the whole time. They were such street rats, so violent towards each other.' There is revisionist disgust, spiked with a shot of residual pride.

'I was just trying to be something I wasn't, like I was some rude girl, speaking like them, dressing like them. At the end of the day there's no point in that whole attitude of

"I'm from the ghetto, I'm so hard", because I've got a nice house and I'm quite obviously not from the ghetto.' She laughs easily at herself. 'The only way I made friends with them was by completely acting like I was someone else.'

But everybody does it. 'It's the culture today. Teenagers nowadays aspire to violence and that's it. They see all these American gangsters and think "that's what I want to be." Boys think they have to fight to prove they're big strong men, and lots of girls fight to look good in front of the boys.'

'They think it's cool, anything American rappers do, all the violence and the money, the way they talk, all the clothes they wear, that whole image of being a pimp and being a gangster.' That's just what boys learn – that the only way to treat women is for sex.

That hoary double standard is astonishingly persistent. 'It's fine for them to have sex all they want, but as soon as there's a girl who enjoys sex she's a slag. They'll ask her to do all this stuff and if she actually does it she's a ho or a slut. She gets a reputation, and once other girls hear about that – girls can be stupid sometimes too – they'll beat her up. But if you don't do something with a boy then the boy will get pissed off with you and go round saying you're a slag, so you get the reputation either way.'

There's a desultory acceptance of the status quo. And Laura has met a new boy, called Kevin. It's not a very nice name, she says hastily. Kevin is seventeen, and he's at some music production college. They're going out, so she's spending quite a lot of time with him. Sometimes friends will set you up with a boy, but usually if you're flirting with someone, it's meant to be the boy who makes the first move. You think boys are more confident but recently they aren't like that. It's usually the girl who has to be quite forward.

'I think boys are more insecure than they let on, and I definitely think women are getting more and more confident.' But there's a vivid dissonance between that and the 'ho' culture. 'In one way you think that women are becoming much more powerful, with *Sex and the City* and women being portrayed as so independent. But the stuff that's being most projected towards teenagers, the music videos and rappers, you watch any of those videos and it's literally like women standing there in their underwear dancing for men. And then you turn on the female singers like Beyoncé and she's just writhing around in her underwear. If girls are just going to stand there and look like all they have to offer is their bodies then you can't really blame men for treating them that way.'

When Laura dresses up she can look fairly Beyoncé-esque herself. A few weeks later, it's midday, and she's just come in from a night at Kevin's. She looks dewy. She's wearing a short black skirt, a stripey off-the-shoulder top and heels. Her limbs seem airbrushed. Two long diamanté threads hang from her ears. Aside from a faint haze of self-consciousness, she might be twenty. She rearranges her legs, and fashions her arms into a cradle for one knee.

Kevin doesn't know a lot about her history. Only recently she told him about being depressed and going to hospital. He doesn't ask too many questions, and she likes that. She sniffles. It's hay fever. She's been seeing Kevin for nearly two months now and it's fine. They see each other a few times a week, which is better than when she went out with boys at school and you'd see them every day at lunch-time.

Her mum is OK with her staying over at his place. She was a bit weird about it at first. 'Some of my friends' mums are completely fine, and my friends have boys to stay at their house all the time, and some of my friends' parents are really strict. So I think my mum didn't really know which kind of mum she should be,' she explains indulgently, 'but she trusts me.'

It's fine to stop when you want. 'I think Kevin lost his virginity to his last girlfriend, and the first time I stayed at his house he didn't know me that well, and he didn't know that I was a virgin so he tried to have sex with me. But I'm quite scared to lose my virginity so I think he understands that and he doesn't really mention it now.'

Of the nine girls in her friendship group, three have lost their virginity, but one of them only had sex once. Some of them don't care, some of them have real principles about how long you should wait, and some of them are just really scared.

There are lots of reasons why Laura hasn't done it yet: 'I'm scared 'cos everyone says it really hurts the first time. I know that when I wear outfits like this' – she gestures to her trouble-making skirt – 'it seems like I'm really comfortable with my body, but I'm not that comfortable being naked around boys. There's not that many things in life that once you give away you can never get back, but I think my purity, my inno-cence . . .' – the thought gets a little tangled – '. . . I could never say I was pure again.' She shakes her head. 'It sounds a silly reason.'

Most of Laura's friends have experienced some sort of miserable time. One took a small overdose; another used to be bulimic and now she never eats. The friend under discus-sion calls on the mobile at just that moment: 'Jessie, hey baby, can I call you back in half an hour? Love you.'

She didn't appreciate the scale of adolescent unhappiness until she got there herself. 'When I went into hospital I started hearing about how many teenage psychiatric units there are, and how there's this underworld of depressed teenagers,' she says. 'Everyone in these different units knew each other, and there was this whole scene of depressed people. So maybe it is happening more, and our culture alienates a lot of people too, people who don't want to be part of that gangsters crowd and can't find any other good friends. Loads of teenagers don't really know who to try and be.'

In 2004, the Nuffield Foundation published a detailed assessment of the mental well-being of three generations of fifteen-year-olds. The most authoritative study of its kind to date, it found that behavioural problems had doubled between 1974 and 1999, while emotional problems rose by 70 per cent. Comparable work in the United States and the Netherlands has not identified similar trends.

The deterioration of children's mental health in the UK has been stark. Since the mid-1980s, emotional problems like depression and anxiety have increased for both girls and boys. Adolescent conduct disorders showed a continuous rise over the whole twenty-five-year period, though the study found that this related to non-aggressive behaviour such as lying and disobedience, rather than fighting or bullying. The researchers ruled out the possibility that these results were attributable to changes in the thresholds for what was counted as a problem. Teenagers were not simply being rated as more disturbed; there were real changes in the numbers experiencing poor mental health.

The Nuffield researchers offered a range of possible causes for their findings. While expectations of academic achievement have increased, opportunities for children who struggle with testing have been restricted. Young people are finding it harder to enter the job market, which may affect how they see themselves and their economic role.

As young people spend many more years in full-time education, and remain financially dependent on their parents for longer, the transition to adulthood has become increasingly mutable. Perhaps we parent differently from families in other countries, the researchers suggested. Or maybe something has changed in non-familial socialisation over the past twenty-five years.

Identification of risk factors is at an early stage. But the Nuffield study did conclude that family breakdown and poverty made only modest contributions. Although children in step-families and single-parent families are unhappier than those with two natural parents, mental health has become dramatically worse in all three categories, and the deterioration has in fact been fastest among children in conventional families. Similarly, although teenagers from wealthier backgrounds had better mental health, the decline was significant across all social classes, and particularly for middle-class children.

The psychiatrist Professor Peter Hill, who worked at Great Ormond Street Hospital and is now in independent practice, notes that although children's experience of physical abuse and deprivation has decreased over the generations, 'other more shadowy influences, certainty of personal identity, security of career structure, have taken their place'. In particular, he points to work carried out in the United States, which found that adolescents who were able to adopt a social or professional identity handed down to them by their parents tended to be happier.

'We are more alert to young people's distress now, and more inclined to see it as distress rather than as reprehensible behaviour. But,' he cautions, 'we don't like children in this country, even though we're going to be so dependent upon them with the current demographic shifts.' He argues that the position of the Children's Health Tsar has been serially emasculated, and that we need a Children's Minister in the Cabinet with the power to veto.

Despite the Nuffield study's gloomy prognosis, Hill remains hopeful about this generation. 'I think that today's fifteen-year-olds are much more impressive than fifteen-year-olds in the 1950s. I don't think that they are less resilient, but that they are more emotionally literate. Soap operas, for example, have been wonderful for that. Young people are much more aware of the impact of arrogance and prejudice, and much more able to be sensitive to those sorts of things.

'The problems arise when other influences make them less likely to display that. For example, the amount of alcohol consumed by the young is terrifying, and once you're drunk it's hard to be sensitive to other people.'

Hill says that one of his greatest concerns is the abuse of skunk. 'It's emerged in the past three or four years as a major problem, and I don't think that parents realise that they didn't smoke the same stuff that's around now. I've seen a number of youngsters going quite seriously mad on it, and the parents are indulgent because they think they know what their children are buying.'

The increase in alcohol and drug abuse, especially of the stronger types of cannabis now available, must certainly have an impact on mental well-being. A variety of other factors also play their part. Hormonal changes are generally thought to have a small impact, though they can be significant for a minority, and research continues into the effect of adolescent brain development on mental health. Deteriorating diet may have a direct biological impact. In one study, young offenders who were given multivitamins and fatty acids over a two-week period showed a 34 per cent drop in antisocial behaviour.

Parenting clearly makes a major contribution to children's psychological well-being, particularly the quality of care received in the earliest years of life. There is also

ample evidence that increased consumer choice and affluence has been accompanied by a general decrease in levels
of satisfaction.

Like all young people, Laura and her friends are bombarded
with messages about celebrity and wealth. She says that
'loads of teenagers don't really know who to try and be'.
The tyranny of absolute choice can make the universal struggle for identity feel like a personal failure. And the people
who teenagers best know how to emulate are those they
watch on MTV, guiding them round their luscious
mansions. When expectations reach this level of extrava-
gance, the ordinary disillusionments of growing up become
infinitely harder to bear.

Gender is another factor. As a middle-class female, Laura
may be particularly vulnerable to psychological distress. In
a study of fifteen-year-olds over a twelve-year period,
published in 2003, the Medical Research Council found that
girls with professional parents were more stressed, particularly
in relation to their academic achievement, than those from
the lower social classes and boys. It suggested that these girls
were doubly disadvantaged by a combination of newer
educational concerns and more traditional worries about
personal identity, in particular body image.

Now it would seem that girls, especially middle-class
ones, expect to excel at school, to go on to university, and
to control their fertility whilst advancing in a more equal
professional environment. But the advances of feminism
only take young women so far. They have to wrestle not
only with the extended pressures that these possibilities
bring them, but with a culture that tells them they must
still look and behave – particularly sexually – in a certain
way in order to be truly successful. There are so many more

hurdles to leap over in order to achieve perfection that the race must feel never-ending.

Laura's mum has been abroad for a conference, so her dad has been staying in the house. She prefers living with her mum but she does get really stressed and she only buys healthy food. 'I think I'm as close to my dad as you could be to a dad, but because we don't live together there's not as much tension.' She sniffles again. The pollen is high this morning.

'I don't like when people say, "Oh she comes from a broken family", because it's just stupid. I think it's one in three or two in three people get divorced now. It's not like any of us are hard done by 'cos we still see my dad on a regular basis. I think my sister was a bit upset when they got divorced but I was too young. It doesn't really matter to me at all. I can't even imagine my parents being together.'

Laura admits that she's kind of given up on school. She has been offered a place at Fitzroy House in September and, when she turns sixteen, she will apply to the London School of Beauty where you can learn to be a make-up artist. She's really looking forward to that, because make-up's something she really wants to do. 'I think if later on in life I need GSCEs or A levels I can go back and do them 'cos there are all sorts of colleges for that. I'd like to get a job related to beauty and make-up. If not I'd like to have something to do with writing. I might be unfulfilled by just being a make-up artist. Ever since I was really little I wanted to write novels and stuff.' What would be ideal would be writing for a magazine about beauty. There are many contradictions in Laura's world.

It is now later in the summer, and she has been on holiday to Cuba with her mother, sister and mother's friends. It was nice, but her tan is fading. The builders are here, and the front of the house is encased in scaffolding. There are dust-sheets all the way up the stairs and a van blocking the back driveway. One of their jobs is to convert the attic into a new bedroom for Laura, with a private bathroom. She is wandering around, half-dressed, in shorts and an airtex vest. It's weird having all these workmen in your home.

She hasn't seen Kevin for ages, because she went to Cuba and now he's gone to New York. But he said that he was missing her so much that he's changed his ticket, so he's coming back a whole week early. Laura wraps her arms around her bare legs and stares ahead, preparing her caveats. 'It's cute but – not in a mean way, it's probably just me being an idiot, I really like him – I feel like being single. But now because he's paid £150 out of his own money to come back early . . . you can't break up with someone after they've done that.' Her voice will always be light, but today it has gained some resonance.

Laura missed her last appointment with the psychologist. She has her own problems within the system, but for many others a postcode lottery of services means that they are never referred in the first place. The National Collaborating Centre for Mental Health estimated in 2005 that only a quarter of children with a depressive illness were receiving treatment. Although one in ten school-age children has a diagnosable mental disorder, a minority are seen in specialist out-patient clinics, and referrals are driven largely by how much trouble the child, or its parents, are causing to other people.

Until very recently, drug prescription to children has been escalating. At the end of 2003, more than 50,000 children were taking antidepressants. Prozac is still approved for use with young people, although, in the autumn of 2004, other antidepressants of its kind were withdrawn after concerns were raised about their side-effects, including self-harm and suicide.

Then, in the autumn of 2005, the government's National Institute for Clinical Excellence (Nice) responded by telling doctors to stop prescribing antidepressants to people under the age of eighteen. (Previous Nice guidance had already cautioned against using antidepressants as a first resort.) Children with mild to moderate depression should be given advice on diet and exercise, the guidance told GPs. In moderate to severe cases, a three-month course of individual cognitive behavioural therapy or family therapy should be offered, with psychotherapy provided for the most serious instances. Only if there has been no improvement after four or five sessions should the doctor – and by this stage it would be a psychiatrist – consider prescribing a fluoxetine such as Prozac.

Although welcomed by campaigners, health professionals have pointed out the significant shortage of trained NHS staff to provide these therapies. The availability of drugs had, one psychiatrist suggested to me, made doctors less willing to consider the complexity of a child's individual situation. Drugs are far easier to prescribe and control, and much less expensive, than cognitive behavioural or talking therapies. Similar criticisms have been made regarding the use of Ritalin to treat ADHD, and some believe that it is over-prescribed because adults are prepared to tolerate an increasingly narrow band of behaviour in children.

When Laura talks about her suicide attempts it is as though she is describing another person and, she would argue, she is. 'It just occurred to me one day in school. I was sitting in Spanish and I was thinking sad things, and it just snowballed. So I thought "I'm looking ugly today", and then I thought, "I bet everyone else is feeling really disgusted by me", and then slowly it goes into "No one really likes me, my family doesn't like me" and you can't see any way out.'

Her mum's been really good lately. 'Sometimes she gets too worried about me, checking in my room all the time, or calling me every five minutes.' Laura takes a moment to connect why her mother might be especially concerned about her youngest daughter. 'You'd think someone who took an overdose would think about what their family were feeling. But I just thought I was going to die and I didn't think of anything else happening. I woke up the next day and I was really confused. I didn't understand. I did feel bad about them. They were crying and stuff.'

It's a sunny lunch-time and despite, or perhaps because of, the builders' presence, silence covers the house. Laura talks about the second time she tried to die. 'That time, it was in a back alley. I was on observation, but the staff nurse must have forgotten and she let me out. It was actually really bad because the chemist is only supposed to sell you thirty-six paracetamol but they sold me two boxes of thirty-six which is actually illegal,' she notes primly.

She was throwing up loads. 'Because that time it was just paracetamol but the first time I didn't know anything about overdoses and I was taking antibiotics and hay-fever tablets and that's why I messed up.' She yawns discreetly, covering her lovely mouth.

Autumn arrives early this year, and on my next visit the builders are still here. The fire is flickering in the sitting-room, and Laura is making herself tiny in the corner of the sofa, hugging a russet cushion into her chest, chewing at the corner like a comforter. Her skin is terribly pale. It's a working day, but her mother is at home, offering her daughter tea, juice, the yoghurt she likes. There are invisible eggshells in this house today. Laura doesn't say that she tried to hang herself at the weekend.

She watches the rainy day through the front window and says she feels cosy. She's started at Fitzroy House four days a week. They have school in the morning, though it's really basic, and then therapy in the afternoon. She's had a couple of one-to-one sessions, and then they have all these different groups, when they just talk: cooking group, girls' groups, one called 'problems on a plate'. At least it's something to do with your mind, though they gave her a book to read at home that was for ages twelve and under. She's been accepted on to the beauty-therapy course. So that's really good, she says, as though uttering it will make it so. She wants to start in January but might have to wait until next September because she's too young.

She split up with Kevin. It had been up and down for ages, but he was really sad and that made her feel a bit guilty. He's got loads of mates, but they're boys so they don't really talk about girl stuff, she whispers. Her voice has been charmed away again. 'Me and Kevin, we were breaking up and getting back together so much I don't feel sad about it any more. I'd been expecting it for a while.'

Laura isn't sure what shape this season will take. 'Keep going to Fitzroy House, do my room.' The thought of her room, her turret at the top of the house, enlivens her. 'I want it to be all white. Me and my mum have already bought a really nice bed and a nice wardrobe. I'm going to have it white but flowery in places, quite girly. I'm going to have just floorboards, and a really, really, really nice but really expensive dressing-table I've seen. It's white, and it looks really antiquey, and it's got curved legs and then two upright wooden poles with a big swing mirror in between them. It's £400 but I'm going to get it for my birthday from Mum and Dad.'

This birthday, Laura will be sixteen. 'I always think I'll feel different after birthdays, and sixteen does sound a lot different to fifteen with it being like growing up, and not being a little girl any more. But then I always think that and when it gets to my birthday I don't feel any different. I already smoke, I don't have sex, and I don't really care about driving.'

Laura says she just wants to stop being unhappy. 'Like when I had my first meeting with my therapist [at Fitzroy House], they said that you have to get worse before you get better, and that I'd probably be OK by January. But I want to be better before then.'

Any society's well-being can be measured according to the gap between the aspirations of its members and their attainability. Such invidious comparisons dominate the contemporary understanding of what it is to be happy. The economist Richard Layard explores in his book *Happiness* what he calls 'the First World paradox' of a society which seeks and delivers greater wealth than ever but is little happier. He argues that the gospel of individualism has proved to be a false one. It is based on the self-defeating notion that having more than others makes you happier, which then conversely makes those others unhappier. Layard advocates a return to the Benthamite notion of 'the common good', but how might that be achieved in a society adrift from shared moral or spiritual values?

Freud believed that the two central components for a happy life were love and work. A few years ago, the psychiatrist Anthony Clare offered an interviewer a more detailed prescription for happiness: 'One, cultivate a passion. How important it seems to me in my model of happiness to have something that you enjoy doing. Next, be a leaf on a tree. You have to be both an individual, you have to have a sense that you are you and that you matter, and at the same time you have to be connected to a bigger organism, a family, a community . . . My third rule, avoid introspection. Next, don't resist change. Change is important, people who are fearful of change are rarely happy. I don't mean massive change, but enough to keep your life stimulating. And finally, live in the moment, live now.'

Many childhood psychiatric disorders are eminently treatable, and doing so can furnish young people with skills that will serve them a lifetime. A more holistic approach to mental health, placing it on equal footing with physical well-being, would pave the way to a better understanding of how psychological distress affects other problematic aspects of growing up, like criminality or educational underachievement. But improving children's mental well-being requires much more than action on specific risk factors, like diet.

There is wide consensus amongst practitioners that a crucial policy improvement would be the provision of universal parenting skills training, ideally making it a compulsory part of the curriculum. They emphasise the need to prepare for the transition to parenthood from birth. In Canada, a classroom scheme called Roots of Empathy has had a dramatic effect in raising school children's social and emotional competence. A local baby visits the class with her parent every three weeks over the school year. Pupils are encouraged to observe the infant's development, interact with her and learn about her needs, while a specialised curriculum teaches them about child safety and development and responsible parenting. But the current failure to provide even basic sex education in many UK schools doesn't bode well for this aspiration. Parenting is included in the PSHE curriculum but, if it is dealt with at all, is usually framed in terms of discouraging teenage pregnancy, not encouraging the psychological flourishing of the next generation.

What about Anthony Clare's injunction to be 'a leaf on a tree'? In order to offer young people an alternative to the misery of meaningless choice and inflamed expectation we may have to reconceive childhood itself. Some of the emotional distress that many young people feel must surely be based on their experiences of marginality and exclusion. The UN Charter lays down every child's right to protection, provision *and* participation, but that third right is rarely acted on. We can help adolescents to develop a more coherent social identity only by allowing children genuine involvement in the world they are growing up in.

In an essay on fostering resilience, Sebastian Kraemer of London's Tavistock Clinic writes, 'In a world in which individuality is acknowledged, even celebrated, resilience is best understood as the experience of agency: that what you do or say makes a difference, that it is worthwhile making plans for your life, that you are not simply a helpless victim of forces entirely beyond your control.' But children, he argues, are still relatively powerless, 'at the mercy of our adult terror of helplessness'.

'When we talk about children we talk about everyone, yet there is . . . a subtle but pervasive contempt for children, often disguised with condescending words, as if they were a different species. Quite apart from the scandalous levels of poverty in one of the richest countries in the world . . . there are still far too many neglected children, at all levels of society . . . After sexism and racism, we still have to confront "childism".'

Referring to the work of John Bowlby, Kraemer concludes that all those who come into contact with children and young people need 'the reflective skills that make all the difference between power which is abused, and authority which is necessary. It is no good arguing for resilience based on secure attachment if we do not also argue for a society that welcomes it.'

Almost a month later, on another damp day, Laura is explaining why she doesn't want to go back to Fitzroy House. The builders are nearly finished, and her room is all but complete.

'I dunno,' she says, 'I didn't feel like I needed it. I didn't like it there, and compared to some of the people there I don't feel like I'm that ill any more. They won't discharge me for another month, and I'll have to go there twice a week for a meeting where they'll basically try to persuade me to go back. But I didn't go to my meeting this Monday, and I've got another one this Friday. I don't think I'll go back.'

She is relentless. 'Their routine is that you get worse before you get better. They want to break you down, and find out all your problems. They want to go into your childhood, and I don't think I had any problems in my childhood. It's not for me.' Laura says she isn't like the other people there. 'Not like really ill, really quite disturbed. There's one girl just always takes her top off and her bra and everything, she can't help it, and everyone's got to stop her. I'm not like that.'

Her parents think that she should stay there until December. She presses her point. 'I don't feel high risk, like I would want to kill myself or anything. I do still feel really ugly but I think every teenager feels like that sometimes. It already takes a lot less time to do my make-up when I go out.'

So why is she still considered high risk? She talks about the last time, just before my previous visit. 'I felt really sad and really lonely, and I was in the house all alone and I tried to kill myself but it didn't work. Even that was better than the first time,' she insists, 'because I never used to give up. When it didn't work I just kept trying and trying. I tried to hang myself, but the cord thing broke. I tried a couple of times and then just gave up.'

'That seems like quite recent, but you know when you just feel something inside yourself changing? But I can't really say because everyone at Fitzroy House is so convinced I need their help. I can't say I don't feel suicidal any more because they're like, "Well you say that now but then a month ago you tried to kill yourself, na, na, na, na." But I just know. I feel more in control of myself and more – I don't really know how to explain it.'

Neither do I. Even at the worst of times, Laura has always remained supremely lucid about the agonies and absurdities of her adolescent universe. At times like now, when her voice is tough and certain, her frame not limp but upright with energy, you want to believe every word. But if psychology is silly, and therapy delves too deep, can it all be left to how Laura feels on sad afternoons?

She is particularly resistant to her new therapist's emphasis, as she sees it, on her early childhood experiences. 'I think people always like to blame their problems on their parents. Everything about you pretty much is from your upbringing, but I know lots of people take any little problem they have and blame it on "when I was five my dad didn't do something . . ."'

Laura believes her depression is all to do with what happened at school. 'There's some stuff. Like my brother and sister used to be really best friends, and they wouldn't speak to me because I used to get on really well with my mum's boyfriend and they didn't like him. I wouldn't say that made me depressed, but it did make me feel left out and like I was always second best. But I think that's the only thing my family did.'

She flexes her fingers. Her nails are so neat. She's got some white nail polish that glides on really easily so she can do a French manicure at home. She used to get fake nails but they cost twenty-five pounds for a set, and when she smoked they'd go all yellow so she wound up biting them off.

Beyond Fitzroy House, Laura would like to get a job, but she's aware that no one trusts her to turn up on time every day. She doesn't want to leave home. 'I've got my new room being done. Mmmm,' she makes the sound of a satisfied cat. 'I can't imagine myself leaving. It's a bit scary really. My brother and sister are still here.'

Becoming an adult, Laura says, is about recognising the fleeting nature of happiness. 'When you're younger, you're kept happy all the time. When you're not happy you cry and your parents do something to make you happy. But when you're a teenager it's not so easy. If you're even a bit insecure then you compare yourself to other people and think their lives are perfect, and you feel bad for it.'

Laura read something the other day that one in three people have depression in their lives. 'When you think of happiness you think, "Oh there'll be a point in my life when I have everything I want and I'll be happy and it'll stay that way for the rest of my life," but you forget that circumstances change. Like say you expect you'll go to secondary school, you'll get all your good friends, you'll get a boyfriend and you'll just be happy for the rest of secondary school. But you forget that your friends might turn on you, your boyfriend might dump you and you'll stop going to school. You don't expect that to happen so you think, "I'll just be sad for ever now."'

Laura employs her favourite disclaimer: 'Not in a mean way, but I think that stupider people find it easier to be happy.

Not like stupid and clever in an academic way. But simpler people who don't think about stuff as much find it easier to be happy because they don't sit and analyse the bad stuff. If you're simple and careless you just take life as it comes.'

The cleaner comes in. She needs to vacuum the sitting-room. So Laura climbs the stairs to her new bedroom, past mother's, brother's and sister's rooms and up a newly conjured staircase. She pads across the varnished floorboards. It smells of dry paint and young wood. The wet sunshine streams through the skylight. Up here in her tower, Princess Laura will sleep, until the enchantment is broken, until the mirror on the wall tells her a kinder story. Out of the window there's a view right across the city.

Majid

'They can't decide who lives here and who doesn't.
It's their country, yeah, but it's a free world.'

Majid and his mother were on the bus. This woman was
going to get off and she said to his mum, 'I personally don't
think you should wear the headscarf because it doesn't
matter what your hair's like.' Some people think it's just to
hide the hair or not show yourself in front of men. That's
a different thing to how Majid understands it. His mum is
a believer in Allah and she wears the headscarf to respect
Him.

Majid is thirteen years old. He lives with his parents and
younger sister in a sprawling suburb of a large multicultural
city. Their airy, bright-tiled flat is a thoroughfare, where
uncles and cousins and toddlers tarry. He speaks Arabic at
home and, though his English is fluent, on occasion he adds
a non-native flourish, like a strictly grammatical expansion
of a tense.

He is slight of build but expansive in gesture, with a wide
mouth and mobile eyebrows. Majid is a declaimer. He
delights in florid description, especially when he's detailing
the playground battles that leave him exuberantly bruised.

There's lots of ethnic minorities in Britain, he says, that
all get along. He qualifies his optimism. On the other hand
you have some people that think it's wrong [to welcome

different races]. It's not really pressure, but the war gets to you, so do politicians, drugs, the bad influences.

Majid's family is Iraqi, and his grandparents still live in Baghdad. His parents came here two months before he was born, to escape the Kuwait war. His father fought in the Iran–Iraq war. 'They came out through Syria, and then they came to Britain, then they had me, then they had my sister, and a couple of months after that my dad got stabbed in the chest.'

He was about two at the time. His father was attacked on the street, apparently at random, and the police never caught his assailant. Majid can't remember much about what happened, but it remains an important story to tell about his early life. His dad was in a coma for two weeks. He used to be a mechanic, but now he can't work, because he doesn't have the stamina.

There have been lectures about the aftermath of war [the US–British-led war in Iraq, which began in the spring of 2003 – these interviews took place in the spring of 2005 when the country was still in turmoil and occupied by foreign troops]. Majid has gone to some of them with his dad. 'People were very angry because they said we were better off with Saddam without the bombs, at least we could go out. They said it was better with Saddam than what we have now, and everyone agreed. Then they made accusations, who is doing this and who is making all this happen? And why Bush did want to actually go to war.' He thinks Bush is an idiot.

Majid is staunchly male: noisy, rambunctious, crackling with energy and outrage. He is alive to injustices big and small: the treatment of asylum seekers, the teacher who tells him off for calling out *when he knew the right answer!* He balances rights and responsibilities: his right to play on the street with his need for protection there; his responsibility to behave in class with his desire not to be seen as sissy.

Previously, I discussed Sebastian Kraemer's belief that resilience, a quality essential to mental well-being, is best understood as the experience of agency: that what you do or say makes a difference, that you are not simply a helpless victim of forces beyond your control. He argued that only by correcting the imbalance of power between adults and children might we effectively foster resilience in childhood.

But this imbalance runs as a seam through children's lives. They are granted rights in principle by the UN, but refused many of them in practice. They are denied responsibility over their own education, health and welfare, then punished when they behave irresponsibly. They are excluded from the political process then berated for their apathy. At a time when adults' perception of childhood is fraught with contradictions, young people's own potential to balance them is seldom considered.

Majid's auntie works for Alfayhaa, an Arabic-speaking satellite station based in Kuwait. This weekend she reported that they had captured some bombers in Iraq, and most of them were Syrian, Saudi Arabian and Sudanese. These suicide bombers are sad low-lifes, says Majid. 'Most of them are people from foreign Arab countries that don't want Iraq to evolve. Some of them are Saddam's people, and others are just people that have been threatened.'

'Most of the people that are killed are the Shia not the Sunni. There's kind of a racial thing, like a civil war. But I'm a Muslim.' He slaps his chest. 'I'm not Shia or Sunni. I believe in one god, Allah; I believe in the prophet, and I believe in his followers.'

Majid doesn't go to mosque regularly, but he attends with his family on special occasions, like Eid. He goes to the lectures and he's been on a few marches. He prays five times every day, and he fasts.

The prayer in the afternoon is one or two o'clock, but he prays when he comes back from school instead. 'I don't pray at school because you have to make *wudu* [washing] and the toilets are dirty.' He knows some Muslims who pray at school, but they pray in a different way, and he gets confused. Most of Majid's friends at school are Christians. He's not a racist person.

Majid says that he's religious, but he's not extreme. 'It's like McDonalds. I don't know how they kill the chicken, but I still eat it.' It's certainly an arresting analogy. 'I pray, but I'm not *extreme*, extreme. 'Cos some people try to make up their own rules, and I think it's wrong. Like one of the lectures I went to, he said that listening to music is wrong. And it's true, but then again it's just a little beat with words that rhyme.' That's what he thinks.

If Majid had a vote, he'd vote Labour, because for now they're the safe side. 'Greenpeace, they want to make things like flying more expensive. And Conservatives, they say every man for himself, people won't get educated if they can't afford it, no free dental, no free doctors, that's not fair. If someone's life could be saved just for money, that's not fair.'

He thinks that the way politicians talk about asylum seekers is disgusting. 'They can't decide who lives here and who doesn't. It's their country, yeah, but it's a free world.'

Majid isn't certain whether his own parents sought asylum in Britain. He thinks they were granted British nationality because he was born here. He says it's kind of sad. 'It's not their choice. People that have to run away from home, they don't want to, but they have to leave to live. That's not fair,' he refrains, getting louder and more urgent. 'And then people say we don't want you here, go back home and die.' He points to a dictatorship in the corner of the room. 'That's not fair. It's like execution, just a longer way. The thing about this country that's nice is that every race is accepted. It lets a lot of people in. That's good.'

Majid didn't used to care about things like this. He wasn't that much interested in politics until the war started. When Pokémon cards were out, he just used to worry about them, and his dad would say, 'Look what's happening in your country, and you want to buy Pokémon cards!' He never knew what was going on.

He last visited Iraq two years ago. It was a relief to see his family. 'No matter how many poor people there were, everyone was helping each other out, so everyone was happy and sad at the same time. And you saw everyone unite, not like now when everyone's against each other and they're all trying to kidnap children to get money.'

One third of the British Muslim population is under the age of sixteen, and is more likely to grow up in poverty and to leave school without qualifications than average. This is a critical cohort. Many are third generation and negotiating in their daily lives the opposition between Islam and the West that has dominated world politics in recent years. Although research into the attitudes of young British Muslims is minimal, and only beginning to distinguish by faith rather than ethnicity, those working within the community testify that, like Majid, their children have been brought directly to consciousness by events like 9/11, the bombing of Afghanistan, and the war with Iraq.

My interviews with Majid took place before the London bombings of July 2005. Carried out by four young British Muslims, this act of terrorism placed younger members of the community under even sharper scrutiny. After the bombings, according to the Muslim Safety Forum, the total number of faith-related attacks in the capital rose by 500 per cent compared with the same period the previous year.

Shareefa Fulat is the director of the Muslim Youth Helpline, the country's only support service for young Muslims. Dealing on average with one hundred clients each week, it aims towards the 16–25-year-old age group, although it has taken calls from children as young as twelve.

Fulat says that she did not notice a significant increase in calls after the July bombings. In a sense, the problems that young people bring to MYH are no different from those encountered by their non-Muslim peers – relationship worries relating to family and friends, exam stress, bullying and depression.

But the charity's online discussion forum was frantic with debate following the London attacks. Fulat has seen an increasingly assertive Muslim identity developing amongst the younger generation in the last five years, which she explains can be a powerful tool to combat cultural assumptions about the role of childhood: 'But it can mean that young Muslims find themselves caught between a traditional community which views most youth issues as taboo, and a mainstream secular society, which fails to provide appropriate support.'

Young people are expected to be deferential to their elders to the extent that they cannot express what they really think. 'Some have resolved that by turning back to Islam, to find out what it really means rather than accepting their parents' cultural interpretations,' she says. Girls, for example, have discovered that their faith encourages female education. 'Others have gone in the opposite direction and rejected Islam out of hand.'

Fulat is convinced that this new assertiveness is a direct

response to the political climate: 'Young people are more conscious of their Muslim identity than ever before. Even if they're not practising, they still identify themselves as Muslim when they wouldn't have done five years ago. There's a sense of victimisation, and a fear that people are going to assume you're a terrorist simply because of your faith.'

This is also the experience of Anjum Anwar, who co-ordinates the Understanding Islam project across the north-west of England. A post-9/11 initiative, the project works with schoolchildren and teachers, as well as local community organisations, presenting Islam 'as a body of lived experience'.

'The youth is much more aware of its own faith,' says Anwar. 'There is so much anti-Islam feeling across the media and they want to understand why their religion has attracted it. Younger Muslims are investigating Islam, and discovering that it's not the faith itself that preaches violence, but rather that certain people within it do.' Young people are returning to Islam, she says, because they want to be able to challenge the misrepresentations they see.

She finds the media invention of young Muslims as violent jihadists vexing. 'They're playing a very dangerous game because the general public who don't understand the Islamic faith are influenced by it. They see the youth as dangerous, as causing problems for the security of the country. They think that wherever you have two or three Muslim boys talking they must be planning something.'

It is important to understand that Islam is a monolithic faith, says Anwar. 'If something happens to a Muslim in Timbuktu it still affects British Muslims. Everybody feels the pain.' She believes that the young people she works with have a genuine sense that Islam is under attack. 'They are angry. And they are also coming to terms with the need to be the people Islam wants us to be, rather than just ritualistically praying five times a day. But they need some sort of outlet for this. Now mosques are moving into the twenty-first century and working very closely with schools.'

Anwar describes a generation existing at a complex cultural interface, where every decision – from how to dress in the morning to who to marry – has a Western as well as an Islamic resonance. Young people are reaching for a European Muslim identity, she says. 'We can't impose the identity of the parents on their children, and we can't expect parents to change overnight. But young people have to forge new identities.'

Anwar suggests that this quest for identity should be supported by schools as well as by older Muslims. 'The curriculum needs to be widened, because it tends to miss out the contribution made by other civilisations. I know schools which are 100 per cent Muslim, and there the priority must be that they are taught about their own faith, and taught the Arabic language. If you teach a child about his own history you increase self-esteem and knowledge becomes relevant so they work harder.'

For Anwar, the perceived radicalisation of Muslim youth is a welcome development, encouraging dialogue and growth within the community. She is aware that not everyone interprets it so positively. But the Islamophobes have to understand that this generation is firmly embedded in British culture, she says. 'This is their home. They will protect their home, but they won't give up their faith, and they can still support Manchester United at the same time.'

It is not only Muslim children who have been radicalised by recent world events. In the spring of 2003, in the first days of the invasion of Iraq, this country was witness to a new kind of protest. In the most significant child-led campaign for a century, schoolchildren as young as ten walked out of their classrooms to attend what were, for most, their first political demonstrations. But they weren't just trotting alongside older activists, or parroting the slogans of their parents. These young people were organising and leading their own protests, leafleting at school gates, recruiting via email networks and cultivating the media.

Adults struggled to identify the root causes of this surge of activism. The younger generation was perceived as apathetic, children as small-visioned and self-interested. Kids cared about whales, recycling and the occasional prisoner of conscience. Adolescent idealism was as much about the self-definition and challenge of proclaiming one's vegetarianism as it was about genuine belief. It was easily dismissed as a short-lived trendification of protest, fuelled by mass hysteria and the lure of legitimised misbehaviour.

On Thursday, 20 March 2003, the country awoke to the news that Operation Iraqi Freedom had begun. I spent the day in London's Parliament Square, reporting on the school walk-outs for the *Guardian* newspaper. By late afternoon, several thousand young people had amassed there. I spoke to Muslims and Christians, public school rebels and – granted fewer – working-class kids, a fair number of chancers, and many more true believers. There was an adult presence too, but they certainly weren't taking the lead. Many of those I interviewed had finely tuned critical faculties. Their assessment of news sources and their alertness to propaganda was impressive. These children were sceptical, but not cynical, and mainly well-informed about why they were there.

Over the coming days, the scene was replicated across the UK – 5,000 in Birmingham, 3,000 in Manchester and Edinburgh, 1,000 in Sheffield. Condemned by the police and teaching unions, many of the youngsters who took part were marked down as truants, with a significant number of absences resulting in suspension or expulsion.

Michael Lavalette is an expert in the sociology of childhood at Liverpool University, with a particular research interest in the study of popular protest. He suggested that this wave of collective action bore many similarities to past youth protests. 'They all happened in a particular context of general unrest across the country,' he told me. 'In 1889, 1911, during the 1970s and again in the mid-1980s, over short periods of two to three weeks, large numbers of children walked out of their schools.'

In 1911, for example, at the time of the Great Unrest, a wave of school strikes affected some sixty towns and cities across the country. Students walked out in protest at the brutal corporal punishment then meted out by teachers, and called for free access to education for all. 'They were affected by the rebellious spirit of the age,' said Lavalette. 'Many had seen their parents out on strike. They were extremely well organised and quickly established a national set of grievances and demands.'

Lavalette was dubious about the suggestion that the anti-war protests were incited by adult campaigners seeking to bolster their own agenda. 'With any form of collective action, politicians always like to blame an agitator. It turns everyone there into sheep, and it's incredibly patronising to the children. They may have taken their tactics from adults, but these actions were led by the young people themselves.'

Citizenship education, aimed at 'improving political literacy and community involvement', became compulsory in the autumn of 2002, the year before those protests. It was suggested at the time that children's new-found engagement was a direct result of these classes. But later research would appear to contradict this. The largest ever survey of pupils' opinions on their citizenship classes, published three years after their introduction, found that, while most enjoyed the subject, 67 per cent of students questioned said that they remained uninterested in politics.

This was inevitably construed as further confirmation of young people's apathy. But a less cursory examination of the results reveals another dimension. What the survey actually showed was that young people continued to mistrust politicians and had minimal interest in participating in conventional politics. But this did not translate into apathy.

Although the majority of students in all year groups said that they did not support any party, less conventional forms of participation were far more popular. More than half had taken part in a range of political activities, including signing petitions, attending public meetings or taking part in demonstrations. Seventy-five per cent of Year 12 children indicated that they intended to vote in the future, and 68 per cent read a national newspaper, while a fifth used the Internet to look up current affairs.

Perhaps the disparity between interest in world events and interest in conventional politics comes down to language. The very mention of 'politics' puts off many young people. It is worth noting that *Newsround*, consistently the most watched terrestrial children's programme, seldom uses the P-word or reports on the day-to-day running of Parliament, concentrating instead on single issues.

Kierra Box was seventeen at the time of the anti-war protests in 2003. Along with two friends, all pupils at a north London comprehensive school, she organised Hands Up For Peace, an Internet-based campaign which invited children across the country to decorate a single handprint with their name, age and a message of peace. On the day that the war began, they planted some of the 2,500 hands they had received on sticks in the grass of Parliament Square. The organisation has since re-invented itself as Hands Up, and continues to support and connect young activists.

Box, now studying English and history at university, was never convinced that citizenship classes were contributing to young people's political awareness. 'The educational establishment pushes you all the time: "You should be interested in having debates about sex, about drugs, because that's what we need you to be aware of. You must be informed about these young people's issues." But then there was the firemen's strike, the teachers' pay dispute, tuition fees and the war, all of which were far more relevant to our lives. Yet we were told to ignore all of that, and just concentrate on not getting pregnant, not taking an overdose and getting a job with good prospects.'

The war provided unusual public exposure for youth activism, she says, as did the G8 protests in July of 2005. 'There's still of lot of interest and passion, but it's gone underground again, because there generally isn't space in mainstream politics for young people to get involved. The war made them realise that they could set up organisations on their own. They're still doing it, but now on a local level. It's there all the time, but there isn't the same media interest now.'

Recently, through Hands Up, Box has come across a group of children who campaigned to save a bus route that took them to school, and another who had successfully fought the deportation of a refugee family. 'With G8, again it was seen as coming from nowhere. But people don't get politicised in a week before a big event, or because pop stars tell them to. They start out thinking locally, and then when the chance comes to affect something globally they take it.'

*   *   *

For his part, Majid is not purely an ideologue. Football matters too. He learnt it on the streets, he says mightily. If he had the chance, he'd play football twenty-four seven. He supports Manchester United, and he likes strong defenders who will really go in there and take a beating.

When he's older, he wants to move to Spain, so he can train to be a footballer. But he'll have to do university first, business or mechanical engineering. He's good at science. He's in the highest group.

This week, he's later coming home because he has a science revision class after school. We are in the sitting-room, while his mother prepares dinner in the kitchen. Next week he has tests in French, science, English and maths. He doesn't feel nervous because he knows he's worked hard.

Teachers are a variable tribe, according to Majid. 'You have teachers that are very good at it, and you have teachers that just can't control anyone. It really depends. We had this one teacher, he left us a term ago, but he was loose, he would act higher than us, but not so high, and we would understand.'

Some teachers don't let you get out of your chair, they're proper, proper strict, and others are a bit more flexible. Majid says he will always talk, and be a bit loud, but work at the same time.

Some teachers find it really hard to control his class. 'Like at science a week ago a boy in my class he verbally abused the teacher, he said, "I'll get my dad to rape you".' He thinks she called his parents. 'But people think if they're rude to teachers, they can't do nothing to you.'

It's less of a big deal to be rude to teachers at secondary school. 'When I was in junior school, you had the most respect for teachers, but on my first day [at secondary school] I saw year sixes and they're calling a teacher a female dog. I'm like,

"Wow! This has never happened in my life!" and people just pick up on that.'

The girls in his class, everyone thinks they are the good ones, but they are devils. He wrinkles his nose at the maleficence of the opposite sex. 'They will bitch about one another, they will talk about each other, they will make noises to annoy the teacher. In PE we are the best behaved because the boys are split up from the girls. It's the girls that start things.'

Status is carefully calibrated, and it is not always obvious how to acquire it. 'There's this girl that thinks she's so popular, but she is not. She's been trying hard to get with the really popular girls, but then this new girl just made friends straight away with the popular girls and the first girl bitched about her and it became this big fight. She said, "Oh my God, how come you can get with them and look at my standards?" and everyone was like, "Look at your own standards!" In slang we have a word called "beg" and she begs a lot.'

Neither is status a constant. If you don't stand up for yourself, explains Majid, you will eventually lose power. 'Like, me and my friends have play fights' – he rolls up his sweatshirt arm to display a ladder of bruises. 'There was this one boy, he came at me when I was at my uncle's house, and I was like, "What? What?" and I had to blow him twice in his face and he hit me once.' He executes a pair of upper cuts whilst he's talking.

But with boys, in contrast to girls, everyone's equal. 'There's this one boy, he's grown very big. But we don't pick on him, we all make fun of each other. We're like brothers, but the girls are always bitching about each other.'

The true depth of this brotherly intimacy is unclear. Angela Phillips, who has written widely on the young male experience, points out the poor fit between boys' sense of loyalty to one another and a group culture that is contemptuous of close relationships.

In interviews with thirteen- and fourteen-year-olds about attitudes to schooling, she found that although the boys were aware that girls had more intimate relationships, they were suspicious of them. Many were preoccupied with girls' 'whispering', implying that this made them sneakier and less honest than boys. Phillips suggests that this betrayed their own feelings of exclusion, when traditional masculinity demands that they forge an identity beyond the warmth and intimacy of the female family circle.

She discovered that, in the classroom, much of this 'whispering' was in fact collaboration over school work, something which boys found embarrassing. 'Somehow the idea of helping each other has been tied up in their minds with this feminine intimacy,' she writes. 'Helping is something that mothers and girls do so to help others would open them up to accusations of being soft – like a girl.'

Majid says nothing much else has been happening lately. 'Just getting beat up!' he says cheerfully. He says the bruises don't hurt. 'I always take them down with me, start hitting their legs, then get up and run. That's what you do.' His strategy is all worked out.

When he misbehaves at home, he says it's mostly to do with his sister. 'And I'm the one that's always to blame 'cos she's younger, so it's my responsibility to look out for her and not abuse her. We play-fight but then it gets real. Last year I was jabbing her with a comb and she moved her head down and it went into her ear, nearly deafened her! She went to hospital. I was just shaking!'

Sometimes Majid has trouble starting sentences because

there's so much to convey, and the syllables tumble over each other. He's noticed a big change in himself over the past few years as he's become a teenager. 'Before I wasn't very hygienic, I used to sleep in my same clothes, I didn't care, I never used to do my sheets, never used to do anything for Mum. Now I do my bed every day, change my clothes. I never used to like outdoors much. Now I really, really like going out.'

Majid's specific trouble with really liking going out is that his mum worries. She doesn't let him go out in the evenings, even though all of his friends are allowed. 'But my mum thinks that I'm too young. I say to my mum, "Please!" She thinks I might get kidnapped, but I'll be with a big group of people. She thinks I might do drugs, but I've been offered millions of cigarettes before and I said no.' He thumbs his chest. 'I can handle peer pressure!'

Drugs and cigarettes are so stupid. His dad used to smoke the long shisha pipe. 'I used to say,' he sneers into a baby voice, ' "When I grow up I want to be like Dad and smoke." And I'd be putting everything in my life at risk, for what? None of my friends smoke. We beat up people that smoke. Round the back at school, we steal their cigarettes and beat them up. Smoking, look where it gets you – not just heart disease but bruise disease,' he scoffs.

He's seen a few people smoking weed. He makes a face. 'Stinky, expensive, fake. Yeeeuh!' Alcohol is against his religion.

But he's not that sensible, he appends. 'I have a big mouth. I speak a lot. I never used to do that before.' He's more confident now. 'I have to look out for my sister. Like she was in an argument with some girl in her class the other day and I had to sort it out. 'Cos the brother of the girl and me, we're friends, so I spoke to him, sorted.' He crosses his arms, a man.

Majid thinks it's easier to grow up as a boy than as a girl. ''Cos girls do a lot of make-up and stuff, and, "Ooh, does this boy like me?" As a boy you don't *care*!' He spits the word out like a bad taste. 'As a Muslim girl, my sister can't go swimming, but I can. She has to be careful who she talks to, what she does, how she reacts.' Does he think that's fair? 'It's a way of respect. You don't want her becoming one of those girls that dresses in miniskirts.'

Majid doesn't worry about what girls think of him. 'No! I just judge them, whether they're nice or not.' And does he ever wonder about marriage? 'I'm not even thinking about that right now!' He seems stranded between girl-hating and girl-desiring, not quite sure which way to jump. Would his future wife have to be Muslim? Yes. Who practises? 'Not necessarily,' he says. 'I'd turn her into one.'

As Laura observed in the previous chapter, 'loads of teenagers don't really know who to try and be'. If adolescence induces the struggle to fathom identity, how much harder has that become for boys, now that the male role is so in flux? The 1990s witnessed anxious debate about 'the crisis of masculinity'. It seemed that boys were struggling more than girls to adapt to the major changes taking place in society, falling behind at school, falling into delinquency, unable to imagine their place in a new economic landscape that valued feminine skills more than traditional masculine ones. Negative portrayals of men in the media, unsuitable role models and single mothers were all variously accused of contributing to a lack of confidence among young males.

Meanwhile, lingering conventional expectations of what it is to be a man can narrow the range of boys' responses to these challenges. In their book *Young Masculinities*, the psychologists Stephen Frosh, Ann Phoenix and Rob

Pattman describe this process: 'The ways in which masculinities are "policed" by peers and adults communicate to boys a message that alternative . . . ways of being are abnormal for males – that they are girlish and hence subject to opprobrium and exclusion.'

The book is based on an extended research project, interviewing 11–14-year-old boys in London schools over a number of years. The authors found that their subjects characterised masculinity as involving 'toughness, footballing prowess and resistance to teachers and education'.

They saw how boys' behaviour and appearance were powerfully regulated by a set of gendered contrasts. 'Boys were seen, by boys themselves and to some extent by girls, as "naturally" active and energetic, physically tough, easygoing, funny, brave and sporty, while girls were passive, fragile, obsessed with their appearance, easily offended, emotionally weak and academic,' they observe. These contrasts were assumed to be present in all activities, and so the performance of boys and girls 'was constantly examined by their peers for signs of gender conformity or deviance.'

One form of 'deviance' to which the boys in the study frequently referred was homosexuality. Calling somebody 'gay' was a generic insult, rarely based on any concrete evidence about a person's sexuality. Often being gay and being girly were seen as interchangeable. 'Homophobic and misogynistic repetition,' note the authors, 'may be understood as a continual attempt to construct an ever-elusive masculine ideal.'

They described the ubiquity of homophobia among the boys they spoke to, and the way in which they used it to publicly assert their 'normal' masculine identity. When I broach the subject of homosexuality with Majid, his reaction is immediate: laughing, cursing, embarrassed. 'It's wrong, really wrong!' he cries. 'I'm racist against it!' At school, if someone says you're gay it can mean something else, not in a homosexual way, like you're annoying.

What would he do if one of his friends told him that he thought he was gay? He points to his father's walking stick, which is leaning against the fridge. 'Take that,' he says deliberately, 'bring it down on his head.' Even if he was your friend before that? 'It's WRONG!!!' he shrieks. 'God made man and woman for a reason, not man and man. It's going against the rule of nature.' If a gay person told him they couldn't help it, he'd tell them to get a doctor. Doesn't he have any sympathy for them? 'Hell no! Eeeyeuh.' He squirms on the settee, tugging at his tracksuit leg in agitation, disgusted.

Like Majid, many of the boys in the *Young Masculinities* study used the football pitch as a site for exploring their male identity. When comparing themselves with girls, an important difference they highlighted was that they were more interested in sport. Like the boys that Angela Phillips spoke to, they expressed bafflement at what girls actually did during the lunch-hour when the boys were playing football.

The authors describe the 'opposition between the active and productive use of time in playing football, characteristic of boys, and girls' aimless sitting, walking and talking . . . "Just" talking was understood as talk for its own sake, as having no other purpose and therefore as pointless and obsessive. When boys talked, it was for a reason.'

The following week, Majid's been up late watching a video. It was about a good president and an evil president, and there's this guy who has to take out the evil one.

His exams were quite easy, apart from English, which was hard. 'They gave us this text and most of the questions were based on opinion so we had to use PEA: point, evidence, analysis. It was about being watched all the time. Somebody wrote a book in 1948 called *1984*, "Big Brother's watching you" kind of thing. The second part was "how do you feel about CCTV?"' Majid doesn't have CCTV in his block, but they're getting an entry gate because there are loads of druggies downstairs.

There have been more fights, he laughs, showing off a fresh crop of purplish bruises. 'Yesterday I got taken down by *eight* people! It was a play-fight. My friend started it off, he kept cussing all these people, and I went to join in for my friend, then he just ran and I had to take on eight people that were strong! They kicked me down but I was kicking back and they said, "This one's a warrior, keep him alive."'

The distinction between play-fights and real ones is subtle, but significant. He had a real fight on Thursday. One nine-year-old and one eleven-year-old, they wanted to have a go at Majid from when they moved into this block [of flats]. He said, 'No, 'cos I'll get in trouble, but they kept on: "You're scared", other language, bad language. Then on Thursday, they started fighting me, and they hit me in the face which hurts a lot 'cos I have braces and it cuts your cheek, then one of them punched me so I ran after him and I punched him in the face but he was wearing glasses so it cut his eye.'

His mum was very angry. 'She said, "You're stupid, you're older than them, you could have put him in hospital."' But it wasn't Majid's fault. He had to defend himself. As punishment, he's not allowed to play football downstairs for a year. He doesn't care. He doesn't want to play down there anyway.

There are a lot of play-fights at school, but some of them are serious, and the teachers break them up. Sometimes you just get an incident report and it goes into your record. Sometimes you get held back after school.

The worst punishment Majid's ever had was a phone call home which was for swinging on his chair and for calling out. His voice rises in indignation. ''Cos some teachers, I hate them so much 'cos they know you want to answer the question, they know I want to do it right and they don't pick me for the fun of it. They see me getting frustrated and they want me to get in trouble, 'cos I have this urge to call out, and it's their fault if they don't pick me!'

His teachers think he's naughty but they think he's all right. 'I'm intelligent, but I'm naughty.'

Over the weeks that Majid had been discussing his school – the boy who made the rape threat, the good teachers who are flexible, the bad ones who pick on you for calling out – a minor wave of child-panic about classroom discipline was sweeping the country.

In April 2005, Channel 5 screened a documentary by the film-maker Roger Graef, who had equipped a supply teacher with hidden cameras to expose the extremity of insolence and disruption she encountered. The National Association of Head Teachers condemned irresponsible parents who sent children into school lacking basic social training. New figures revealed that the number of physical assaults on teachers had doubled in the space of a year. At the beginning of May, Education Secretary Ruth Kelly called for 'zero tolerance' of disruptive behaviour in the classroom, while the Conservatives offered up the dubious panacea of fast-track expulsions.

In the same period, the annual report from the chief inspector of schools, David Bell, received selective coverage, fuelling the impression that the nation's schoolchildren were beyond control. But, as Fiona Millar pointed out at the time, Bell actually reported that discipline was satisfactory or better in the majority of schools, and poor in 1 per cent of primary schools and 9 per cent of secondary schools. 'In short,' she concluded, 'there is a chronic problem in several hundred schools, most of them secondary schools with an above-average number of children on free school meals.'

Since leaving Downing Street, where she worked as an aide to Cherie Blair for many years, Millar has proved herself a passionate but cool-headed advocate for the state education system. She noted that, while many schools with generally good behaviour did suffer the kind of low-level disruption that the education secretary was talking about, blaming parents was not the answer.

'Most parents of low-level disrupters are doing their best,' she wrote. 'They can be let down by an unstimulating curriculum, headteachers who don't manage behaviour consistently and teachers who can't hold their pupils' attention.' Which is certainly Majid's experience. 'A programme of behaviour initiatives won't work without acknowledging that children also have rights: to be well taught in schools where expectations are clear.'

It is hardly surprising that teachers, as well as pupils, struggle with the imperatives of standardisation and centralisation, though many continue to create stimulating learning experiences in spite of the strictures of the National Curriculum. Latest educational theory is moving away from grading, towards a more comment-based approach, and the Department for Education and Skills' own five-year strategy emphasises that the child is 'a partner in learning, not a passive recipient'. But in socially and ethnically mixed inner-city schools, where the aim is to get all children – no matter how unable or unwilling their parents – to a useful level of literacy and numeracy by the time they leave, perhaps a degree of plodding is inevitable.

While Majid may not be exemplary in class, he has the sense and the family support to work hard when it's important. When he grows up, if Spanish footballing doesn't work out, he says he'd like to get a job with cars, designing them. And he'd like to open a restaurant, or a business of some sort. 'The thing that I would want is a McDonald's that is hallal, 'cos you'd get much more custom. The Muslim people that go to McDonalds, they only buy the Filet-O-Fish [he pronounces it the French way] which they don't even like. But if you do it the hallal way you'll get much more profits.'

The following weekend, it's the beginning of the spring half-term holiday, and Majid is planning to play football all day every day. His mum says she's going to feed him like a pig! He's too skinny. Sometimes I wonder if his noise and bluster are an attempt to take up the extra space he'd like his body to. But the thing is he's fussy about food. He doesn't like fried onions and he doesn't like aubergines and they're in Arabic food a lot. So he eats junk food, but they say that it makes you obese, and he's *still* skinny. He pats his slim tummy.

He's already had some of his exam results back. In maths he got two down from the very top grade. But he failed his art. 'I don't care about art! I've got no *passion* for it!'

At school this week there was excitement over crutches. 'My friend, he broke his leg. He fell on the stairs with his bike. He came in yesterday and everyone started borrowing his crutches and fighting with them! And in my history lesson, I was just playing with his crutches and I got in trouble! For no reason!!' Majid has an unsurpassable talent for this.

He has some homework to do this week too: a thousand-word essay for geography on ecosystems; some maths questions; and for English they have to make a holiday brochure about a city. But mainly he'll be in the park. Sometimes when he's playing football, older people come and play with them. It's like a manhood connection.

'If I wanted to I could just deceive my parents and say I was going to the park then go to Oxford Street. When my parents let me do something, I don't take advantage of it. I do the thing I told them I would.'

Majid isn't sure whether children deserve more rights. 'Yeah and no. Yeah is because when I went to a funfair I wanted to go on the bumper cars but you had to be fourteen. Little minor things like that. But no for major things like drinking and smoking.'

He thinks that if children had proper rights they would go over the limit. 'But sometimes, because they're children, people say they can't do stuff. When we play football in the park, if there's adults they say, "You can't join us 'cos you're too little", when we're sometimes better. Or in Apollo you can't buy DVDs 'cos you're under sixteen. And you can't pay for petrol in the petrol station for your uncle when he's in a hurry. There's an airline called Ryanair and you can't travel by yourself if you're under sixteen.'

Majid shows little confidence in his peers' capacity for moderation. 'As things are going now, it's kind of corrupting, with drinking and that. Some people, their parents smoke weed and then they get into it. Or some music has songs about violence, saying you have to do it. They think if you're being bad you get respect. They're all in groups, they all look like they're going to pull something off.'

Majid says he feels unsafe on the streets. 'Anyone could come and jump you.' He acted it out in drama yesterday, because it happens all the time. 'My friend who was on crutches, I was in his group. My and my other friend, we acted as we were brothers, we jumped him and took his phone. My friend on crutches went to his dad, then my other friend who acted as his dad came to get us, and he beat me up. And then my friend who had crutches came and beat me up for real!' He rotates his arm to show the latest bruises. 'He jumped me for real in front of the teacher, and she thought it was acting.' He chuckles noisily. Once in drama they pretended to be Taliban and beat up the Americans!

Children's confinement has reached troubling levels in recent years, but being outside can have consequences too. It is other children, not adults, who are mainly at risk from young people's antisocial behaviour. Young males in particular are more likely to be victims than perpetrators of street crime. Increased surveillance of childhood has not resulted in increased security. Majid has the right not only to be outdoors, but also to feel safe when he's there.

Many of the policies that most curtail children's rights, like curfew orders or ASBOs, may also be seen as an avoidance of adult participation in socialising children. What used to be the responsibility of a whole community is now left to parents and, *in extremis*, the police. While adults invest hugely in their own offspring, they have neither energy nor inclination to get involved in the upbringing of other people's children.

It follows that children's rights cannot be exercised in isolation. Their rights to provision, protection and participation laid out in the UN Convention on the Rights of the Child must be balanced with adults' responsibility to facilitate them, and children's own responsibility to exercise those rights with consideration for others.

But children's rights need not be an affront to adult authority. As Mary John, a developmental psychologist widely recognised for her work on children and power, writes: 'Children are not out to grab some of the action of invested power. What is involved [is] changing the relationship between adults and children so that, through participation and voicing, each person works towards understanding and respecting each other's realities.'

Betrand Russell issued the challenge that 'no political theory is adequate unless it is applicable to children as well as to men and women'. But it is a far more paternalistic philosophical tradition that has prevailed in modern times. John Stuart Mill insisted that children should be 'protected against their own actions as well as against external injury'. Liberty was only an inalienable right in the case of adults. For children, well-being – achieved through altruistic adult interventions – took precedence. And Kant denied that children had the 'reason' that affords individuals the ability to make rational choices for themselves.

In some ways, this is akin to how women's and ethnic minorities' rights – or lack of them – used to be framed. Indeed, it has been argued that children are now in the position once occupied by the idealised bourgeois wife and mother, as historian Harry Hendrick puts it: 'pampered and loved, an essential ornament serving as testimony to domestic bliss, but subservient to male power.'

In his introduction to *The Children's Rights Handbook*, Bob Franklin offers a number of sensible grounds for rejecting this paternalism. Firstly, plenty of research evidence exists to show that children can make informed decisions and do reveal a competence for rational thought. Secondly, if children are not allowed to make decisions because they have no experience, then how will they ever get started? 'It does not follow that children should not make decisions simply because they might make the wrong ones. It is important not to confuse the right to do something with doing the right thing.'

There is nothing wrong with making mistakes, according to Franklin, nor are adults universally skilled decision-makers. Fifthly, 'allocating rights according to an age principle is incoherent and arbitrary, with different age requirements for adult rights applying in different spheres of activity.' Sixth, he argues that rights should be allocated according to individual competence rather than limited to the developmental hierarchy of age and stage.

Seventh, the denial of participation rights to children is unfair because they can do nothing to change the structures that exclude them. And finally, writes Franklin, 'to define everyone under eighteen years of age as a child, or more accurately as a "non-adult", obscures the inherent diversity of childhood and attempts to impose a homogeneity upon children which the plurality of their intellectual and emotional needs, skills, competences and achievements undermines.'

The crux of the matter is whether adults and children are ontologically different. If children are regarded as 'naturally' incompetent, do adults have a 'natural' right to exert power over them? The Norwegian academic Jens Qvortrup, one of the pioneers of children's rights theory, has argued that, to justify this position, the actor-status of the adult must be qualitively more important than that of the child. It must also be beyond doubt that adults will always behave in the best interests of children. 'It is more likely,' he concludes, 'that the adult world doesn't recognise children's praxis because competence is defined with reference to adults' praxis.'

Despite their potential, children's rights are poorly served in the UK. Children can, by law, be assaulted by their parents if it meets the requirement of 'reasonable chastisement'. A young offender can be tried in an adult court and named and shamed in newspapers. And the widespread use of curfew orders allows police to pick up people under sixteen who are out after 9 p.m. without a supervising adult.

Meanwhile, across the globe, children are proving themselves time and again to be thoroughly competent. Ten-year-olds head households in war-torn African states. Child labourers unionise in India. One study found that three-year-olds could plan, budget for, buy and cook a midday meal at their playgroup. Because children can doesn't always mean children should. But ordinary children in extraordinary circumstances are continually revealing capabilities that remain unexplored in their more fortunate peers. The possibilities offered by a rights-based approach need not deprive children of their childhoods nor dissolve into a *reductio ad absurdam* of votes for toddlers.

Lowering the voting age to sixteen is regularly proposed as a way of increasing young people's participation in civil society. In February 2006, the report of Helena Kennedy's Power Commission suggested as much, and was endorsed by Gordon Brown.

It has been argued that lowering the voting age would simply increase the proportion of those who don't vote. Certainly, there seems to be minimal public support for the move – polling by the Electoral Commission, which in April 2004 recommended that the voting age remain at 18, found that only 25 per cent of the public wanted the age reduced. Nor do young people's voting habits suggest otherwise. In the 2005 election, national turnout was 61 per cent, compared with 37 per cent amongst 18–24 year olds – down 2 per cent from 2001.

But others counter that only by giving young people the vote at sixteen will their democratic engagement increase. By treating them as citizens, they will they act as such. Research into how people develop voting habits has found that 'vote early, vote often' holds: those who are old enough to vote while still at school are more likely to vote again than those who have to wait until their twenties for their first chance. In the 2001 election, for example, turnout amongst 27-year-olds was 49 per cent, compared with 65 per cent among 28-year-olds who had been old enough to vote in the 1992 election.

It does seem absurd that sixteen- and seventeen-year-olds who can serve in the army, marry, work and, above all, pay taxes should be denied representation. And citizenship education might be taught to better effect if it was addressing how students were imminently to use their first vote.

In her brilliant essay 'Thinking About Children', the philosopher Judith Hughes plays with the idea of extending suffrage to children much younger than sixteen. She argues that advocates of children's political participation have failed to address the realities of childhood, because they hold to a model which demands that any difference between childhood and adulthood is construed as an inferiority on the part of children. 'Must what is insulting to an adult – being treated like a child – be insulting to the child?' she asks.

She uses the example of a toddler who yells 'I hate you!' at a parent while in the throws of a tantrum. The parent does not interpret this as a genuine expression of loathing, nor do they believe that the child means it in any lasting sense. But to respond to an adult's 'I hate you!' in a similar fashion would be paternalistic. And so, she writes, 'This is part of what treating someone as a child is; not denying that he thinks or feels but rather not leaving him in the loneliness of his judgements until he has learnt much, much more about what that involves.' An adult who fails to respond to the anger of a two-year-old as the anger of a two-year-old is himself immature. 'To treat children as equals here would be a monstrous form of oppression,' she concludes.

Of course, toddler suffrage is a philosophical trope. Even the most radical proponents of children's rights do not suggest that they should be at the ballot box before they can write their own name. But the point Hughes makes is a critical one: at times it is only by failing to treat them as equally responsible agents that adults can teach children how to assume responsibility for themselves. This is not to say that children are always without capacity, but that the changing relationship between adults and children which Mary John writes about must incorporate a respect for incapacity and dependency too.

Majid would vote at sixteen if he could. You can change the Prime Minister here, so there is a point voting for the future of this country, but it won't change anything in another country. He's stopped going to the lectures about the war lately. They're boring. It's depressing. They talk about the new government, what they should do, but no one's going to hear them so what's the point?

Something serious happened this week, that seems to have left him feeling a little hopeless: 'They bombed ten metres away from our house in Baghdad. Nobody was hurt.' He calls to his mother in Arabic for more details: 'Who bombed Bibi?' His cousin wanders in from the hallway to hear the story told again. He's drinking Tango and his tongue is bright orange.

'Many people died, a hundred people,' says his mother. She speaks in angry fragments, apologising for her English. 'They want to attack any people. My mum we call her, we call her every day to see what's happened to them.'

'They stole my cousin.'

'Hostage,' prompts Majid.

'About two days ago. They wanted £20,000, that's not normal. How they get this money? Go sell your house, sell anything you've got, after twenty-four hours we go kill your son, and the son is twenty-one years old. It's terrible! Now they tell me, they sent him back, he's scared of *everything*. They beat him with the gun. It's terrible our country. They say it's government, but there's no government.'

It depresses his mum, says Majid, and he doesn't like to see her upset. His dad gets upset too. 'He cries when he watches the news. He gets angry about how many they kill. They say it's bin Laden or Syria or al-Zaquarwi. They say it's jihad. There's no such thing as jihad! Their jihad is to kill. Our jihad is to do what Allah wants. Allah says thou shalt not kill.'

Majid suspects that America is sending these suicide bombers to Iraq. ''Cos half the Arab population are American dogs, they're puppies. They say, "Go fetch, go kill." They say, "We conquered the country, the country's yours".'

Somehow, his holiday week hasn't been as much fun as it should have. He's been trying to play football every day, but it's been raining hard. Majid says you can get bored really easily. He's very vocal this morning, full of exaggerated phrasing and noises, and though the unused footballing energy is finding other ways to expend itself.

His girl cousin is playing with his sister, making regular trips to the kitchen for chocolate fingers. He admonishes her for taking too many. He says he knows most about the Middle East, but he knows something about Africa too. 'To tell you the truth some parts of it are really, really bad, worse than Iraq. Some people only have a tiny bit to eat. They're malnourished. Their heads are big but their stomachs are flat in. Woah!'

'I say thank God for every morsel I have. I say I'm going to eat every morsel on my plate, then I can't! I don't know what's wrong with me!' He riffs on his inability to grow fat one more time. 'I say I'm going to eat it but I have about a quarter and then I can't eat any more.'

He doesn't know who could make things better in Iraq. His uncle says that Bush had the right idea, and then he messed it up, but now he says there's hope. Sometimes Majid feels hopeful, and sometimes he doesn't. 'All these bombers, they're catching more every day, but I doubt they'll catch all of them.'

Sometimes Majid agrees with what his father and his uncle think, and sometimes he argues with them. 'I just believe what I hear on the news. My uncle says there's hope, my dad says there's hope; I say, "OK, there might be hope." The only thing I want to do is go back to my family. I want to see my grandparents, and take care of them.'

He brings through a snapshot that is normally stuck to the fridge door – of him and his mother with his grandmother and cousins on his last visit to Iraq. They are making bunny-rabbit ears behind each other's heads, and grinning wildly.

Majid says he doesn't feel British, even though he was born here. 'I feel Arab. I don't think anyone's got the right to say where you can live and where you can't, what you can feel and what you can't. My blood is Iraqi Arab but I live here. Everyone has pride in where they're from.' He has pride in Britain too, though he doesn't like the mice.

He thinks that when he's an adult the world's going to be very hi-tech and very chaotic. ''Cos if you look at the teenagers now, what will they be like when they have all those privileges?' And politicians will still be dogs. 'I don't know why I'm stuck on politics,' he sighs. 'I get too involved in it.' He doesn't know anyone else his age who is as interested in world events. 'That's the stupid thing about me, I like getting into adult conversations. I love talking to peers my age, but I want to get into adult conversation too. It's trouble.'

Ashley

'I don't really think you could grow up normal in Peckham. You'd still have a little mad thing about you.'

It's a mad life. When you're on the road, it's like you're two people. There's the kind one. And then there's the poor one, the one that's got no money, that has to go out and hustle. Ashley plumps up cushions and arranges them tidily on the sofa before settling himself in this corner of the cacophonous youth centre. He is fifteen. He's been drinking hot chocolate with spoonfuls and spoonfuls of sugar stirred in.

'I reckon that people just see us as thugs. They don't know where we're coming from. It's not like you mean to go on the street and rob someone. It's 'cos you ain't got no money, you get me, no one's helping you, you get me, it's just you alone. You see people with flash phones in flash cars, you think, "They've got it, why can't I have it?" They take certain things for granted, like they've got a big Rolex but it's nothing to them. They can go and buy another one.'

Money is everything. 'You need money for clothes, you need money for food. When I see that they've got money, and they can do all that, and you have to have egg on toast for your dinner because you ain't got money to go shopping, or go to the sweet shop and get some sweets, and you can get arrested for that, for thieving a chocolate bar.' He shakes his head.

Ashley is an honourable thief. He doesn't go for people that don't have much because if he robs them they're going to be in the same situation he is. He robs the people he knows can replace what they lose. He walks up and down the road half an hour and sees a man that's got a nice watch: two people haul him up, run through the estate, go to the pawn shop.

He was nine when his dad moved out. He's an alcoholic. His parents were always fighting. His mum's white and his dad's from Barbados. He says there's no point in calling himself mixed race, because there's black and there's white in this world, and he's more black than white.

Ashley likes to keep his baseball cap on at all times. He has yet to shed his little boy's body, but his frame is poised for broadening, and he will grow a little taller. He must be aware that he's handsome. With his smooth vanilla skin and dark eyes, he looks like he could get away with murder.

It's years since Ashley went to school. 'I get with a couple of my friends and they'd be like, "You want to eat?" We used to go to Bermondsey a lot, pull people out their cars and drive off. Or if there's someone walking down the road with their trousers halfway down, pull off their trousers, you've got their wallet, everything, they run off in their boxers. Bare madness. Stealing cars to get police chases, just for fun. If there was more for people to do, but in Peckham it's just full of crackheads. There ain't too many parks where kids can go and play.'

Sometimes he feels guilty; it depends. All sorts of things go through his mind. He can't sleep sometimes. He might stay awake all night because he thinks police are going to come to his house. He sets out the realities of this mad life quietly, with precision. His voice is low and insistent. His speech has a rhythmic quality, 'like' and 'you get me' punctuating the phrases into a musical metre.

Ashley has grown up on the estates of Peckham, an area of south London made infamous at the turn of the millennium by the murder of ten-year-old Damilola Taylor, who bled to death after being stabbed with a broken bottle on his way home from an after-school computer club. (In 2002, four teenagers were cleared of the killing, following a much-criticised trial. The case remains open.)

Ashley is one of the un-children, doubly excluded by society, once for the fact of being a child and twice for failing to conform to the narrow ideology of contemporary childhood. Childhood is supposed to happen inside society, inside the family, inside the school gates. Any child whose experience falls outside these strict parameters is denied the respect that they are so often charged with denying to others.

The current climate of child-panic deems that all children are vulnerable – to sexual predators, commercialism, media violence and so on. But in doing so, it has pushed the truly vulnerable minority – the un-children of the underclass – beyond this blanket sympathy. Children who express their vulnerability through antisocial behaviour, crime and violence are primarily considered a threat to social order and to the formation of economically productive citizens. The majority of interventions are based on society's needs – for conformity, obedience, a future workforce – rather than their own.

The Children's Commissioner, Al Aynsley-Green, marked his appointment by warning of a national ambivalence towards children, with adults investing enormously in the young people with whom they are intimately involved, while remaining equivocal about those growing up on the margins.

In a paper written two years before his appointment, Aynsley-Green suggested that British society is currently experiencing a turbulence similar to the upheaval of the Victorian era. He argued for a recreation of the reformist 'movement for children' that characterised that age. But if the immediate needs of children like Ashley might be met by a legion of modern-day Dr Barnardos, they will only thrive in a country that ceases to demonise the poor and the angry.

As Stanley Cohen noted in his acclaimed book *Folk Devils and Moral Panics*, first published in 1972, recurrent moral panics in Britain since the Second World War have related to deviant youth. Subcultures – like the Teddy Boys, Mods and Rockers, skinheads and hippies – have occupied a constant position as folk devils, he writes. 'The identities of such social types are public property and these particular adolescent groups have symbolised – both in what they were and how they were reacted to – much of the social change which has taken place in Britain over the last twenty years.'

But in devoting so much attention to the shapes that these folk devils can assume, the media and politicians may well amplify the original problem. Cohen explains: 'An initial act of deviance, or normative diversity (for example, in dress), is defined as being worthy of attention and is responded to punitively. The deviant or group is segregated or isolated and this operates to alienate them from conventional society. They perceive themselves as more deviant, group themselves with others in a similar position, and this leads to more deviance.'

Put simply, if all young men wearing hooded tops are treated like violent thugs, they may well start acting that way. The present government's 'respect' agenda could well amplify divisions instead of healing them. But demonisation of youth has a racial as well as a class context. Cohen was writing when analysis on grounds of race was in its infancy.

But one of the most potent folk devils of our times is surely the young black male – a boy like Ashley. If there is a continuum from GCSEs to the prison cell, black boys are over-represented at every wrong turn, in school exclusions, in stop-and-search cautions, on remand and in custody.

Ashley's mum's got three operations coming up. She's got polio in her left leg, she's got cancer, and a couple of other sicknesses. She needs a new knee and a new hip. Because his mum's sick, he's got to move with her, look after her. She just got moved to Catford, but Ashley's not from Catford. Catford's classed as ghetto, and he's from Peckham, so the people don't mix. There's a lot of trouble when he goes home on the bus.

His mum doesn't drink. She smokes loads of menthol cigarettes, and she smokes a bit of hash now and again, but that's for the pain. 'Me, I smoke skunk. I've been smoking skunk since the age of nine, when there was all the family trouble. I'd get pulled by the police, but when I was younger I didn't get a criminal record. They'd usually just tell me off, make me sit on a detention bench in the police station.'

When his dad moved out, his mum found it hard because she didn't have the money, and his dad wasn't giving any. Ashley's got seven brothers, six sisters, and loads of foster brothers and sisters because his mum used to be a foster-carer. He's the youngest. Only him and his two closest-aged brothers are his dad's children; his other brothers have a different father, so they're half Turkish. At the moment it's just four of them living at home. Though he usually sleeps in Catford, Ashley still spends his days in Peckham, but it's getting harder because he's got to check on his mum and he has a lot of appointments to keep. He's a very busy boy.

'On the estates it's every man for himself but my friends,

they're like my family. You can't be my friend unless I know you've got my back. If I've got trouble or beef, you won't run off.' When his father left, and his mother couldn't support them all, his friends would help him out. 'I'm not a charity, you get me, but when we'd go out, do whatever we're doing, steal cars, make a bit of money, if they got a bit of money they'd give me some; if I ain't got weed, they'd give me weed. Now I do the same.'

When he found out that some of those friends were smoking crack, he stopped seeing them. Ashley has a strict policy on drugs. Smoking weed, he's not doing anyone wrong. But he always said from when he was little that he would never smoke crack in his life.

If Ashley's on the road he must get pulled by the police six times a day, or more when he's in a group. That's how it is. He's used to it. He's been in trouble so much, the police know him and his brothers.

Race comes into it. 'If you're in a group and it's a group of four black youths, you're definitely going to get pulled. Say you was with three white boys, you've less chance of getting pulled. But if one white boy was walking down the road with three black boys, the police go up to him, ask him what he's doing, are we trying to rob him.'

Street robberies are always blamed on black people, he says. 'There's a couple of times I've been arrested and my friends that were also involved were white, and they get treated completely different. Even in the police station.'

Ashley first got properly arrested when he was twelve. But the first time he got pulled over he was eight. To begin with it was mostly stealing cars, driving underage. He learnt to drive watching his big brother, who taught himself from go-karting. Now the police stop him because they know he smokes.

Ashley has a lengthy record, and has been identified by the courts as a persistent young offender. He's been held on remand, but says he's never actually been convicted. 'I've been in court for burglary, handling weed, assault, robbery, just petty stuff. But they couldn't find me guilty.' Like Macavity, sometimes Ashley wasn't there. 'Most of them I was there but I didn't do nothing, you get me? I was just part of the group, but they held me responsible for what the other boys did.'

The police aren't there to protect people, trust him. 'Any time I've got arrested, it's bare abuse. All that police brutality, it's true. When they've got their uniform on they think they're above the law. I takes the piss out of them. "You think you're bulletproof because you've got your uniform on? If you was out of clothes walking in Peckham I'd shoot you, I'd stab you, anything could happen",' he brags.

Ashley used to carry a Rambo knife – he parts his palms – about that big. He has a replica 9 mm handgun and a starter pistol. 'I've seen loads of guns. When I was little and people were talking about guns I was like "Yeah, you're on it!" Now it's an everyday thing. I see guns everyday, I see weed every day, I see crack every day.'

His friend Lizzie brings him a cheese and white bread sandwich that she's made in the centre's canteen for lunch. He gets up to eat it at the table. He's thought about how it must be to grow up in a middle-class family in a nice area. But he wouldn't like it. 'Not now I've grown up seeing almost everything.'

'I wouldn't like it because of the way they talk, the way they look down at people. Me, I don't look down at people, I don't look up at people. I just see them for who they are. If I think that you could be my friend I will make conversation and when I find out a bit about you I can choose, will you get me into trouble or are you too posh for me?'

Not now that he's grown up seeing almost everything. Talking to Ashley, the question arises: is he telling the truth? Does that even matter? It's his story, the way he wants to tell it. Some of the things he describes, one would rather he had embellished. But Ashley won't be teased into revelation. When probed, he looks down and his face contorts with a twisty sort of smile. He says, 'Leave it at that.' When Ashley says he's seen it all, unfortunately, I believe him.

It's a few weeks after our first meeting, and Ashley says that in the interim he's been trying to sort out his education. He needs to get a copy of his birth certificate. He's had a lot of appointments to keep. He's a solicitous creature, opening doors for me first, greeting friends with handshakes and kisses, sitting down at our table last. 'I got kicked out of my first school in Year 7 [the first year of secondary school] for behaviour and stuff, like fighting, and for other reasons.' He won't be drawn on what those other reasons were. That twisty smile appears.

'Then I come here to Kids Company and did education, and then they got me a place in a centre. But I lost my placement 'cos I didn't attend too tough, 'cos it was just *shit*. It was a house, and break-times and lunch-times you weren't allowed out and they didn't do hot meals, just sandwiches. And the lessons, they were forty minutes each and they didn't make it interesting, so unless you knew what to do with the work . . .' The tirade drifts. 'Like, I had a bit of trouble with the work.'

Kids Company, the centre where we are meeting, and which Ashley visits almost daily, has been caring for the street children of south London since 1995. If the Children's Commissioner is seeking a contemporary Joseph Rowntree or

Elizabeth Fry, he could do worse than look for them here. The charity was set up by Camila Batmanghelidjh, an Iranian-born psychotherapist who previously developed the in-school counselling service The Place2Be. Batmanghelidjh is a charismatic character, fond of turbans and bright scarves, devoted to her kids as they are devoted to her, and remarkable for the immediacy with which she cuts through street swagger to reach the unhappy child. She has been criticised over the years for her unconventional methods, and her refusal to countenance the bureaucratic strictures of state care that can hamper swift intervention. But she knows how to get things done.

Kids Company exists for those children – of whom there are more than adults would imagine, particularly in inner-city areas – who have slipped through the attendant nets like shrimps. Young people refer themselves to the service. The majority have not been parented in any conventional sense, and many are homeless. Ashley started coming here six years ago, after his brother told him about Camila. He says she's like his second mum now.

Batmanghelidjh estimates that as many as 500 children visit each year, the majority of them black, male adolescents, excluded from education and finding their only status or security in gang culture. Open six days a week, the centre offers a mixture of emotional and practical support. The children can get daily meals, clothes and basic necessities, as well as counselling and education, all under one roof.

Following the death of Damilola Taylor, Kids Company was praised by senior government figures as a potential model for dealing with hard-to-reach young people across the country. But despite this, and high-profile supporters like Cherie Booth and Prince Charles, the charity has been threatened with closure a number of times, and only recently received a government grant of half its budget over three years, which it must match through its own fund-raising initiatives.

Luckily, when it comes to fund-raising Batmanghelidjh has a flair for spectacle – including an art exhibition at the Tate Modern which garnered a heap of publicity for its simulated crack-den, an installation to which Ashley contributed. But the day-to-day running of the centre is far from glitzy. Many of those who attend are extremely volatile, and staff are regularly threatened.

Batmanghelidjh identifies a state of emotional coldness in the children she works with. Their experience of growing up in chaotic or abusive environments has led them to close down. Feeling neither pain nor empathy, they will carry out a violent mugging without compunction. And they are unreachable through traditional methods of sanction because they have nothing to lose.

'A child who has been terrorised and neglected isn't going to feel threatened by punishment,' she says. 'Loving care surprises them more and has greater impact on minimising negative behaviour.' But policy makers, she argues, are reluctant to take on the reality of unparented children.

Batmanghelidjh attests to her frustration with the under-funded and over-stretched government agencies she deals with. This was echoed in the finding of the inquiry into the murder of Victoria Climbié, which recommended structural reforms of children's services in order to prevent vulnerable children falling through the gaps in the care system. Under the 2004 Children Act, councils and primary care trusts will have to establish children's trusts to co-ordinate local child-welfare services – including health, early-years and careers advice. The consolidation is due to be completed by 2008, but while three quarters of councils continue to report difficulties recruiting children's social workers, standards are unlikely to be raised.

Everyone wants a fairy tale, says Batmanghelidjh. People want to see an out-of-control child transformed by a simple rescue package into a model citizen. 'It never happens like that. The only power you have over them is the power of love. They want love and for that they will work, and that's the power that people don't understand. They don't know how to manage disturbed children like that because they're so preoccupied with punishing them and taking revenge.'

Ashley left his pupil referral unit two years ago. Camila has tried to get him back into education but is now looking for a private tutorial college place because none of the local authorities have found anywhere that will take him. In the meantime, he's been going to one hour's education a day at Kids Company.

Ashley would like to learn. But the schooling process has left him ambivalent: 'At the unit, it was more like the kids disciplining the teacher. He was a dickhead. At school, I had one or two good teachers, they would just keep it raw, and instead of sending you home they give you a cooling-off period.'

'It's hard for teachers,' he grants, 'because some kids have problems and they ain't got the time to spend with the one student. They've got a class full of students, but the ones that find it hard to work they say they don't want to help because they've got all the other kids.'

Just before Ashley got expelled, at the age of eleven, he had an operation on his ear. 'I was deaf in my left one, and they got told to speak louder, but none of the teachers did. I was trying to explain you need to talk up, but I got sent out of lessons most of the time 'cos they thought I was taking the piss.'

Of prime concern in the ongoing debate about discipline is

the behaviour of boys. As the world-renowned parenting expert Steve Biddulph observes in his book *Raising Boys*, in the classroom 'girls ask for help, but boys often just act for help'. Indeed, Biddulph traces this back to the very beginning of boys' schooling, arguing that they should start education a year later than girls, because of their slower cognitive development.

Some researchers have questioned the accuracy of the prognosis that all boys are falling behind, arguing that the majority of middle-class boys continue to do well, while certain groups like working-class boys and those from African Caribbean, Pakistani and Bengali backgrounds have always struggled. It is probably more accurate to say that the progress of boys in all classes has remained stable, while recently girls have surged ahead. Amongst middle-class children, girls have caught up with boys, while in other groups they have surpassed them.

The common problem is that educational achievement is still seen as 'girly', which prevents working-class boys in particular from progressing. The authors of the Young Masculinities study believe that 'as educational demands have shifted and increased, boys' ways of expressing masculinities have become less compatible with the gaining of educational qualifications.'

In their interviews with London schoolboys, they discovered that to be 'cool' and popular entailed challenging adult authority in the classroom. The boys were anxious not to be thought of as 'swots' or 'boffs', though the most common strategy was to negotiate a middle way where they did do schoolwork, 'but not so single-mindedly that they came to other boys' attention as over-studious.'

Another of their findings calls into question how productive the focus on boys' attainment has been. 'Boys are well aware of their standing as socially and educationally problematic and resent this,' wrote the authors, who went on to suggest that sometimes a vicious circle occurred where boys acted up as a way of expressing frustration at feeling 'written off' – particularly those from ethnic minorities. This sense of injustice translated into a belief that they were treated unfairly by teachers in comparison to girls, who could get away with more bad behaviour. A number of academics have pointed out that white working-class boys, and some Asian boys, face similar pressures to black boys in the education system. The broad categories used in ethnic monitoring fail to show up differences within them (for example, Indian boys fare much better than Pakistani boys, though both are considered under the generic category 'Asian'). But the fact is that when people talk about boys failing, they are usually talking about African-Caribbean boys and – in a roundabout way – the particular resonance that their failure has in the Western psyche.

It's a resonance that has much to do with the threat of black male success. This historic anxiety was best articulated by beat poet Leroi Jones in his writing about the boxer Sonny Liston, the Mike Tyson of his day. He described him as 'the big black Negro in every white man's hallway, waiting to do him in, deal him under for all the hurts white men, through their arbitrary order, have been able to inflict on the world . . . the bad nigger, a heavy-faced replica of every whipped-up woogie in the world. He is the underdeveloped, have-not . . . backward country, the subject people, finally here to collect his pound of flesh.'

Gus John, who published his influential study of black youth in Britain in 1981, believes that the way that young black masculinity has come to be constructed has much to do with how the white population saw their parents and grandparents. 'In the fifties and sixties when the first generation of post-war immigrants arrived, British society didn't confer them any status,' he says. 'Black males were seen as coming off a Caribbean plantation. Over time, as a result of under-employment, doing manual jobs, and constant prejudice what built up was the idea that the black male was not up to much. Wind forward to the 80s, with black school leavers still not getting decent jobs, and that whole period when the police were using stop and search to criminalise young people. It's very difficult to cultivate high aspirations in the face of such a debilitating stereotype.'

In his 1971 pamphlet *How the West Indian Child is Made Educationally Subnormal in the British School System*, the Grenadian academic Bernard Coard identified three factors that were causing black boys to fail: 'Low expectations on his part about his likely performance in a white-controlled system of education; low motivation to succeed academically because he feels the cards are stacked against him; and low teacher expectations, which affect the amount of effort expended on his behalf by the teacher and also affect his own image of himself and his abilities.'

Coard was one of the first in this country to raise the issue and, more than thirty years later, he has said that he believes the problems have become entrenched. While overall pupil performance has improved, according to the latest statistics only 33 per cent of African-Caribbean boys gain five A*–C grades at GCSE, compared with 51 per cent of white pupils, and they are twice as likely as white boys to be excluded. In the 1970s, Coard urged black parents to set up 'supplementary schools' for their children, presaging the suggestion by Trevor Philips, current chair of the Commission for Racial Equality, that black boys be taught separately for some lessons.

The sociologist Tony Sewell has written about the way that

black boys exploit popular conceptions of their masculinity, behaviour that is often self-defeating because it serves only to reinforce teachers' stereotypes. He identifies the way that African-Caribbean boys position themselves as superior to white and Asian students in terms of sexual attractiveness, style, creativity and toughness, adopting black masculinity as a collective response to a racist culture.

This response is also examined by the American psychologist Richard Majors, who famously defined the attitude of young black males as 'cool pose'. Majors argued, 'Black men often cope with their frustration, embitterment and alienation and social impotence by channelling their creative energies into the construction of unique, expressive and conspicuous styles of demeanour, speech, gesture, clothing, hairstyle, walk, stance and handshake.'

Sewell accepts that this resistance requires careful management. 'Black boys are aware that their teachers find them threatening, and school is by definition a conformist institution. Boys must be skilled to get the pay-off: to adopt the amount of cool pose that's necessary to maintain street credibility and the amount of conformity that is necessary to continue in education.'

He is unapologetic in tracing the difficulties African-Caribbean boys have at school back to a 'parental crisis' in the community. Forty-eight per cent of African-Caribbean families are headed by a single parent, compared with 22 per cent of the general population. 'What's clear is that our reliance on raising males in situations where they are predominantly taken care of by single females is problematic. It can be done but the question is how can you do it successfully, and how do we bring black men back into the role of nurturing their children?'

Others have argued that institutional racism in the

education and criminal justice systems holds black boys back. For Gus John, it is young people's disconnection from their collective past that renders them vulnerable. 'There's much less emphasis on identity and being competent by virtue of knowing who you are and where you're from. In the seventies there was a confidence in the community that filtered across from the American civil rights movement. Nowadays young people have no idea about that period. For mixed-race children that's even more of an issue. They're at the sharpest end of that dislocation from history.'

Ashley thinks it's true that white kids think black kids are harder. 'If you're in a group of black kids, and you meet a group of white kids, there's more chance they would run off 'cos they think black kids come with knives and stuff.' His friends have told him: 'Never let a white boy take the piss out of you, never let a white boy punch you in the face.' It's not like racism; it's the way they've been brought up. The way Ashley was brought up, it was never let *anyone* punch you in the face.

So it was a concatenation of events that left Ashley walking the streets: his parents splitting up, his operation, the attitude of teachers, his own attitude changing. And it was around then that he started smoking skunk. At first he smoked to be in the gang, to show off and that, but then he got addicted. He's seen skunk turn some people mad, but he can handle it. Crack is ten times stronger. 'If I don't smoke weed my body just feels like shit.' He says he's trying to stop.

His mum hasn't been keeping so well these past few weeks. He's been checking on her a lot. She has her good days and her bad days. He loves his mum, but she can't get about too tough no more, not like when they were younger and she used to take them to the seaside. Now she takes twelve tablets three times a day. She's always telling Ashley to get an education, so that's why he's trying to sort his life out.

'I want to get a better education, I want to get a job, nice pay, something that I like doing, I want to settle down, have a wife. A couple of people have asked me what I want to do for a job, I don't really know. But when I do know, it should be good,' he says gently.

Ashley's dad came over from Barbados when he was sixteen or seventeen. He was working on the buses, but now he's retired because he injured his knee. When he met his mum, she was married to his other brothers' dad, then they separated, and she got with his dad, but they didn't get married.

When Ashley's parents first split up, his mum didn't want him to see his father, but he sees him most days now on the estate. A father can teach a son to be a man. If you've got to teach yourself to be a man it's harder. 'My mum's sick and my dad wasn't there to watch us when we was younger, so we'd just go out on our own. He's your dad, yeah, he's there for a reason. He can teach you things your mum can't. When my dad was around I didn't really get in trouble 'cos I knew I'd get beat.'

He thinks that people should be allowed to hit their kids, but it depends on the way you're hitting them. 'If you just use your hand and you slap them on their arse or their leg, just once or twice to show them it's wrong, but if you're hitting them with belts and things . . .'

There are a good many reasons to rue the glut of reality parenting programmes on our screens. But at least they serve to illuminate an unpalatable reality of many children's lives. I have lost count of the number of times that a toddler has been woefully tendered to a telly nanny as unfathomably violent, only for footage of their home life to reveal that they are regularly on the receiving end of violence themselves.

Despite previous condemnation by the UN Committee on the Rights of the Child, in the autumn of 2004 the government failed to support an outright ban on smacking in the latest Children Act, leaving open the defence of 'reasonable chastisement'. The lacuna on smacking is perhaps the most vivid exemplar of this country's failure to treat all children with the respect they are due. Although over the past generation public opinion has shifted to favour a ban, the significance of the legal position cannot be underestimated.

Just as rape within marriage used to be legally sanctioned because a wife was her husband's property, so smacking maintains children's position as chattels. The underlying message is that adults should not be expected to respond to children with the basic tolerance and self-control they are expected to employ towards people their own age. It reinforces children's lack of rights in the most primitive of ways.

Save the Children has noted that in Sweden, where smacking was banned over a decade ago, child deaths at the hands of their parents fell to virtually zero. In the UK, that figure averages one death a week. As Rabbi Julia Neuberger says in her book *The Moral State We're In*, 'It really makes no sense to allow parents to hit their children when we remain shocked by the deaths of children from violence at the hands of their parents.' Until it is enshrined in law that it is never right to hit a child, one wonders how Britain can ever consider itself a genuinely child-friendly country.

Ashley has friends who are already fathers, but he wouldn't like to have a baby until he's at least in his twenties. He's not old enough now, and he hasn't got money to buy nappies. That's what he's trying to do, sort his life out, and then think about those things. He's got a proper girlfriend now, been going out a couple of months. He can talk to her about his worries.

Ashley goes on to offer his male perspective on adolescent sexual politics. Girls can be either wifies or hos, he explains carefully. 'Most people got their ho. When you're with your friends, what's mine is yours, I'll share everything with you. I'll share hos with you except for my wifie, 'cos that's my girlfriend, and you could go out with her for time, or have a baby with her. But hos, they're just girls that get sexed out for the fun of it.'

'When you meet a girl you think, is she a ho or could she be wifie material? Because there's hundreds of us, and if a girl gets about it gets around to the boys, so it's easy to find out what a girl's like, how many people they've slept with, and that's how you can decide. A girl that has sex with loads of people, people call them prostitutes or slags or whatever.'

Ashley believes it's different for girls, though unlike Laura (in the earlier chapter), he tends towards the anatomical rather than the sociological for explanation. 'Just remember, yeah, it's worse for girls 'cos they've got different things inside. They've gotta be more hygienic. With boys, if they use condoms, there ain't really nothing for them to do after, so they could have sex three times in a night, but with girls they've got to jump in the shower. If they don't do that, they're just nasty.' He tuts fastidiously. He's never, he adds firmly, had a problem with girls.

The first time Ashley had sex, he was ten. But when he proper had sex he was thirteen, thirteen and a half. There's a difference because when you're little you haven't got come, so you can just keep going, but when you've got come you've got to stop. Those early times he wasn't really thinking about it. 'I just wanted to do bare stuff, but when you get older you think: I've done that, I've done that, I've done that. I stole cars, I've had sex, look where it's got me. If you think about things before you do it, it could come out better.'

A week later, Ashley arrives stoned. It's lunch-time. His lids are heavy, but his movements are fidgety. He has to work to stop his mouth falling into a lazy grin. He is rambling about the fakeness of the rap star Fifty Cent with the friend he's arrived with. She wanders off and he gradually straightens out.

His mum's been feeling a bit better. 'Nothing's going to happen,' he says defensively. 'I don't think like that. What I think is that my mum's healthy, even though she ain't, she's really sick. I like to think she's healthy, I'm checking up on her, she's got all the help she needs, she just lives until her life's done. Everyone's gonna die, but I don't hope or talk about what's going to happen. I just wait till it comes.' This weekend, he wants to take her to the seaside with his brother. She's got a car on disability so she can drive them there.

He doesn't spend time at friends' houses, though he might drop in to pick up some clothes, because he hasn't got a lot and they're everywhere. But he's the kind of person that doesn't like to be in one place. There's only certain houses he can stay where he feels safe, like his mum's. 'When I'm there I've got my manners. I'm not saying when I go out I ain't got manners, but when I'm on road I've got different manners. If people look at you the wrong way you've got a different attitude.'

Ashley says that nobody's safe. If he's in his area then he's all right. Nobody troubles him, because everybody knows him. But if he goes into other areas there might be trouble, like fighting, or someone might try to rob you because you're not from there. He's never been knocked out. One time, he got chased by a gang of twenty white kids, with sticks. 'All I'm hearing is, "Come here you black bastard, we're gonna fucking cut your balls off, you this and that"; pure racism.' He just ran.

He stopped carrying his knife because he kept on getting arrested, and if you've got a knife it's worse. He thinks there's a big gun problem in Britain. It's not mostly street gangs, it's people in their twenties. Street gangs are made up of people his age, up to eighteen or nineteen. They're 80 per cent black kids, and the rest are the roughest white kids, the ones that won't have it from nobody. Gangs are just about where you grow up. When those teenagers get older, it depends what happens next. 'They either move on or they move up in the game. They get bigger, the money starts rolling for what they're doing, shotting [drug dealing], or whatever.'

There remains a lack of authoritative research to indicate whether youth crime is rising or falling. While it is true that adolescents do commit a disproportionate number of crimes compared with adults, the trend is for them to grow out of it as they get older. And it is still the case that most young people do not get involved with the criminal justice system, while the majority of those that do commit non-violent offences.

But a glance through the newspapers any given morning would suggest otherwise. Children, in particular adolescent males, have faced growing demonisation since the beginning of the 1990s. Young people's appearances in the media are now almost entirely related to criminality – be it deliberate commission, or 'status offences', like underage sex or alcohol and drug use. A select few remain 'angels', but they must be chronically ill, heinously abused or – ideally – dead to warrant that epithet.

Bob Franklin, an expert in media coverage of childhood, believes that the trial of Robert Thompson and Jon Venables for the murder of James Bulger in 1993 marked a crucial watershed. He argues that three responses were triggered by the vindictive media frenzy that followed their conviction: 'First, the earlier romanticised social construct of children as innocent "angels" was challenged, toppled and reconstructed in more sinister guise.' Thompson and Venables were described as 'fiends', 'devils' and 'little bastards', language that was soon extended to other, lesser, child offenders.

'Second, the reporting of the Bulger case provided additional impetus to the existing media-generated moral panic about children and crime,' says Franklin. 'Finally, the Bulger case seemed to legitimise the increasingly authoritarian criminal justice policies of successive governments.'

He traces the shift in public perception and policy reaction to the present day: 'At the beginning of the 1990s, in the wake of widely publicised inquiries into the deaths of a number of young children at the hands of their parents, as well as events at Cleveland, children were victims and society was shaping policies designed to protect them. [Now], society is designing policies to protect the community from unruly, criminal and antisocial children.'

There is much to be said for the presentation of children as individuals of average virtue, rather than wholly blameless victims. But the media pendulum has swung to the opposite extreme, caricaturing 'teens from hell' and 'imps of Satan'.

In 2004, Shape, a forum on youth crime organised by young people, conducted a detailed analysis of the print media over a three-month period. It found that most vitriol was directed at white, working-class boys. In crime reports, young people were described as 'thugs', 'yobs' or 'louts' far more frequently than as 'young offenders'. The voice of the child who had committed the offence was seldom included, unless to emphasise their lack of remorse.

The Shape report found that, in the majority of coverage, no space was given to mitigating factors which might have made children more vulnerable to offending. This is despite the fact that, according to recent figures, 40 per cent of young people entering care with no previous cautions or criminal convictions had one within six months of living in a children's home, while 54 per cent of those referred to youth offending teams have experienced the death of a close friend or family member in the past two years, and the majority of young male offenders have been excluded from school.

Across the tabloid press, Shape identified as a central theme the demand that the criminal justice system be tougher on children in trouble. Particular derision was reserved for the use of 'soft' community sentences, and the 'pampered' conditions inside young offenders' institutions.

Orchestration by the media of public unease is hardly a new phenomenon. Nor does describing something a 'moral panic' imply that public anxieties are entirely spurious. But policy responses based on a few exceptional and highly reported cases can only lead to injustice when they are applied to the mass.

Following the Bulger trial, the Conservative Prime Minister John Major launched his 'Back to Basics' crusade, insisting that society should 'condemn a little more and understand a little less'. The welfare-based approach to youth crime, with its emphasis on diversion, decriminalisation and decarceration, was effectively abandoned. Michael Howard, then newly appointed as Home Secretary, introduced privately run secure training centres for 12–14-year-olds, based on US military-style 'boot camps', and increased the maximum sentence of detention for 15–17-year-olds. Between 1993 and 1998, the number of imprisoned teenagers doubled.

After Labour's landslide victory in 1997, Howard's successor, Jack Straw, was quick to condemn the 'excuse culture' of youth justice. The subsequent 1998 Crime and Disorder Act overhauled the system, most significantly abolishing the ancient presumption of *doli incapax*, which held that the prosecution must prove that a child under fourteen was aware that their actions were seriously wrong, rather than simply naughty.

The abolition of *doli incapax* was in direct contravention of a UN recommendation that the UK give serious consideration to raising the age of criminal responsibility and bringing the country into line with the rest of Europe. Britain's unusually low age of criminal responsibility means that children from the age of ten are now treated as having the same criminal intent and maturity as an adult. It would seem that the only time we're prepared to treat children equally to adults is when we're punishing the most vulnerable amongst them.

Another crucial element of the 1998 act was the introduction of new powers, including child-safety orders, local child-curfews and an early version of the antisocial behaviour order, that did not require the prosecution or even the commission of a criminal offence. As criminologist John Muncie notes in an essay on children's rights and youth justice, this programme of early intervention – which has become increasingly authoritarian in recent years – is couched in the language of crime prevention and child protection, and so 'erosion of civil liberty is presented as an enabling, new opportunity'.

But it is a programme above all driven by coercive powers, he writes. 'Civil orders are backed up by stringent criminal sanctions. Similarly, by equating "disorder" with crime it significantly broadens the reach of criminal justice to take in those below the age of criminal responsibility and the non-criminal as well as the known offender. Above all the number of young offenders incarcerated has continued to grow.'

Under New Labour, policy has continued to emphasise the containment and control of young people. The UK incarcerates more of its children than any other country in Europe. Between 2000 and 2005, twenty-seven children killed themselves in custody, some of whom were being kept in adult prisons, while young offenders institutions are rife with bullying and self-harm.

There is ample evidence that this policy does not work. Eighty-four per cent of juveniles released from prison in 1997 were reconvicted within two years. But the addiction to custody shows no sign of abating.

Youth justice policy has historically been manipulated for short-term political expediency and electoral gain. But it is the antisocial behaviour order that has proved the nadir of this tendency.

In June 2005, the report by the Council of Europe's Human Rights Commissioner Alvaro Gils-Robles – condemning the British government's record on children's rights – was particularly damning of the government's 'ASBO-mania', stating that 'it is difficult to avoid the impression that the ASBO is being touted as a miracle cure for urban nuisance'. At the time, almost half of all antisocial behaviour orders were being served on juveniles.

Gils-Robles was especially concerned about the broad

definition of anti-social behaviour (anything likely to cause 'harm, alarm or distress'), the ease with which ASBOs were obtained, and the 'naming and shaming' of children. This civil order, which relies on a lower standard of proof and can be granted on hearsay evidence, reverses for the first time in almost a century the presumption of anonymity for children appearing in court. A juvenile convicted of murder cannot be identified, while one exhorted not to swear in the street may find his local council posting cards bearing his image and details of his ASBO conditions through his neighbours' letter-boxes.

As Shami Chakrabhati, director of the human rights group Liberty, has observed, whether ASBOs lead to vigilantism or become a perverse badge of honour, 'it's a situation not a world away from the mob justice of the medieval stocks'.

At the time of writing, no central records exist for the kinds of behaviour that are considered to merit ASBOs, nor for breach rates, though from the evidence provided by 'naming and shaming', it would appear that the majority of children given ASBOs are from poor backgrounds.

Early assessments suggest that the breach rate is higher for juveniles, and concerns have been raised that the orders will serve as a fast-track to prison for young people. Others believe them to be a counter-productive addition to the framework that already exists for dealing with criminal children.

Marian Fitzgerald, professor of criminology at the University of Kent, conducted one of the first analyses of ASBO use for young people in the summer of 2005. She expresses deep concern at the 'net-widening' effect of the orders, and found that pressure on police to meet targets and the practice of bolting-on ASBOs to other sanctions was resulting in serious up-tarriffing, whereby even first-time offenders were ending up in custody.

That is not to suggest that persistent young offenders should go unpunished. But those sanctions already exist. The pernickety conditions peculiar to ASBOs – not to wear a hat, not to use a certain swear-word in public, not to meet a particular friend – are surely setting young people up to fail.

As Terri Dowty, director of Action on Rights for Children, says, 'The problem with ASBOs is that they are too weak an intervention for lost boys, and they are too harsh for those who hang around the edge of danger. They do not discriminate between a young person in need of massive containment, and one in need of an adventure playground and a good youth service. They trivialise serious delinquency, and criminalise aimless boredom.'

Critics of ASBOs have been dismissed as 'Hampstead liberals', blind to the way that gangs of hardened youngsters can place neighbourhoods under siege. Of course, there are grim pockets of ever-diminishing public housing where local authorities have no choice but to concentrate anti-social families. Of course, life there can be intolerable, and will not be improved by building a youth club. But the Children Act of 2001 already provides a range of responses, including ones for children whose behaviour is out of control but not criminal in nature, and does so within a far more progressive framework.

Combined with curfew powers that allow police to chase young people off the streets after 9 p.m. whether or not they are known troublemakers, it is not an exaggeration to suggest that children are now criminalised purely by virtue of their age. Their right to inhabit the same public spaces as adults has been utterly violated.

Surveying some of the more absurd uses of the order, it is hard not to come to the conclusion that ASBOs are also being used to punish what adults find annoying rather than threatening. In one case, a fifteen-year-old boy with Asperger's syndrome, which can manifest in obsessional and repetitive behaviour, was given an ASBO with the condition that he was not to stare over his neighbours' fence into their garden. In another, a child with Tourette's syndrome was ordered not to swear in public.

The incivility of some young people is appalling, but it is not illegal. If they are acting it out on the streets, it is usually because they have nowhere else to go, so the legislation favours children who can afford expensive leisure activities or have parents willing to chauffeur them to friends' houses. All that rackety posturing is more often evidence of extreme insecurity – the hooded top a desperate attempt to cover acne – than it is a precursor to robbing pensioners.

The following week, Ashley arrives with his seventeen-year-old brother, who's been banned from the building for threatening behaviour. When the security man keeps him out, he kicks off again, screaming obscenities and trying to ram the door. He's high and enraged. Ashley's bothered but too stoned – and too used to it – to engage. His skin is pale, with a waxy sheen to it.

He slept at his sister's last night. He did manage to take his mum to Margate on the weekend. She enjoyed herself, he says softly. He's been tired this week, so he's slept quite a lot.

Does it bother him, always being half-cut? It's a habit, so it's not easy to stop if you've been doing it for years. If he had the chance to go back in time he wouldn't start smoking because over the years it does show on you. And if police know you smoke it's easier for them to catch you because they know you're going to be out of breath quicker, he adds mordantly.

'But I'm the same person,' he insists. 'I don't switch. It's hard to relax when there's so much going on around. I get into stupid stuff and there might be people out for me. Weed just keeps me relaxed so I don't think about it too much. It just motivates me through the day.'

If you're smoking considerately, not taking the piss, it just keeps you mellow. 'I don't smoke to get a buzz during the day, I only get buzzing at night-time. If I'm doing stuff in the day I might smoke three or four spliffs. Say I'm doing education, I might smoke half a spliff, go in, do my lesson, come out halfway through, smoke another half, do another lesson. If I'm at home in the evening, watching TV or something, I smoke a spliff every two hours.' He estimates that he gets through about twenty pounds' worth of skunk each day.

His brother is still screaming outside: 'I'm gonna fucking kill you!' Ashley explains that he's got an ASBO. He's got ADHD so he's hyper, and when he gets arrested they're not allowed to lock the police cell door because he's got mental problems. He can't really help it too tough. His brain ain't ticking, so he sees red, and when he's angry it's harder to calm him down. People tell him he acts a lot older than his brother. He feels very responsible for him, tries to keep a close relationship.

He's sweet on his brother. 'He's just hyper, he's had a hyper life, so he's going to be more up for doing things. If you're on road and someone says let's steal this car, he's up for it. He's first one to say yes and the last to say no. It's because he's got ADHD so he likes being in mad situations.' He wants to be a stunt man when he's older.

Ashley explains the fine distinctions of the street community. 'There's stupid kids, and there's kids that are trying to make money, and then there's kids that are crackheads and whatever. The stupid kids, they're just watching

TV and they want to be bad on purpose.' They're also mostly white.

He has no time for people who don't make the most of their chances. 'I know a couple of kids, they walk around the same as me but they're wealthy. They've got all the new Nike, but they're just following fashion. We look like thugs 'cos we ain't got many clothes. They've got a wardrobe, we've got a couple of tracksuits.'

These are the stupid kids. 'They weren't brought up [on the street] but they want to be like that for some reason.' He thinks it's a respect thing. 'Me, I've got a lot of respect. No one will trouble me, but I've had to earn it.' Those stupid rich kids think they can have everything because they've got all the stuff, all the clothes. 'But you've got to start at the bottom. I've earned my respect over the years, got to know people, done things for people. I've been brought up with the same kids, same surroundings, so I know what it's like.'

Ashley understands that strangers look at him and see trouble and, on occasion, he is. But what frustrates him is never being given the benefit of the doubt. 'We're not always out to cause trouble.' He lays his hands wide. 'You could just be playing out. But even when we're trying to be good, we're still getting pulled over by police. The majority of the black kids, we've got a police record, but if you go through it you see it's NFA, no further action, but it's still there on your record, so it just builds up and builds up.'

It's a lot to do with colour, he spits. 'It's just history. I say the world's fucked up.' (Ashley very rarely swears in front of me.) 'If there was no slavery and everyone was to just get on, there wouldn't be problems now, 'cos there's still people that want to carry on the racism.'

Ashley says he's not a racist boy. 'When I say colour comes

into it, I don't really see why we should go without and they should have. When you look at it properly, you see it's more white people that got and black people that haven't got, like Africans starving and here you've got us with just enough money to live.'

On the estates, there aren't places for kids to go. 'There ain't no youth clubs so there ain't much for kids to do but play out. There are crackheads who draw kids in, you see them a couple of days later, thinking what is he on, is he smoking crack now? Bare little mad things.'

This week, in May of 2005, a shopping centre in Kent has banned teenagers from wearing hooded tops on its premises. Ashley thinks that's silly. 'I know what they're saying 'cos people use hoodies for doing street crime 'cos if you put your hood up you won't get seen on camera. But there's no point banning it 'cos it's not hard to make something to cover your face. It's just clothes.'

So has the incidence of antisocial behaviour amongst the young increased in recent years, or are we simply more aware of it? To an extent, this is symptomatic of the growth in adult surveillance of childhood. The noisy posturing and petty misdemeanours, the self-conscious boundary testing, the moments when good lessons are learnt from bad behaviour; these things no longer occur behind the proverbial bike sheds.

Even very young children are not exempt from centrally sanctioned surveillance. The government-funded RYOGENS (Reducing Youth Offending Generic Solutions) project is being piloted by a number of councils across the country. This 'early warning' system asks nursery staff to identify children who display bullying behaviour or have a history of criminality in their immediate family in order to target potential offenders.

At the end of 2005, the youngest person entered on the system was just nine months old.

By no means all antisocial behaviour can be explained this way though. Plenty of incidents are far from petty. In the same week as the shopping-centre hoodie ban, a father of four was severely brain-damaged after being attacked when he confronted a gang of youths who threw a stone at his car. A sixteen-year-old schoolgirl was knocked unconscious and suffered temporary paralysis when she was beaten up by fellow pupils. In a craze known as 'happy slapping', her assailants recorded the attack on a mobile video phone and circulated the footage around her classmates. And three more youths from Peckham were arrested for the murder of Damilola Taylor.

But what is significant is that these crimes – assault, GBH, murder – are now viewed as part of a continuum of juvenile behaviour, so unruliness or incivility is infected with criminal intent. Yet the majority of young people, it bears repeating, do not commit crimes.

Also that same week the Prime Minister, Tony Blair, dedicated his government in its third term of office to fostering 'a culture of respect'. This has been a recurring theme of Blair's. In his disasterous Women's Institute speech of June 2000, amidst the cat-calls and slow hand-claps, he urged, 'Respect the old for what it still has to teach, respect for others, honour, self-discipline, duty, obligation, the essential decency of the British character.' Now respect, and children's supposed lack of it, has become locked into social policy, culminating in the launch of the 'respect action plan' in January 2006, which includes plans for a national parenting academy, new powers to impose parenting orders on those whose children are deemed 'out of control' and possible fines for young people under the age of sixteen.

* * *

The culture of street respect Ashley describes is far removed from New Labour's rhetoric. But it is a highly nuanced and, in its way, coherent system. It may be mired in violence and drug-dealing, it may limit as much as it liberates, but it does have an internal logic of loyalty and apprenticeship.

Ashley cares a lot about manners, those quotidian rituals that smooth minor human exchanges, so often judged wanting in young people. 'Most of my people got respect for our elders,' he says, before adding, 'but it depends on how they're showing us respect, because if they don't respect us they don't get respect back.' Fair exchange is no robbery, after all.

He recognises too how much middle-class children covet his kind of respect, and why they will never – fortunately for them – be able to earn it. One could argue that this envy is the inevitable result of Ashley's 'cool pose'. But it's also possible that children find an authenticity here that they do not find in the selfishness and venality of much of contemporary adult culture. Maybe they find little worth respecting in the popular injunctions to put self-love first, or to dismiss gradual graft in favour of instant celebrity.

Adult society has rightly jettisoned the traditional requirements of deference to others on account of rank or status. Yet it presumes that children should continue to defer to their elders, purely on account of their difference in age. This must be deeply confusing for young people, at a time when adults are still seeking a more equitable formula for conferring respect on one another.

It's a presumption that is based on the idea of children as incomplete adults. This country's record on children's rights provides another stark indication of their lesser status. So is it any wonder that children find it hard to respect their elders when those elders seem consistently to disrespect them?

The corrosion of adult authority is hugely problematic for teachers and parents who wish to provide children with the structure and example from which they can develop their own criteria for respect. But adults have to accept their own part in the diminution of deference.

Whether coveted by middle-class children or lived by un-children, Ashley's system of street respect does not offer a genuine alternative. The American sociologist Richard Sennett might well have been describing one of Ashley's associates when he wrote about a young man called Robert in his book *Respect: The Formation of Character in an Age of Inequality*. Robert, a drug dealer from a black ghetto in Philadelphia, who was imprisoned as a teenager, struggled in forfeiting the respect of his gang in order to go straight and build a business selling fruit and hotdogs.

Sennett describes how Robert had to recast the ghetto rituals of toughness and manhood in order to survive and keep out of trouble. 'He uses street smarts – from turns of phrase to threatening physical gestures – in order to make a turf for himself which is "clean"; eventually he earns a respected place in the community for this toughness, now put to decent uses.'

Robert was no longer dependent on others for his self-respect, but learned to manipulate 'the mutual exchanges which generate black brotherhood' in order to become a puppeteer of the code of the street, rather than a puppet.

Here Sennett observes a tension, between self-respect and mutual respect: 'Ritual exchanges build mutual respect . . . so deep is this power of expressive exchange that it can be turned to the most contrary ends: inequality can feel good . . .' He concludes: 'The art of expressing respect . . . does not imply justice, truth or goodness. And as Robert's experience on the streets of Philadelphia makes clear, expressing mutual respect can do an individual harm.'

Sennett's remarkable book is devoted to exploring the ways in which respect can forge bonds across inequality. He believes that there is disparity inherent in the ways that contemporary society confers respect, critiquing in particular what I described as the 'excuse of exceptionalism' in Allana's chapter. This is the idea that, through talent and determination alone, children can transcend their circumstances, so avoiding any wider interrogation of social exclusion.

'The structural problem is that modern institutions are bad at dealing with individuals who are ordinary – at according them respect even though they are nothing special,' Sennett wrote in an article assessing the government's 'respect' pronouncements in May 2005. 'Schools and workplaces are obsessed with discovering exceptional talent . . . The social issue concerns what happens to those left behind. The meritocrats are held up as an example to the losers. The very word "losers" denies the masses their dignity.'

Ashley says that it's impossible to legislate for respect. 'They can't make everyone in London respect each other.' He has little time for politicians. 'It's them that made us like this, 'cos they're in control of us, they're up that high, we're down there. And they still don't give us enough to live on.'

Here he touches on another of the factors identified by Richard Sennett as diminishing respect – that society struggles to accept the just claims of adult dependency on the welfare state, while refusing to allow people to participate actively in the conditions of their own care, thus confusing caring with controlling. He suggests that the belief that any kind of dependence demeans arises from a concept of adult-hood in which dependency is viewed as an incomplete state, only acceptable in children.

Sennett's ideas about dependency dovetail neatly with the thoughts of the American political theorist Joan Tronto, who argues in her book *Moral Boundaries* for a new moral and political 'ethic of care'.

Tronto believes that the 'threat' of dependency on others has been greatly exaggerated, suggesting that the human condition is best understood in terms of interdependency: 'People are sometimes autonomous, sometimes dependent, sometimes providing care for those who are dependent.'

This notion of interpendency confronts what Tronto describes as the 'liberal fiction of the rational autonomous man'. And it finally grants status to a central but devalued aspect of human toil. 'Because our society does not notice the importance of care and the moral quality of its practice, we devalue the work and contributions of women and other disempowered groups who care in this society,' she writes. 'Only if we understand care as a political idea will we be able to change its status and the status of those who do caring work in our culture.'

Naturally, raising children is a significant element of care. Perhaps by recognising dependency not as an incomplete state but as a universal one, we can raise the status not only of those who care but of those who are cared for. Thus we raise the status of children, and finally grant them the respect they are due.

Ashley says he doesn't remember much from his early child-hood. He's sitting at a rickety table in the centre's art room. In primary school, he was good. He never had a bad report. But as he got older, his behaviour got out of control. He used to like playing football. And he learnt to play pool from when he was eight or nine, because he went to the pub with his dad.

He trawls for an earlier memory, grins. 'Before that I used to go to work with him. I would ride on the buses with him all day. I would get my *own seat* on the bus, 'cos my dad was the conductor. I used to enjoy it. And lunch-time we'd go to this baker's shop, the same baker's shop, and get the same thing: steak bake, and then a cream roll.'

He's got a couple of teddies still. He hurries out the denial: 'I'm not a little boy no more, I don't cuddle them, I just keep them there for decoration.' It makes him feel warm, he says. 'I've got a dinosaur, I've got a big Pikachu, I've got a kangaroo, a Tigger, a Winnie the Pooh, and a Scooby-Doo.' The Pikachu is the oldest. It got a couple of holes in it, so he had to stitch it. This is the first time that Ashley has done anything close to giggling.

He says he was a fearless child. 'From little I ain't been scared of nothing really. The only thing I'm scared of is dying, but everyone's going to die so I don't talk about it.' No one wants to die really.

Does he mean that he's put himself in danger in the past? He churns in his seat. That pained, twisty smile reappears. 'Some of them . . . but that's why I've stopped it, why I'm trying to fix up my life. There's a couple of things I've done, leave it at that.' His flat palm skims across the table surface.

Ashley's silences are tender and protective: of himself, of his family, of the friend who was murdered when he was still at primary school, of the consequences of his brother's crack habit, of the times – and I surmise there have been a few – involving guns and drugs and imminent threat to his young life. What he doesn't say is far more unsettling than what he does.

Yes, he feels different from most people. 'It's different 'cos I can't do certain things they can do. Like, say my mum had a bit of money, life would be a lot easier. But it's a lot harder when you're brought up on loose change.'

'If you've got an easy home life, there's no fighting in your household on a regular basis, it would be easier to get on in school. But if you're going through a mad life then when you come to school you're going to be upset from what's happened. You might get into a fight at school, then they cuss your mum, but they don't know what happened at your house, so you're angry and you do something you might regret.' He might even be talking about himself.

'When I was little I wanted to be a judge or a lawyer or a barrister,' he says, out the blue. 'But it will be harder for me 'cos I'm coming from Peckham. Peckham kids, there's not many of them in schools.' He can't even remember why he wanted to be a lawyer. But from little, he did well in school. 'My mum used to tell me she wanted one child not to get a police record. But I flopped it for myself, I got myself arrested, all them times.' He shakes his head, defeated, mumbles: 'I just flopped it for myself.'

Told across the table, Ashley's story is hard to hear. But somehow it's not the sort that would satisfy the voracious public appetite for tales of early misery, which has flourished over the past decade. Stories that prompt thoughts, rather than feelings, are not so palatable. So the contemporary experiences of un-children remain untold, while the bookshops are clogged with more easily digested trauma.

In the months that Ashley was talking to me, the bestseller non fiction charts were dominated by: *Just a Boy*, by Richard McGann, whose mother was the first victim of the Yorkshire Ripper, 'a graphic account of how four children lost not only their mother but their childhoods'; *Sickened*, by Julie Gregory, whose mother suffered from Munchausen's by proxy, 'a harrowing but compelling account of the way her mother stole her childhood'; *One Child*, by Torey Hayden, 'educational psychologist helps an abused child back to life'; and *A Brother's Journey*, by Richard Pelzer, brother of Dave.

Dave Pelzer, the million-selling memoirist, has been described as 'one of the most severely abused children in California's history'. His own trauma tale, *A Child Called It*, which he followed with *The Lost Boy* and *A Man Named Dave*, documented his early childhood with a mentally disturbed and alcoholic mother, who fed her son from a dog bowl, ritually humiliated him and forced him to sleep in the cellar.

In the introduction to his beautifully executed memoir *Experience*, the novelist Martin Amis wrote: 'It used to be said that everyone had a novel in them . . . [now] you would probably be obliged to doubt the basic proposition: what everyone has in them, these days, is not a novel but a memoir. We live in an age of mass loquacity . . . Nothing, for now, can compete with experience – so unanswerably authentic, and so liberally and democratically dispensed. Experience is the only thing we share equally, and everyone senses this.'

But the most successful childhood memoirs are not written by the already famous. And, while the occasional few have attracted literary esteem – like Andrea Ashworth and Frank McCourt, or the cheekily subversive Dave Eggers – the majority trade on crude honesty rather than stylistic ability.

It has been estimated that one in fifteen adults in Britain has read a book by Dave Pelzer. Why is it that we would rather learn about a corrupted American childhood from the mid-1970s than contemplate how children live in the UK, here and now? Perhaps it is because such tales are only appealing after the fact, when they have been strained through the muslin of hindsight and spiked with psychobabble, providing the reader with a flavour of catharsis or there-but-for-the-grace gratitude, in a culture where voyeuristic maundering passes for emotional literacy.

Reviews of Pelzer's work on the Amazon website are instructive. There are many postings from people who were abused as children themselves, and who have found his model of healing through self-expression useful in their own quest for equilibrium. But while these books may offer individual succour, they are usually void of any lesson beyond the personal, suggesting no broader political imperative to prevent future harm.

The popularity of these memoirs cannot be explained away by shared experience alone. As effusive in their praise on Amazon are those readers whose lives were untouched by maltreatment, who simply relished a book that made them cry and cry.

It is plausible that, for sanitised Western adulthood, where encounters with the extremities of birth and death, insanity and cruelty, are strictly monitored, these memoirs – like horror movies before them – provide a last forum in which to explore collective fears.

This is surely not what Amis had in mind when he wrote of the unanswerable authenticity of experience – titillation by artlessly rendered trauma. For the majority of readers who have not experienced abusive extremity, there is an ugly, near-pornographic component to this hanky-clutching appreciation.

These testimonials of triumph over tragedy turn the capacity to survive into a moral imperative. We valorise the formerly abused who visibly triumph, just as we resent a child like Ashley who exposes how early damage can dislocate. Such books confirm adults' preferred rear-view of childhood, whereby it is less challenging to interpret the antithesis of innocence as guilt, which we can easily attribute, than as knowledge, which might take us anywhere.

Adults tell expurgated versions of their own small time to friends and strangers all the time, to seduce or to supplicate. Even an ordinarily unhappy childhood can provide a comforting rationale for adult failure as well as adult success. Perhaps these memoirs soothe our fear that no story of childhood ends well. Because it always ends up right here in adulthood.

The following week, there's more trouble at the door of the centre. Ashley's brother is high again, threatening to stab the security man in the eye with a pen. He loses patience, and calls the police. Ashley waits passively, goes to the shop to buy Refreshers. On his return he distributes them to everyone who has crowded round, except for the security guy and the two newly arrived policemen. Despite the warnings, his brother was here yesterday, and he'll be back again tomorrow. There's nowhere else for him to go.

Ashley is back in the art room, pondering how he drums up twenty pounds every day to buy skunk. 'It's either money I'm making myself or if I get a bit of money from my mum or dad I put it towards it.' If you can't support your habit then don't smoke, that's how he sees it. But he's got enough to get his draw every day. And how does he make his money? 'It's bizznizz, innit?' Leave it at that.

A couple of weeks ago, he talked about 'moving on or moving up in the game'. It depends on your line, he says. If you've got a lot of customers you move up. If you're not making enough then you're back to square one, living off the government.

But it's not really possible to live on benefits. If you want to make extra, you either get a job or find something else to do to make more money. He doesn't know many people who don't have something else going on. 'My business, I'm looking to stop it soon, but for the time being it's all right. I'm making the money but it's nothing big.'

Ashley delineates clearly between crime for its own sake and crime to earn. He is derisive about kids he knows who shoplift sportswear. ''Cos you shouldn't thief clothes, that's one thing I wouldn't do. I just wouldn't lower myself to that level. They're not selling the clothes and making a business. They're stealing them 'cos they want them that bad.'

It's not stupid to steal wallets, or things you can pawn, because you're making money. 'If you were going to prison for robbing a bank then good on you 'cos at least you tried.'

There are other things he wouldn't do. 'I don't do kids' stuff any more, I don't rob cars, I don't rob wallets. I just do one thing. I would say it's all right to sell weed, it's not all right to sell crack. If you're selling crack it's a hard thing to do 'cos crackheads just go mad for it. It's mostly Yardies that sell crack, and it's mostly kids that sell weed.'

He blows through his lips. 'I don't know, like, I don't really think you could grow up normal in Peckham. You'd still have a little mad thing about you. It's not that you're going to turn into a crackhead or nothing, but the kids in Peckham, the community, we ain't got much, we have to make do.'

'Yeah, you're a bad boy, but I wouldn't really call it that. You're just out there, trying to make paper. People are gonna get in your way then.' He grimaces, gestures with one hand: 'Just push them aside.'

Nothing surprises him. No. He can't imagine anything that would shock him. No. He's laughing now. Is that a good thing or bad thing? Bad. The laughter evaporates. 'I've seen too much.'

Ashley scratches his crown, removing the baseball cap that is normally welded there. His hair is soft and curly. He looks much younger. He says he's never without his hat. Only when he's had a haircut. He likes a number one. Couldn't he just get a pal with some clippers to do it? No, he says, appalled. 'I've got my barber.'

He has a lot of support right now: his mum, his girlfriend, Camila. He wants to do his education, he says, like he always does. And there's one special, shining hope: 'Barbados.' He treats the word delicately, in case it dims with overuse. Then it all falls out in a rush: 'I ain't been there but I'm going there probably the end of this year or the beginning of next year, and I might be living over there. My mum's gonna start saving the money and I'm gonna go over there for perhaps six months. I'm going to live with my godparents, and if I choose to stay I'll stay. My mum's planned it for a couple of years, but bills and that come up. She just wants me to get out of this life, misbehaving and that. She wants me to have a better life.'

He reckons he'd enjoy it in Barbados. He doesn't know no one over there, so it means he'd have to start new friendships. And if he goes to school, they're still caning people. He laughs, his lovely face bright with a huge, unfettered smile. 'I'd probably beat up the teacher!' In his dreams. 'They're brought up getting caned so they're not thinking, "Who is this teacher?" They're scared of the teacher. Trust me,' he articulates slowly, for effect, 'when he picks up that cane and slaps it down!' He bangs the table with his palm. 'My dad said he used to be *shook*!'

He doesn't know how much his mum's got saved. 'She ain't even looked at the flights. I think she's going to do it when my passport comes through, and then she's gonna find it on Easyjet.' Ashley says he likes the sunshine.

Lauren

'They get it all wrong. They think that if you're fifteen you can't look after yourself let alone a child.'

Lauren's hands are blue. She's designing a shoe for her textiles course and the dye gets everywhere. It's going to be work, work, work for the ten GCSEs she's taking this summer. The school told her she could drop some, but she didn't want to. Lauren's favourite subject is English. She loves literature – Dickens, Steinbeck – and that's what she's going to do at university. She's been making this blue shoe as one of her final pieces for submission. She says she needs three sketch books too. Ollie, her baby son, who has been fidgeting amiably on her lap, is suddenly sick, and Lauren shouts to her mum in the kitchen to bring through the wet wipes please.

It's January now, at the long dark end of a short wet day. Lauren sits back on the living-room sofa in jeans and a jumper, her long blonde hair loose around her broad shoulders. She gave birth to Ollie on 5 August last year, three months before her sixteenth birthday. In the womb, he had been an unobtrusive passenger: 'I wasn't being sick, I'd only put a little bit of weight on, physically I felt fine. That was why I only found out when it was that late. Five months!' She says it quietly now, disbelieving.

'It was dead weird. I went after school to one of those clinics for young people in Manchester. I went for a test, when I would have been six weeks pregnant, but it said I wasn't, so I just went with that. And then I kept going to the toilet all the time, and my friend said to me, "You'd better go for another test." The doctor felt my belly and said, "I think you're about four months," and I was like' – she makes a wide open mouth – 'God!!!' A surge of noise pounds through the ceiling. Her thirteen-year-old sister Danielle is up in her bedroom and she's got her moshing music on. The four of them – three women and a baby – live together in this new-build council house in Gorton, Manchester. Down here the lights are low, and Lauren lays Ollie prostrate in his buggy for a nap.

Lauren is a child who is also a parent, a totem for liberal despair and conservative vitriol. There is no more resonant a position in the current climate of child-panic. It is the ultimate adult encroachment, as well as a profound statement about what a young person is capable of. Her dual status attacks not only the idea of what it is to be a child, but also what it is to be a parent.

The UK currently heads the European league table for teenage pregnancies. Should we blame poor sex education, a decline in moral values or a grossly sexualised culture for Lauren's pregnancy? Is it worthy of blame in the first place?

Lauren's mum found out that she was pregnant two weeks after she did. She guessed of course. 'I felt like I'd disappointed her – 'cos I'm the one in the family, "Oh Lauren this, Lauren that." I'm good at school, I'm good at sport, I sing and that – and I cared what she thought. I didn't care what other people thought, just my immediate family, but they was all right.'

Lauren doesn't know whether she'd have had an abortion

if she'd found out earlier. You can't really say, can you, unless it actually happens to you. By the time she knew she had three weeks left, because the limit is twenty-four weeks isn't it? And her mum said, 'You can still go back to school,' so it didn't bother her. Now her mother looks after Ollie during the day, and on Saturdays her nan takes him until about six o'clock, so she can catch up on her homework. 'I do make sure I go to school,' she says seriously. 'I don't like to have a day off.'

At school, everyone was all right to her face. 'I don't know if anyone slagged me off behind my back, but most of my friends said they knew already. They were like, "Oh can I feel your belly?" And the teachers were really good. I think if I'd been someone who was really naughty it would have been different, but I get on with them. They all love me. I love them too. They always stay behind to help me. When the baby was born they bought him lots of stuff.'

Lauren's boyfriend, who is two years older than her, was living here at the time, because he was having problems at home. He was really, really good, she says fondly, and he was there when Ollie was born, but then about two months ago he went a bit weird. 'Like, I would go out on a Friday night and he was supposed to mind the baby but then he would just go out, and I found text messages on his phone from other girls. So I said, "Don't you think you should just move home and we could spend some time apart?" and then after that I realised that it was better so I told him and then we split up.' He still sees his son, but she doesn't like to see him because he gets jealous when she goes out.

Lauren gets out once a week, usually on Friday nights. It's just nice to go and sit in someone else's house and not have to be a mum and changing nappies. She knows she's a mother but she's doesn't always think of herself as one.

'And then I have one of my friends sat next to me, and she's so young!' She gives it a Mancunian plosive 'g'. 'She's the same age as me and she hasn't one responsibility, and the difference from her to me, it's hard to believe. But you get used to it.'

Perhaps it's a redundant question to ask, why parents have children. Relationships happen, conception happens: the template of partners and progeny is what we have always built societies around. For any culture to survive, it must promote the act of replenishing its members, and teaching them the social and economic skills necessary to progress as a community. For most people, the grouping we call family is the best way to carry out this task.

It is not just the community as a whole that needs children, writes the philosopher Thomas H. Murray in *The Worth of a Child*. Individual adults need children for their own flourishing. 'Children have helped to meet a variety of adult needs: economic needs, as household workers or as support in old age; emotional needs for intimacy and affection; and developmental needs, for maturation, for ripening of the virtues appropriate to adult life.'

Do adults have children solely in pursuit of their own fulfilment, or can it be a selfless act? 'The old, familiar moral categories of altruism and selfishness seem to be jumbled up in well-functioning parent–child relationships,' says Murray. And whatever framework we choose to assess the worth of children will have to encompass an assortment of paradoxes.

'[W]e celebrate individualism, yet we find meaning in family relationships; we cherish freedom, yet we have children whose needs constrain us profoundly; we want the liberty to get up and go whenever it suits us, yet our flourishing depends on lifelong commitments and enduring, steadfast relationships; we exalt choice and control, yet families are built largely on acceptance of people as they are, with all their imperfections; we participate in a vigorous commercial culture, yet we cherish and protect a sphere in which interactions are regulated by values alien to the world of commerce and markets.'

British adults are having fewer children than ever before. Indeed, nowhere in the European Union does the current birth rate approach the level needed to keep the population stable. In this country, it is predicted that by 2014 the over-sixty-fives will outnumber the under-sixteens for the first time. Demographers warn of a fertility crisis that threatens economic growth and social welfare. In France and Italy, governments have offered financial incentives to procreate.

The trend towards having fewer children later, if at all, is largely a middle-class phenomenon. With success in the workplace – and the material benefits that brings – increasingly considered the measure of bourgeois fulfilment, it is unsurprising that some are unwilling to contemplate lowering their professional and consumerist horizons in order to raise children. Where once we debated how to make our children happy, we now discuss as much whether they can make us happy.

As Laurie and Matthew Taylor point out in their book *What Are Children For?*, 'What explains the gap between the reality of declining real costs and increasing opportunities for parents and the perception of growing burdens and choices denied, lies in a very different, less tangible and less easily articulated sense of sacrifice – the loss of those modern absolute values: autonomy and freedom and individualism.'

But there are other reasons why middle-class women are pursuing their careers into their thirties, enjoying economic independence and professional fulfilment while controlling their fertility. They are unwilling to sacrifice their hard-won status in the public sphere because they are all too aware that having children will penalise them far more than it does their male colleagues.

Feminism has often been described as a movement against nature. In her tome *Sexual Personae*, Camille Paglia wrote: 'The more woman aims for personal identity and autonomy . . . the fiercer will be her struggle with nature – that is, with the intractable physical laws of her own body. And the more nature will punish her: "Do not dare to be free! For your body does not belong to you."'

It is not only nature that punishes women who hold back from childbearing. The only group as embattled as working mothers are childless women in their thirties, who are continually bombarded with doomy predictions about diminishing fertility and wasted ova. Yet little is done to shape the workplace to fit any life other than that of a male without child-care responsibilities.

Meanwhile, an expanding range of birth technologies that promise to ease later conception suggest that having children is an alienable right, provided one has sufficient resources. Despite the 75 per cent failure rate of IVF treatments, or the profound emotional consequences for child as well as parent of using donated eggs or sperm, there is a subtle implication that any woman can be a mother if only she tries hard enough.

That many more women say they are choosing not to have children confronts the notion of a 'natural' maternal drive. It is certainly arguable that childbearing is as much of a social imperative as a biological one. But 'choice' here is a tricksy concept. Life is not all about choices – when to work, when to fall in love, when to procreate. In fact, much of our time is spent on these things that won't – or can't – be facilitated alone. Women do not remain childless for longer just because they're holding out for a fatter pay cheque.

Former tabloid editor and media commentator Amanda Platell has written movingly about her own childlessness. 'I've spent my life with people assuming that I placed ambition above motherhood,' she wrote in a column for the *New Statesman* magazine. 'Well, call me selfish, but I only ever wanted to be a mother one way, with my own child born into a loving relationship with its father. I never thought that being a mother was just about my fulfilment.' She concludes: 'Not being able to have kids has not defined me, but it has defined my life.'

Lauren thinks people have children for different reasons, some because they're lonely, some because they want to make a family. It does change you. If you're young, you have to grow up fast, because you're not just looking after yourself any more. She thinks it's made her a better person, though it might not look like it when she's tired and stressed. It's made her more understanding.

From this time last year to now, everything and nothing has changed. Her plans are the same really. She was hoping to go to Bristol Uni to see another city, but now she's going to one in Manchester. And obviously she'd thought she'd settle down with her boyfriend, but now she thinks it's better this way.

Ollie, who has been dozing in his buggy, wakens. Lauren picks him up again and sits him on her knees. He beams her a look of absolute adoration. She's wearing a baseball cap. 'Lookin' at me 'at,' she says, but it sounds like 'heart' and that seems appropriate too. Lauren thinks babies have dreams because sometimes you see them jump in their sleep. She was going to name him Oliver, but she thought that everyone was going to call him Ollie for short so she'd just use that in the first place. It's the same sturdy pragmatism that runs through all her choices.

A few weeks further into January, Ollie has caught a cold. He snuffles while Lauren feeds him his bottle. She's only just back from school, and still in her uniform of black blazer and trousers, white shirt and tie. Her hair is tied back in a ponytail, and she is wearing a lick of mascara. MTV is on in the corner. Danielle is upstairs in bed. Everybody's tired this afternoon.

It's good being back at school, says Lauren. She's leaving in five months, so there's a lot to do now – finishing coursework, getting ready for her exams in May. She's taking maths, English, science, RE, PE, art, textiles, music, geography and graphic design. She's most worried about maths. 'I'm really good at it but as soon as I get into an exam my head just goes blank. Because you have to remember all the methods. I'm all right at it though. I'm expected a B.' Ollie chews on her blazer shoulder, soaking it.

He sneezes. Lauren's mum took him to the doctor's today but they weren't much help, she says. What's the point of sitting for hours on end if they're just going to tell you to give him Calpol? Ollie is experimenting with a new noise at a higher register. 'Aweh, aweh,' he calls to Lauren. He gets so excited when she comes home from school. Even though he's ill he's got a big smile on his face.

Ollie dribbles on to his chest. Lauren takes his top off in case he's too hot, then wipes his mouth with it. 'Mum, he's got warmer.' She comes in from the kitchen and checks his forehead. She was there at his birth, along with his father.

Labour was horrible. Lauren had gas and air and then the epidural. It took eighteen hours. The first time she saw him she was just shocked. 'I said, "Isn't he small?" I didn't know what to do. He was just there in me arms. He wasn't crying at first, that scared me, then he started crying and I knew it was going to be all right.' Someone brought her tea and toast but she took one bite and she was sick all over him. She laughs. Lauren laughs a lot.

Ollie does a big burp. Lauren's rested him on the sofa, and he's trying to sit up but can't quite. He rolls over on to his front instead. She was trying not to get pregnant. She laughs again. 'Not as much as I should have! I was on the Pill, but I forgot to take it. I never even wanted kids. I don't want any more. I just wanted to do normal things, travel, do my job first.' She hasn't travelled much, though she did go to Malta with her netball team for a competition. They won. 'I wanted to live somewhere, anywhere that wasn't England. My auntie lives in Oregon, Portland, but I've never visited because it's too expensive. I'm still going to college though.' She repeats it like an affirmation.

She sent the application off to Stockport College this week. She chose it because it's got a crèche. She's applied for the English language course. It's about how language evolves and how babies learn to speak. It'll be useful because she wants to be a primary school teacher. That way, she'll get all the same holidays as him.

Lauren isn't sure what advice she'd give to someone who found herself in her position. 'I don't really have a right or wrong on abortion. I think it's every person's choice. Everyone's different. They might not have the support I've got. It's hard work. But as they get older it does get better, and little things that they do make it worth it. Like when he first rolled over. But it is hard. All these girls that get pregnant on purpose. I don't know why they do it.'

She doesn't know people like that personally, but there was a programme on TV about two teenage sisters who got pregnant deliberately. It was probably because they were lonely, or for attention. 'You get some people who are just really obsessed with babies,' she notes with derision. Lauren doesn't like the phrase 'teenage mothers'. 'It's a bit of a cliché. People have this really bad perception. I did, really, until it happened to me. I thought, they're stupid, it's their own fault. You get it from media. They always put it so it looks bad. Nobody agrees with it really.'

People seem to think that teenagers can't look after babies, she says. 'But they don't think that about a first-time mum who's thirty. They get it all wrong. They think that if you're fifteen you can't look after yourself let alone a child. A woman of thirty could have a baby and cope worse than I have, but some people would think that she was more right than me just because of her age.'

It is widely assumed that a young mother will be a bad mother, or at least that early motherhood is bad for teenagers. Certain newspapers delight in highlighting atypical cases of twelve-year-old pregnancies and fourteen-year-old abortions as evidence of the country's moral unravelling. The distillation of the feckless council-estate teen is Vicky Pollard from the comedy series *Little Britain*, who swapped her new baby for a Westlife CD. Since the 1980s, when the Conservative government specialised in attacks on young mothers, there has been the impression that the country is facing an epidemic of teenage pregnancies.

Certainly the rates are comparatively high, though it is worth remembering that, in 1970, teenagers were twice as likely to become mothers as nowadays. Despite the shock-horror headlines, the teenage conception rate dropped by nearly 10 per cent in the five years since the introduction of the government's Teenage Pregnancy Strategy in 1999.

The rationale for the strategy, set out in a paper from the government's Social Exclusion Unit, aimed to demonstrate that a woman's life chances, and those of her children, were adversely affected by early motherhood. Teenagers in deprived areas are both more likely to become pregnant and less likely to consider abortion. The majority of teenage mothers do live in poverty. They are more likely to be unemployed, to suffer from depression and to become dependent on alcohol or drugs. But so are their childless peers. It is typically poverty, not early motherhood, that truncates life chances.

Clearly, helping more young people out of poverty is a laudable objective. But it is worth assessing whether this altruism is at all motivated by adult distaste for teenage sexual activity, or by a conviction that children are not capable of looking after other children. Vicky Pollard is compelling precisely because she plays on fears of a rampant underclass.

If the decision is made freely, and properly supported, there is nothing essentially wrong with having a baby before you're twenty. Granted, not every teenage mother is as capable and undiminished as Lauren, nor do they all have her support network. But, instead of condemning the root causes – like social exclusion, poor sex education or lack of opportunities – it is the young women themselves who have been continually vilified by the press and politicians as slags or scroungers, despite there being no evidence that teenagers get pregnant to procure better housing or benefits.

And these prejudices can also inform the public service provision they receive. In a poll conducted in 2004, the YWCA found that half of education professionals thought that young mothers were not interested in education, though their research shows that having a child of their own makes them more determined to gain qualifications. Lauren didn't need any persuading to get back to school. Indeed, she didn't miss out on any of her education because, with her usual precision, she gave birth during the summer holidays.

Ollie saw his dad yesterday. He's got his own flat now, but Lauren insists he has Ollie at his mum's. Otherwise she'd be ringing up every five minutes to check on him. He'd be sat there and spark up a cig or something. He's dead dopey, she says, still half-indulgent. There's nothing special between them now, just 'Hiya', just keeping the peace.

Lauren first went out with him when she was about twelve. Then she didn't see him for ages. And then, when she'd just turned fourteen, she saw his brother at a party and got his number again. The next day she dropped her phone down the toilet so she went to his house to say she couldn't call him; he invited her in and that was it.

'He was dead nice. He used to take me out every week-end. He used to buy me little things, cards. But then it was, like, I'd have school the next day and he thought it didn't matter. We were totally different. I'd say a word and he'd be, "What are you trying to speak posh for?" and I'd be, "I'm not." So we just drifted apart.'

But there's one thing she knows, no matter what their relationship is like: he will be a really good dad. Lauren still sees her own father, who moved out when she was nine, regularly. 'Aweh,' Ollie calls. She holds him to her and kisses his neck. She whispers: 'Big love, big love.'

Before having Ollie, she'd never even held a newborn baby or changed a nappy. 'But if you don't do it, there's nobody else to do it for you, so you just learn. And then they start crying and you learn what different crying means and you get used to it. Because nobody knows, do they? It's just like trial and error.'

Her mum has let her find it out all by herself. 'When he was born, everyone was like, "Oh, you'll be taking over, you'll be looking after the baby all the time," but she's never had him in her room at night, not one time,' she says. 'She's let me do it myself, the hard way, but it's a better way. She was seventeen when she had me so she knows what it's like.'

When I next visit, it's still raining. Lauren started Weightwatchers last night. You sign up, they weigh you and then work out how many points a day you're allowed. You follow the points, and lose the weight. Lauren is allowed twenty-two points a day. You pay a fiver a week. And then when you get to your target weight it all changes and you start eating a bit more but not too much so you don't put all your weight back on.

She went with a friend who's a year older than her. 'She needs it more than me. I was twelve stone thirteen pounds. I was shocked! But before I was pregnant I weighed about eleven stone. I want to lose at least a stone,' she says. Like all of Lauren's intentions, her capability is never in doubt. 'I ate like crazy when I was pregnant. I ate for triplets. And now he's getting older I'm starting to think about me again. They say it takes a year for your body to get back to normal.'

Lauren is in the living-room with Danielle. Ollie and their mum aren't home yet. They're watching MTV. They both like rock, but Lauren's tastes aren't as heavy as her sister's. Danielle wears the moshers' uniform of black and boots, a very teenage way of dressing that screams a statement but hides your shape. She gets called names for her outfits at school, and Lauren worries about that.

Danielle adores her sister, and doesn't bother to hide it. She's always trying to get Lauren to sing. Her friend is starting a band, and she wants her sister to record something and send it to him. 'It has to be punk,' she challenges, 'Green Day or something.' All right, yeah, she'll try it. But she's used to singing ballads, Sinead O'Connor or Shania Twain. Before Lauren got pregnant she sang in pubs for a company called Natural Talent. She says she's an exhibitionist. She'd love to go back to it now, but with having him and school it's too much.

It's parents' evening tonight, but Lauren isn't nervous. 'I've never had a bad parents' evening. They always say good things about me.'

Lauren's mum returns with Ollie, but leaves him sleeping in the hall. Lauren says she got most of her ideas about sex from magazines and her mates. She's always been able to talk to her mum, but for some things it's a bit uncomfortable. She's the magazine queen. She started off on *Mizz* when she was in Year 7, and then *Bliss*, *Sugar*, *J17*. She thinks they're helpful. 'I'd rather the information be there than not at all. It should be there because a lot of people don't talk to their parents and feel more comfortable reading about stuff like that in magazines. I think they're really good, them magazines. And it's just one page [about sex] then the rest is different hairstyles and all them embarrassing stories.'

Lauren didn't get more than a biological cross-section during sex education at school. 'Honestly, it was like the drawing – this is a woman, this a man – and we had about two lessons because they had to speed it on that quick. We had PSHE (personal, social and health education) in Year 7 and then they got rid of it in Year 8 because they didn't have anyone to teach it.'

'I just think that they should teach the facts, not "don't do this, don't do that",' she says, 'and early enough, when you're about eleven or twelve. You need a confident teacher, because if the teacher's embarrassed then the kids are going to get embarrassed. And you should split up the boys and girls, so you feel more at ease.'

Lauren's experience of sex education is not unusual. In February 2005, a report by Ofsted found that provision of Sex and Relationships Education (SRE), a component of the non-statutory PSHE curriculum, was poor in many schools and non-existent in others. It particularly criticised the lack of trained staff, with classes seen as an add-on and directed by form teachers rather than specialists.

Despite the widespread anxiety around children's sexual activity, and the fact that most parents say they want more, not less, sex education, it is still not compulsory in our schools. All the curriculum requires is a basic biology lesson. Anything else is optional, and – oddly – decided by the school's governors. Provision has certainly advanced since the moral fundamentalism of the Thatcher years, and policy has attempted to respond to young people's well-documented requests for greater emphasis on feelings, relationships and values.

But New Labour has been reticent in addressing the spectrum of sexual relations. Official guidance remains defensive, and based around a heterosexual and reproductive model – understandable given the right-wing media's delight in exposing oral-sex lessons for ten-year-olds and the like. Although very few do, the fact that parents retain the right to withdraw their children from sex education is symbolic of the general view that young people are incapable of taking moral decisions themselves, and that the private sphere of the family remains the best place to receive sexual wisdom.

While the average age for first intercourse in the UK is sixteen, significant numbers of younger teenagers are becoming sexually active. The Family Planning Association has called on the government to make teaching of PSHE a legal requirement from primary school onwards. But this will require a fundamental change in the way that we view young people's sexual potential.

Children have the capacity for arousal and orgasm from birth, but continue to be regarded as asexual until puberty. Adults are highly resistant to the fact of children's burgeoning sexual knowledge, though the bulk of research shows that from an early age young people have an active curiosity and awareness about sex and sexuality. As the feminist sociologist Stevi Jackson argues, it is one of the first arenas in which children begin to question conventional definitions of right and wrong. But their capacity to manage this exploration is rarely acknowledged, and often stymied by adults' own evasiveness and repression around sexual matters.

In her book *Childhood and Sexuality*, Jackson suggests that there is such a thing as childhood sexuality, but that it exists independently of sexual knowledge. 'If sexuality amounted to nothing more than a series of physical sensations and patterns of behaviour, an outpouring of sexual energies, then it would be possible to argue that children are sexual. If . . . it is something more than this . . . that must be understood in human and social terms, a sexually aware child can only be described as potentially sexual . . . It follows that there is no reason why children should not be sexual. Their sexuality lies not in a lack of capacity, but in a lack of opportunity; their inability to make sense of the world in sexual terms derives from ignorance.'

Jackson concludes that it is sexual ignorance, not sexual knowledge, that is most damaging for the young. 'In attempting to protect children from sex we expose them to danger; in trying to preserve their innocence we expose them to guilt. In keeping both sexes asexual, and then training them to become sexual in different ways, we perpetuate sexual inequality, exploitation and oppression.'

Arguably, it is gender knowledge rather than sexual knowledge that is more damaging to children. Girls learn to embrace passivity and to view their sexuality as having a market value, both in private and public exchanges. They are taught a romantic story of their futures, of which sex forms one element, while boys learn that sex is a discrete act which underpins masculinity. As Laura and Ashley have described in their chapters, the double standard for sexual behaviour is thriving, and it will continue to do so as long as children are socialised in gender from birth, but expected to remain abstinent until the law tells them otherwise.

Today's young women are reputedly the most sexually confident, most sexually active generation ever, yet a third say that they have been coerced into sex and many more express regret at starting their sexual lives so early. Popular culture may offer superficially subversive notions of women as sexual aggressors, but for ordinary children this is far removed from having any practical working knowledge of their own bodies, or the confidence to protect them.

If young women are indeed learning to value bravado over intimacy, and quantity over quality – while continuing to be punished, and to punish themselves, for displays of sexual agency – then feminism has failed to create an alternative to the macho prescription for sexual pleasure and relationships.

The double standard exists not only between girls and boys, but also between adults and children. As professor of criminology Phil Scraton notes in an essay on regulating sexuality, 'The denial of childhood sexuality is an essential component of the broader negation of children and young people as active citizens.' He describes how children are expected to retain a sexual naivety and to be passive onlookers of a highly sexualised culture.

Scraton critiques the biological essentialism that informs the delivery of sex education, which assumes that sexuality is linked to 'natural', developmental stages, and that feelings and knowledge develop similarly to this. 'Sexuality permeates the school environment,' he writes, 'but the ideology of "childhood innocence" rejects schools as cultural sites where emergent sexual identities are formed, reproduced and lived. Also denied is the active engagement of children and young people in the formation of their sexual identities.'

In 2003, the award-winning children's author Melvin Burgess published *Doing It*, an explicit account of adolescent male sexuality. It was denounced by the children's laureate Anne Fine as 'vile, foul and deluded' and was subjected to frenzied analysis. But when I read it, I found it an honest and deeply moral exposition of the charmlessness and vulnerability of teenage desire.

The response was perverse: Burgess was slated for acknowledging that teenage boys can be pretty filthy in their relentless pursuit of a grope. But the same lads could read all about the latest celebrity sex scandal in *Heat*, or assess 'real' women's assets in *Nuts*' 'Street Strip Challenge'.

Most weeks, the newsagents' shelves are heaving with breathless details of Abi Titmuss's filthiest moments, and inventively angled photography revealing what may or may not be Jodie Marsh's labia majora. The acceptable subject areas are closely prescribed: virginity, loss and maintenance thereof; bisexuality (women's); prowess and endurance (men's). For the cohort of pretty girls done good, who rely upon their talent for exposure as much as their talent, such simulacra of sexual honesty become their currency.

In her *Guardian Weekend* magazine investigation into lads'

mags like *Zoo*, *Nuts* and *Loaded* – which are snapped up by teenage boys – media commentator Janice Turner noted: 'Once porn and real human sexuality were distinguishable . . . But as porn has seeped into mainstream culture, the line has blurred. To speak to men's magazine editors, it is clear they believe that somehow in recent years, porn has become true. The sexually liberated modern woman turns out to resemble – what do you know! – the pneumatic, take-me-now-big-boy fuck-puppet of male fantasy after all.'

But for all they are over-informed about how other people do it, this has not brought young men and women any closer to developing a common erotic language. There must be a way to diminish the junk succour of public sex while freeing private appetites. It is only by confronting the same-again sexism of our full-frontal society that we wrest back control of sex, its meaning and its language, from the mainstream pornographers.

In a world where it often feels like every experience has been flayed of flavour through overexposure, sex is one of the few things that retains its tang. But until adults can address the double standard that surrounds young people's experience of intimacy, this will remain a sexual revolution in waiting.

Ollie still hasn't stirred, but Lauren says he's getting better at sitting up now. He's making loads of noise, and he's getting big. Her dad might take him to the pool because he's a good swimmer, and he's got a baby too. She points to one of the framed photographs on the shelves. 'That's my half-brother. He's walking now. He's gorgeous.' There are photographs all over this house, studio poses as well as family snaps. At the top of the stairs there's even a sepia-tinted shot of the three of them posing in Victorian costume, taken at

Blackpool. They are stern-faced because the photographer told them not to smile.

Lauren has another half-brother who's in the army. He's nearly twenty. Lee. He's her dad's son, but he lived with her and Dan since they were young, so she says he's her brother. He comes home every other month. She misses him.

Now she's thinking about tea. 'Are there any points in that ragu? It says "trace fat".'

'You still have to point it,' warns her mum. She's an expert at the Weightwatchers points system. She used to look like a man, says Danielle. Lauren is mock-horrified, but her mum agrees. 'I did! I lost nearly four stone. I used to wear big checked shirts and everything. Then last January I just decided, and lost two stones in a month.' Losing it was easy. Keeping it off's the hard part.

Now it's February, and Danielle is bundled up in Lauren's bed. She spewed up in her own room earlier and she hasn't cleaned it up yet. They're laughing about it.

Lauren says her favourite thing in here is the mirror, ''cos I love looking at meself!' She's changed the room around recently, because she's started to put Ollie in the cot at night.

'Are you leaving the side down?' asks her sister from under the duvet.

'It's easier,' says Lauren efficiently. 'I can just lean over.'

Here's a picture of her mum when she was fat, and here's a picture of her and Danni at the old house when they were younger. And – ohh! – here's this gorgeous boy from a boy band. Don't you think he's gorgeous? Danielle says she's met him, and she didn't think so.

Lauren chose the decor because she loves pink. A set of star-shaped fairy lights loops around the window. On the corkboard by her bed there's a 'Best Friend' poem and a 'Special Friend' award alongside photos of her pals. Beneath them there's a hand-drawn heart that says 'Lauren loves [Ollie's father].' She takes it down and folds it decisively in two. 'I didn't know that was there,' she says. 'It was under all that other stuff.'

Downstairs again, her mum hands her Ollie, nappyless and shrieking. Parents' evening was good, but there's not much else going on. She's concentrating on school really. She's feeling stressed about work. That's why she stayed behind an extra hour today, to get some done. She gets all this work and she thinks, 'When am I going to have time to do it?'

The first week at Weightwatchers she lost two pounds, then the next week she put a pound and a half back on. She laughs. 'I had McDonald's on Saturday, so it's my own fault.' She needs to get Ollie dressed now because she's going out at six. She's been trying on an old jacket to see if it fits. She's going to Asda with her Weightwatchers friend, who wants to buy a fitness DVD. She's not getting anything herself. She's got about six pounds to her name. It's just to get out the house.

Before she had Ollie, she never had money either. 'My mum doesn't just hand it out. The money I get for Ollie I spend on him, and if there's any left I save it, or I might take a tenner. I'm not really bothered through the week, as long as I have money on a Friday night, because that's my night off.'

Lauren would like to have a bit more money – who wouldn't? But the gap between rich and poor is massive. 'You've got homeless people who don't have 20p. And then you've got all the rich people with their homes in Cornwall. And it's not just a gap of money is it? It's a gap of understanding. If a really rich person walked past a person begging he wouldn't even look at them, he wouldn't acknowledge them.'

Ollie is squalling as she pulls on his trousers. She tells him he's a Naughty Boy. He bubbles his spit, and a string of it attaches to one of the rips in her jeans. Lauren lost her virginity to Ollie's father when they'd been seeing each other for about three months. 'Most of my friends think it's whenever you want. As long as you're not with a different boy all the time, then they'd be worried.'

Ollie's fully dressed now, and Lauren talks into his cheek. Virginity makes her snort. 'I don't know anyone who is! Because everything's about sex, innit? Like music videos, it's advertised all over the place, Page Three women. Staying a virgin is a bit old-fashioned. I think it's only the religious people who do that.'

Most girls nowadays think it's all right to have sex when you've been with someone for a couple of months. But sex is different at different times. 'If you've got a boyfriend then it's for closeness and all that, but if it's just a one-night thing it's fun, and it doesn't mean anything. I think if it's with your boyfriend it's making love; if it's a one-night thing then it's just sex.' She thinks boys feel the same, but they're not as open about it. Ollie is manoeuvring a plastic model into his mouth. 'What are you doing, you? You're going to choke.'

Lauren doesn't want to get married. 'Especially nowadays, it's not as committed as it used to be. People have three or four marriages. At the end of the day it's only a piece of paper. And if you love someone and you've been with them for years then what's a piece of paper going to add to it? I'd rather just be loving with someone.'

She calls to her mum: 'Do you think I should get married?' Her mum puts her head round the kitchen door, and pulls a face. 'I bet I get that off you,' Lauren tells her. 'I've never been one to fantasise about weddings and dresses, have I?'

Her own parents weren't married. No, her mum confirms. She was with him for years and she never wanted to.

It's later in February now, and the afternoon light is lasting longer. There's a non-commital drizzle. Lauren's lost six and a half pounds. It was half-term last week, and she got loads of work done. She's got two five-hour exams for textiles coming up, and four weeks to get her final piece ready. When she got back to school she thought everyone else would have done loads more than her, but they hadn't.

Her sister is sitting in an armchair, writing birthdays on to the kitchen calendar. Her mum has just come back with Ollie, and now he's wriggling under the coffee-table, frantically trying to push himself up with his arms.

'He's dead frustrated!' she laughs. 'He's been trying to crawl but not quite mastering it. He's not learnt to co-ordinate his arms and legs yet.' He had a bit of diarrhoea last week and they had to starve him for twenty-four hours and give him Dioralyte powder in water. But since then he's been really good. He's falling asleep on his own now. If he does wake up it's just for reassurance and if you stroke him he goes straight back to sleep.

Lauren itches her eye. Danielle put Nutella on her face this morning and it's all dried up on her eyelashes. She's never been interested in politics, she says. She's interested in what goes on but she's never watched all the debating. She doesn't like Tony Blair because he wanted to send her brother to Iraq. She pauses. 'I've always wondered that, how do you get to be a politician? Is it people that know the Queen? Or people that own businesses?' Danielle says you have to get in the party really low down and then work your way up. 'Oooh, go Danielle!' teases Lauren.

If she was in charge, she'd have more textbooks in schools,

and better sex education. She thinks there should be more support for teenage mothers. 'I was reading a magazine yesterday about two sisters who had two little boys and they were only fifteen and seventeen and one got expelled from school because the teacher said she was a bad influence on the other girls. Ohhhh!' she exhales outrage. 'I was gob-smacked!'

There should be more support, not just money-wise but also day centres where you can go, or groups where you can meet other people your age who have kids. ''Cos my friends, they understand everything about me apart from when I talk about him. And people always talk about it like it's bad. I don't mean, "Oh just get pregnant and we don't care," but things happen and there should be people to help.'

In 1914, the popular child care expert Ellen Key suggested that all girls around Lauren's age should undergo a year's 'social service' – to coincide with young men's military service – in order to prepare them for the challenges of motherhood. This is not so different from the parenting education in schools that has been mooted as an effective way of maintaining children's mental well-being. But for now, parenting skills have become increasingly professionalised.

The boom in parenting TV, for example, had a grim inevitability about it. The makeover genre has made a tidy profit out of soothing collective vulnerabilities with slick transformations. But the methodology is interesting. It is not only that dominatrix of the nursery, Supernanny, who instructs parents to be firm as well as fair. Both on screen and in print, there is evidence of a return to a more disciplinarian approach to child-rearing. Gina Ford is telling Dr Spock to 'take time out'.

Clearly, discipline has its place. All the uncritical praise in the universe will not help the child who has been given no boundaries. And many of those who fill the bookshop shelves and the television schedules are talented professionals whose techniques have proved hugely successful.

But as these manuals and programmes filter down, a strange sort of cherry-picked received wisdom comes into being – a naughty step here, some controlled crying there. It can be accepted as unquestioningly as we believe Trinny and Susannah's advice on what not to wear with fat ankles. It is a truism that every child is different. So why do we go along with those who would limit and standardise the behaviour that is deemed acceptable?

There remains something troubling in the language used here. Are 'out of control' toddlers soon to be villified in the same way that 'antisocial' adolescents are? It harks back to pre-Enlightenment religious notions of original sin and infant depravity, which could only be excised through the strictest of upbringings.

As family and community structures fragment, it is hardly surprising that many parents are forced to turn elsewhere for support. Parenting is not publicly embedded in society. In a largely individuated culture, the emphasis is placed firmly on personal responsibility. For all its Oprah-fication, Britain remains a seriously child-unfriendly country.

It is getting harder to articulate why people have children, in a period when religious conviction and traditional expectation no longer compels us to. And that makes it harder still to formulate a morality of childhood itself. In a later edition of his best-selling *Common Sense Book of Baby and Child Care*, first published in 1946, Dr Benjamin Spock lamented the loss of 'old-fashioned convictions' about what kinds of beliefs we wanted to share with our children.

'We've even lost our convictions about the purpose of human existence,' he wrote. 'Instead we've come to depend on psychological concepts.' Those concepts can sell manuals and gain ratings, but they cannot address the profound confusion about what childhood is and what it could be that presently finds articulation through child-panic.

In this secular society, where adults and children wear the same clothes and read the same books, how do we reach a consensus on the kinds of morals, ambitions and characters we want to have as adults, in order that we may share them with our children?

In a speech he delivered to the Citizen Organising Foundation in April 2005, the Archbishop of Canterbury Rowan Williams argued that if we do not know what moral state it is that we are inducting children into, we cannot be surprised if chaos results. He suggested that the marks of a mature human might include: being aware of emotion but not enslaved by it; being aware of fallibility and death; being sensitive to the cost of the choices they make; and being unthreatened by difference.

But this is wholly different to the version of adulthood that children see reflected back at them through the commercial sphere, or even in their educational environment, increasingly attuned as it is to turning out good producers and better consumers. As Williams noted unhappily, 'When we live in a debased environment of gossip, inflated rhetoric, non-participation, celebrity obsession and vacuous aspiration, it's not surprising that we have a challenge in the area of . . . human formation.'

Responding to the Archbishop's comments, Tim Gill, former director of the Children's Play Council, suggested that we require a fuller understanding of the journey that children must take to become autonomous adults with self-respect as well as respect for the rights and entitlements of others. 'This means giving children more license and freedom to make mistakes and learn from them. It also means confronting children with the consequences of their actions through proportionate sanctions and incentives that nurture a sense of human agency, rather than behaviouristic and materialistic systems of punishment and reward. And it means taking seriously the way children model their values and behaviour on those of adults.'

Lauren doesn't think much of the idea of parenting classes. 'It's just trial and error. You go to parenting class and they're telling you what they think is the right way. But there's no right or wrong way of doing it. At least if you do things wrong it makes things better because you learn from your mistakes.'

She thinks they should just leave you to it. 'It doesn't matter how old you are or where you come from. Although I'm young, and where I live no one knows what they're doing the first time they have a kid. As long as you try your best.'

Ollie will learn the same as what Lauren's mum taught her: 'No swearing, or not in front of me mum; respect, that's a big one, like my cousins are really naughty, and me and my sister don't understand how you can speak to your mum like that. Standing up for yourself, and treating others how you want to be treated.'

Lauren's mum wasn't nasty, she wasn't strict, but she set the rules and if they were broken then something happened. 'Where with my auntie she was dead lenient, so when she said no they thought they'd got away with it before. If we're good for my mum then we get a return. That's why I was always good because something always comes back to you.'

She does worry about Ollie, because he's a boy. You worry about him getting in with the wrong crowd, robbing cars and all that. There's a lot of it round here. 'It's harder for boys at school. A girl can do all her work through the lesson and stay behind, it'll be like, "Ah, you swot", it'll be laughed off, but boys, his mates would just remind him of it every five minutes that he's a geek.'

She lifts Ollie on to her lap, rescuing him briefly from the agony of not crawling. That's better! Danielle wants to know when their dad's birthday is, so she can write it on the calendar. When Ollie grows up, he can be whatever he wants to be. Whatever he wants to do, Lauren says, as long as it makes him happy. 'If he wants to be a belly dancer then he can.' He eases a string of drool from between his lips. 'Or a dribbler!!!!'

Conclusion

There have been times during the writing of this book when I have felt cheerful about children's experience of growing up in Britain today, and other times when I have felt profoundly depressed. I remember walking back from a meeting with Ashley one sunny afternoon, righteously indignant that the rest of the population was going about its business instead of marching on Parliament to demand an end to social exclusion.

When an injustice seems so enormous and intractable, it is inevitable that cynicism and apathy bleed into our understanding of it. Making a difference feels impossible. But that's what is so exciting about the majority of the questions posed in this book. We all know children. They are our fellow passengers on the bus, our neighbours, our flesh and blood. And how we relate to them can and does make a difference.

These nine stories offer a snapshot of the state of childhood at the beginning of the twenty-first century. I hope they show that there is much more to celebrate in the way that young people are negotiating the years before adulthood than there is to fear. And, in attempting to unravel the reasons for those fears, I hope I have convinced you that, while child-panic will always be with us in some shape or form, it is worthwhile interrogating adult anxieties, and examining how they can distort the experience of childhood and shift our focus from concern about genuine threats to an exaggerated obsession with children's well-being.

Of course adults worry about children. Changes in how childhood is lived confront at the deepest level our sense of personal history and our ideas of what makes us human. The work of raising children is love and life-enhancing, but also very difficult and poorly supported.

The nature of childhood has altered fundamentally, but it is not in crisis. Take a deep breath. We are not off to hell in a handcart just yet. Growing up is not how it used to be, nor should it be.

So many of our fears for and of children relate to adult discombobulation at the shape of the modern world, and nostalgia for a time before mobile phones and breast implants and twenty-four-hour advertising. But we cannot force young people to shoulder the burden of adult loss.

Children respond to the circumstances they are born into. If their environment is one of conspicuous consumption, sexual saturation and violence, then adults need to equip them with the tools to cope with this rather than perpetuate the fantasy that it is possible to shelter them from it entirely.

Childhood has never been a time of utter innocence, and experience is not only corrupting. As adults, we need to understand why it is that we continue to idealise childhood innocence, and to be honest about how many of our grown-up needs are currently satisfied by the way we think of children. We need to break with the prevailing ideology of childhood, which constructs young people as needy and incapable at the same time as excluding those who fail to meet its strict parameters.

If we are to reach a consensus on the kinds of morals, ambitions and characters we want our children to have, then we need to return to a notion of common citizenship. It is time to rebel against the modern absolute of individualism. Parenting cannot happen in isolation. As the saying goes, it takes a village. And it also takes a recognition that children themselves can play an active part in their own development.

Children's rights are not a liberal luxury. They are real, and deserved. Children have the right not to be hit. They have the right to make mistakes and to learn from them. They have the right to be consulted about decisions that affect their future. Children's rights are respected in countless ordinary homes across the country. But where they are not, particularly in the case of children growing up on the margins, they must be fought for.

British society needs to change the way it looks at childhood. We need to recognise children's evolving competences whenever possible. We need to challenge a political culture that seems to value children only for their economic potential, and which is taking an increasingly authoritarian line on young people's behaviour. When dealing with disadvantaged children, we have to understand how social inequality works, rather than assuming that they can be lifted out of poverty through parenting or talent alone.

We need to break with our ambivalence, whereby we worry hugely about our own children but feel equivocal about others, especially those deemed 'antisocial'. We need to work as a community, taking an interest in and responsibility for all children, rather than leaving them to individual parents, or, in extreme cases, the police. We need to appreciate that respect cuts both ways, and that a society that does not treat children as full citizens, and that denies any collective responsibility for socialising its young, cannot be surprised when they respond in kind.

A number of immediate policy changes are necessary.

Smacking should be banned. The use of ASBOs must be reined in. A public information campaign about the reality of child sexual abuse, of the kind advocated by the Lucy Faithfull Foundation, would be welcome, along with better provision for the treatment of paedophiles. We need to improve children's media literacy, while finding non-hysterical ways to control advertising to children and screen violence. The number of young offenders and asylum-seeking children who are incarcerated must be substantially reduced. Schools should have the facilities to feed our children properly, and to address bullying. We need to make it easier for parents, mothers or fathers, to stay at home with their children when they are very young. Mental health provision for the young must become more than a postcode lottery. There has to be decent sex education in every school. The government must continue its solid work on child poverty. We have to save the planet for our children's children.

Yeah, yeah, and when we've sorted all that out, we can think about what to do next year. Which brings me back to injustices enormous and intractable, and inevitable cynicism and apathy. But that's the beauty of childhood. Above all else, and in a thoroughly unsentimental fashion, it reminds us about hope. Just by living and loving, parents make a difference every single day. If we were to change the way we think about childhood, if we were all to parent all children, how much more of a difference might we make?

Select Bibliography

The following references relate to books and articles from which I have quoted at length. For all other references, there should be enough information in the text to track them down. Any remaining quotations come from interviews which I conducted myself.

Introduction

Philippe Ariès, *Centuries of Childhood* (Cape, 1962)

Al Aynsley-Green, *Do ye hear the children weeping?* (Great Ormond Street Hospital for Children, 2003)

Sigmund Freud, *On Sexuality* (Pelican, 1977)

Tim Gill, 'Licence and confrontation', in the *Guardian* (13 April 2005)

Alvaro Gils-Robles, *Report, by Mr Alvaro Gils-Robles, Commissioner for Human Rights, on his visit to the United Kingdom* (Office of the Commissioner for Human Rights, 2005)

Barry Goldson, Michael Lavelette and Jim McKechnie (eds.), *Children, Welfare and the State* (Sage, 2002)

Christina Hardyment, *Dream Babies: Child Care from Locke to Spock* (Cape, 1983)

Colin Heywood, *A History of Childhood* (Polity, 2001)

Allison James and Alan Prout, *Constructing and Reconstructing Childhood* (Falmer Press, 1997)

Mary John, *Children's Rights and Power* (Jessica Kingsley Publishers, 2003)

Ruth Lister, 'Growing Pains' (Guardian, 6 October 2005)

John Locke, *Some Thoughts Concerning Education* (Hackett, 1996)

Thomas H. Murray, *The Worth of a Child* (University of California Press, 1996)

Jean Piaget, *The Language and Thought of the Child* (Routledge, 2001)

Plato, *The Republic* (Penguin, 1987)

Jean-Jacques Rousseau, *Émile* (1762)

William Wordsworth, *Selected Poems* (Everyman, 1983)

Viviana Zelizer, *Pricing the Priceless Child: The Changing Social Value of Children* (New York, 1985)

Rosie

Priscilla Alderson, *Institute of Education Centenery Lecture* (Institute of Education, 2003)

Frank Furedi, 'Why are we afraid for our children?', in *Reared In Captivity: Restoring the Freedom to Play* (Playlink, 1999)

Tim Gill, 'Managing Risk' (Play Safety Forum, 2002)

Gunilla Hallden, 'Children's fictions on their future families', in *Children's Childhoods Observed and Experienced*, ed. Berry Mayall (Falmer, 1994)

Mayer Hillman, *One False Move: A Study of Children's Independent Mobility* (Policy Studies Institute, 1990)

Allison James, *Childhood Identities* (EUP, 1993)

Peter Moss and Pat Petrie, *From Children's Services to Children's Spaces* (Routledge Falmer, 2003)

Iona Opie, *The People in the Playground* (Oxford University Press, 1993)

Anthony Storr, *Human Aggression* (Pelican, 1970)

Anthony Storr, *Solitude*, (HarperCollins 1997)

Gillian Thomas and Guy Thompson, 'A child's place: why environment matters to children' (Green Alliance/Demos, 2004)

Barrie Thorne, *Gender Play* (Open University Press, 1993)

Frances Waksler (ed.), *Studying the Social Worlds of Children* (Falmer Press, 1991)

Lois

Roland Barthes, *Camera Lucida* (Vintage, 1993)

J. M. Coetzee, *Boyhood* (Vintage, 1997)

Morton N. Cohen, *Lewis Carroll, A Biography* (Knopf, 1995)

Anne Higonnet, *Pictures of Innocence* (Thames and Hudson, 1998)

James R. Kincaid, *Child-Loving: The Erotic Child and Victorian Culture* (Routledge, 1992)

Susan Moeller, *Compassion Fatigue: How the Media Sells Disease, Famine, War and Death* (Routledge, 1998)

Tom Regan, 'Why child pornography is wrong', in Geoffrey Scarre, (ed.), *Children, Parents and Politics* (Cambridge University Press, 1989)

Susan Sontag, *On Photography* (Penguin, 1979)

David Wilson and Jon Silverman, *Innocence Betrayed: Paedophilia, the Media and Society* (Polity, 2002)

Allana

John Bowlby, *Attachment and Loss*, Vol. 1 (Pimlico, 1997)

A. Caspi et al., 'Role of genotype in the cycle of violence in maltreated children', in *Science*, Vol. 297 (2002)

Brigid Daniel, Sally Wassell and Robbie Gilligan, *Child Development for Child Care and Protection Workers* (Jessica Kingsley Publishers, 1999)

Charles Darwin, *The Origin of Species* (Oxford World's Classics, 1998)

Howard Gardner, 'The Hundred Languages of Successful Educational Reform' in *Children in Europe* (March 2004)

Sue Gerhardt, *Why Love Matters* (Brunner Routledge, 2004)

Judith Rich Harris, *The Nurture Assumption* (Bloomsbury, 1999)

Penelope Leach, *Ensuring Quality Childcare for Babies and Toddlers* (National Childminding Association, 2005)

Mary Midgley, 'It's all in the mind', in the *Guardian* (21 September 2002)

Elaine Morgan, *The Descent of the Child* (Souvenir Press, 1994)

Stephen Pinker, *The Blank Slate* (Penguin, 2003)

Matt Ridley, *Nature Via Nurture* (Fourth Estate, 2003)

Stainton Rogers, *Stories of Childhood* (Harvester Wheatsheaf, 1992)

Steven Rose, 'Natural conclusion', in the *Guardian* (19 April 2003)

Nicholas

David Buckingham, *After the Death of Childhood* (Polity, 2000)

Richard Dawkins, *Unweaving the Rainbow* (Penguin, 1999)

Oliver James, *Britain on the Couch* (Arrow, 1998)

Stephen Kline, 'The making of children's culture', in *The Children's Culture Reader*, Henry Jenkins (ed.) (New York University Press, 1998)

Ellen Seiter, *Sold Separately: Children and Parents in Consumer Cultures* (Rutgers University Press, 1993)

Jules Shropshire and Sue Middleton, *Small Expectations: learning to be poor* (Joseph Rowntree Foundation, 1999)

Sally Tomlinson, 'Inclusion' in the *Guardian* (19 April 2005)

Shopping Generation (National Consumer Council, 2005)

Adam

Allison James, 'Confections, concoctions and conceptions', in *The Children's Culture Reader*, Henry Jenkins (ed.) (New York University Press, 1998)

Ann Laybourn, *The Only Child: Myths and Reality* (The Stationery Office Books, 1994)

Blake Morrison, *As If* (Granta, 1998)

Neil Postman, *The Disappearance of Childhood* (Delacorte Press, 1982)

Juliet Schor, *Born to Buy* (Simon and Schuster, 2004)

Marlene B. Schwartz, 'Childhood Obesity', in *International Association for the Study of Obesity* (2003)

Lionel Shriver, *We Need To Talk About Kevin* (Serpent's Tail, 2005)

Marjorie Taylor, *Imaginary Companions and the Children Who Create Them* (Oxford University Press, 2001)

Marina Warner, *From the Beast to the Blonde* (Chatto and Windus, 1994)

Laura

Anthony Bateman, Dennis Brown and Jonathan Pedder, *Introduction to Psychotherapy*, (Routledge, 2002)

John Berger, *Ways of Seeing* (Penguin, 1973)

Anthony Clare, in Gyles Brandreth, *Philip and Elizabeth: Portrait of a Marriage* (Century, 2004)

Stephen Collishaw, Barbara Maughan, Robert Goodman and Andrew Pickles, *Time trends in adolescent well-being* (The Nuffield Foundation, 2004)

Sebastian Kraemer, 'Promoting resilience: changing concepts of parenting and child care' *International Journal of Child and Family Welfare*, 3 (1999)

Richard Layard, *Happiness* (Allen Lane, 2005)

Katharine A. Phillips, *The Broken Mirror: Understanding and Treating Body Dysmorphic Disorder* (Oxford University Press Inc., USA, 2005)

Patrick West and Helen Sweeting, 'Fifteen, female and stressed', in the *Journal of Child Psychology* Vol. 44(3) (2003).

Naomi Wolf, *The Beauty Myth* (Vintage, 1991)

Majid

Priscilla Alderson, *Children's Consent to Surgery* (Oxford University Press, 1993)

Priscilla Alderson, 'Human Rights and democracy in schools: do they mean more than picking up litter and not killing whales?' in *International Journal of Children's Rights* Vol. 7 (1999)

Allen Buchanan and Dan Brock, *Deciding for Others* (Cambridge University Press, 1990)

John Eekelaar, 'Parental responsibility: state of nature or nature of state?', in the *Journal of Social Work and Family Law* (1992)

Bob Franklin, 'Children's rights: an introduction', in Bob Franklin, (ed.), *The New Handbook of Children's Rights* (Routledge, 2002)

Stephen Frosh, Ann Phoenix and Rob Pattman, *Young Masculinities* (Palgrave, 2002)

Harry Hendrick, 'Constructions and reconstructions of British childhood', in James and Prout (eds.), *Constructing and*

Reconstructing Childhood (Falmer Press, 1997)

Judith Hughes, 'Thinking about children', in Geoffrey Scarre (ed.), *Children, Parents and Politics* (Cambridge University Press, 1989)

Tony Jeffs, 'Schooling, education and children's rights', in Bob Franklin (ed.), *The New Handbook of Children's Rights* (Routledge, 2002)

Angela Phillips, *How Boys Create Barriers to Learning. Challenging the anti-learning culture in school: an action research project* (Goldsmiths College, 2002)

Jens Qvortrup, Marjatta Bardy, Giovanni Sgritta and Helmut Wintersberger (eds.) *Childhood Matters: Social Theory, Practice and Politics* (Avebury, 1994)

Geoffrey Scarre, 'Children and paternalism', in *Philosophy Journal*, Vol. 55 (1980)

Ashley

A Vicious Circle? What the papers say about children in trouble with the law (Shape; National Children's Bureau, 2004)

Martin Amis, *Experience* (Cape, 2000)

Bernard Coard, *How the West Indian Child is Made Educationally Subnormal in the British School System* (Carribean Education and Community Workers' Association, 1971)

Stanley Cohen, *Folk Devils and Moral Panics* (Routledge, 2004)

John Muncie, 'Institutionalised intolerance: youth justice and the 1998 Crime and Disorder Act', in *Critical Social Policy*, Vol. 19.2 (1999)

Julia Neuberger, *The Moral State We're In* (HarperCollins, 2005)

Richard Sennett, Respect: *The Formation of Character in an Age of Inequality* (Penguin, 2004)

Carolyn Steadman, *Strange Dislocations: Childhood and the*

Idea of Human Interiority 1780–1950 (Virago, 1995)
Joan Tronto, *Moral Boundaries* (Routledge, 2004)

Lauren

Melvin Burgess, *Doing It* (Andersen Press, 2003)

David Evans, 'Falling angels: the material construction of children as sexual citizens', in *International Journal of Children's Rights* (1994)

Ronald and Juliette Goldman, *Children's Sexual Thinking* (Routledge, 1982)

Dina Haydon and Phil Scraton, 'Sex education as regulation', in Barry Goldson, Michael Lavalette and Jim McKechnie, *Children, Welfare and the State* (Sage, 2002)

Stevi Jackson, *Childhood and Sexuality* (Basil Blackwell, 1982)

Camille Paglia, *Sexual Personae* (Vintage, 1991)

Benjamin Spock, *Common Sense Book of Baby and Child Care* (Duel Sloane, 1979)

Laurie and Matthew Taylor, *What Are Children For?* (Short Books, 2003)

Acknowledgements

In the two years that it has taken me to write this book, I have incurred a mountain of debts. The greatest of these is to the nine children and young people who have allowed me to tell their stories here. Without their generosity and trust and that of their families, there would be no book. Thank you Rosie, Lois, Alanna, Nicholas, Adam, Laura, Majid, Ashley and Lauren for your insight, intelligence and patience. I hope that you like the finished product.

Unless you are Dan Brown, writing is not an economic pursuit. I am grateful to Georgina Henry at the *Guardian* for facilitating a jobshare arrangement which allowed me to write part-time and still meet my mortgage payments. My desk editor Seumas Milne has been an inspiring and supportive colleague. My thanks also to Ian Katz, my former editor on G2, who first encouraged me to write about childhood.

Many, many people have helped me to hone my ideas over the past two years. Thank you to all those who submitted to interview, dug out statistics, suggested further reading and generally humoured my obsession. I have acknowledged as many of you as possible in the relevant chapters.

More practically, I am grateful to a number of people who helped me to find some of the children that I profile in this book: John Hartshorn, Sarah Anderson and Samantha Bakhurst. For child-catching and much more besides I would also like to thank Camila Batmanghelidjh at Kids Company and Dierdre MacFarlane at the PEEP Project.

A number of experts in their field have taken the time to read individual chapters and offer their comments. Thank you to Priscilla Alderson, Terri Dowty, Tim Gill, David Wilson, Dylan Evans, David Buckingham, Oliver James, Angela Phillips, Phil Scraton and Yvonne Roberts. Becky Curtis and Becky Gardiner nobly undertook to read the full manuscript – thank you both so much.

My agent Tif Loehnis at Janklow Nesbit was an expert hand-holder and panic-manager. Thank you for keeping the faith, especially when I wasn't. Rosemary Davidson and Mary Davis at Bloomsbury were sensitive and exacting editors.

Writing is an isolating business, and I have been blessed with a support group who put up with my tunnel vision and frequent hibernation. Thank you to Sophie Bold, my oldest and dearest friend, Nicola Norton, who lived with the book for a year, Audrey Gillan, Nick Taylor, Amy Owen, and Ros Wynne-Jones, fellow travellers who understand the imperative to put words on paper, Star Molteno, who housed me during my visits to the Bodleian Library in Oxford, Rhidian Davis and Conroy Harris. Old hands Helen Garner and Gyles Brandreth gave me the benefit of their vast experience. Jo Clark helped me with a small victory at the beginning of the project. My family in Australia have been email cheer-leaders. My mother in Glasgow, and my step-father Alistair, provided outings and listening ears when I most needed them.

Any errors or misinterpretations are mine alone.